Nice Is Not Enough

A NAOMI SCHNEIDER BOOK

Highlighting the lives and experiences of marginalized communities, the select titles of this imprint draw from sociology, anthropology, law, and history, as well as from the traditions of journalism and advocacy, to reassess mainstream history and promote unconventional thinking about contemporary social and political issues. Their authors share the passion, commitment, and creativity of Executive Editor Naomi Schneider.

Nice Is Not Enough

INEQUALITY AND THE LIMITS OF
KINDNESS AT AMERICAN HIGH

C. J. Pascoe

UNIVERSITY OF CALIFORNIA PRESS

University of California Press
Oakland, California

© 2023 by C. J. Pascoe

Library of Congress Cataloging-in-Publication Data

Names: Pascoe, C. J., 1974- author.
Title: Nice is not enough : inequality and the limits of kindness at
   American High / C.J. Pascoe.
Description: Oakland, California : University of California Press,
   [2023] | Includes bibliographical references and index.
Identifiers: LCCN 2023006014 (print) | LCCN 2023006015 (ebook) |
   ISBN 9780520276437 (cloth) | ISBN 9780520396753 (ebook)
Subjects: LCSH: High school students—Political activity—United
   States—21st century. | Equality—United States—21st century. |
   Education, Secondary—Social aspects—United States—21st
   century. | Kindness.
Classification: LCC LA229 .P346 2023 (print) | LCC LA229 (ebook) |
   DDC 373.011/50973—dc23/eng/20230301
LC record available at https://lccn.loc.gov/2023006014
LC ebook record available at https://lccn.loc.gov/2023006015

Manufactured in the United States of America

32   31   30   29   28   27   26   25   24   23
10   9   8   7   6   5   4   3   2   1

For Barrie Thorne, who taught me that we need to listen to kids.
Their voices matter.

I hope I made her proud. I listened as hard as I could.

Contents

Acknowledgments

Writing and researching a book is a collective process. Writing a book in a pandemic is also a deeply isolating process. So I'm grateful for the friendship, collegial support, and intellectual generosity that shaped this text.

I'm eternally appreciative to my editor, Naomi Schneider, for her patience and support. Naomi took a chance on my writing when, while I was still in graduate school, she agreed to publish my first book, an experience that changed my life and the trajectory of my career. She has patiently been waiting for this book, with its delivery delayed again and again by academic moves, parenting more children than I had planned on having, and, in the end, a global pandemic. Thank you for your support and belief in this work.

Audiences at the University of Sydney, the University of British Columbia, the University of California Berkeley, the University of Indiana, and Kent State University, as well as several anonymous reviewers, offered thoughtful feedback on the initial ideas that cohered into this text. The research and writing of this text was supported by the University of Oregon Fund for Faculty Excellence and the David M. and Nancy L. Petrone Faculty Scholar award. Debbie Lewites carefully transcribed many of the interviews that appear here. Ken Hanson and Gracia Dodds provided much needed research assistance for the book. Lynda Crawford, Kirsten Janene-Nelson, and Joan Shapiro thoughtfully copyedited and indexed the text.

Two writing groups provided vital intellectual community through some of the loneliest days of pandemic writing. The members of these groups—Melanie Heath, Sarah Diefendorf, Caitlyn Collins, Amy Stone, Tey Meadow, D'lane Compton, S. Crawley, and Lisa Wade—gave generous feedback and a lot of laughter during the writing process. Michela Musto, Lisa Stampnitzky, Rebeca Burciaga, Jill Harrison, Anthony Ocampo, and Jessica Vasquez all shared expertise on youth, schools, securitization processes, kindness, racial inequality, and organizations that helped me to work through the wide range of literature with which I needed to engage to make sense of what I was seeing. Peggy Orenstein not only shared her expertise on youth but also numerous writing pep talks during key moments in the writing process. Amy Best, Margaret Hagerman, Tey Meadow, and Paige Sweet took the time to provide extensive and invaluable feedback on the entire manuscript, feedback that shaped the contours of this book. Finally, I want to express deep gratitude to Bowman Dickson for the gift of the book's title, a gift born of his deep reading of the manuscript and his own years of experience as a teacher.

When a talk I had been slated to give at Columbia University was cancelled at the last minute as the COVID-19 shutdowns began (and after I had landed in New York!), my friends Teresa Sharpe and Adam Reich had me give my talk in their living room to an audience of two, and provided five pages' worth of feedback on the chapter that eventually became the Politics of Protection. Dear friends like them kept me afloat (and put up with cancelled and rescheduled hangout times because of the weird schedule of an ethnographer) through this research and writing process. Ande Reisman, Teresa Sharpe, Youyenn Teo, Rebeca Burciaga, Jill Harrison, Jocelyn Hollander, Ellen Scott, Chris Halaska, Leia Mattern, Aaron Gullickson, and Ryan Light all kept me laughing, made me food, and put up with me prattling on about this other world in which I was immersed.

Megan Sheppard and Sarah Diefendorf have both read this entire manuscript several times over. I think I'm not lying when I say that just about every page bears their collective intellectual imprint. Through marathon instant-message sessions, multiple-hour Zoom calls, Door Dashing each other chocolate, and weekly long-distance runs, Sarah and I supported each other through our tandem processes of ethnographic research and book writing, a support that became essential and life affirming during some of the toughest, most isolating days of the pandemic. Megan, my partner of twenty-five years, has been with me now through two book length ethnographies, one coauthored book, and two edited volumes (not to mention an MA, a PhD, three children, two academic moves, and the tenure process). This book would not be what it is without her insights, insights born of her years teaching middle school students, and her insistence that I write something regular people can read. And, of course, a huge thanks to our kids, who grew up with this book and put up with me asking them relentless questions about youth culture, school, and being a kid these days. Their insights and patience shaped this text.

Finally, I want to thank the teachers and students of American High. Adolescence is a particularly fraught time. A stranger hanging around, taking notes, and asking questions probably did little to make it less fraught. So thank you. Adults (and I'm well aware that most of you will be adults by the time this comes out!) have left you a world on fire. It was an honor to document the way you demanded and continue to demand change by those in power. Keep doing it.

Thank you to the staff at American High who not only talked to me but let me into their classrooms at a time when teachers themselves were increasingly under surveillance. You not only gave me advice about this book, but changed who I am as a teacher myself. It's not every fieldworker who gets to say they became a better teacher because of their research, but I did. Sitting in your classrooms taught me firsthand about the importance of care in the classroom. Not only are we not taught how to teach in the PhD process, we are not taught about the importance of care in the classroom. In fact, I think we are often taught the opposite, that emotion, connection, support, and care have little place in the academy. Thank you for letting me learn from you, not only in terms of writing this book, but about what it means to be a good teacher.

Young folks, staff, and parents alike told me that American High was a "special place." It became a special place for me as well. I hope that I have done justice to the stories you shared. I hope these stories can help others make and remake this world into one that works for all of us, one that is organized not around competition for scarce resources, but around care, care for each other, ourselves, and those to come.

Preface: American High School

Almost two decades ago I went back to high school as a late twenty-something. From the outdoor hallways to the adversarial relationships between the school staff and students to the casual sexism and homophobia that permeated young folks' conversations, the school I returned to, "River High," in some ways felt a lot like my own high school. I even looked so young at the time that the hallway monitors would yell at me to display my hall pass. However, some important things had changed since I had been in school. When I came of age in the late eighties and early nineties everyone was homophobic, basically. There were no out gay kids at my Southern California high school. It was the height of the AIDS epidemic in the United States and the religious right set the pathologizing parameters for discussions of queer lives. For fun, boys from my high school would drive up Pacific Coast Highway to a small artist enclave that had a thriving gay community to spray fire extinguishers out of their cars at men they thought were gay. One classmate even ended up in prison for a brutal attack on a gay man.

And the sexism? We didn't even know the phrase sexual harassment. When my algebra teacher said, in front of the entire class, "Cheri, if you wear those leggings again, I'll grade the next test on a curve" to student laughter and cheers, all I knew was that it felt awful, not that there was a name for it. Instead I wrote him a scathing letter telling him, "I expect this behavior from teenage boys, but not from a teacher," which speaks volumes about how much harassment we girls endured as a part of daily lives. After all, we had been told over and over again by popular movies (think here of *Say Anything, Footloose,* and the entire John Hughes oeuvre) that stalking was love, sexual harassment was funny, and our "nos" meant little. Only in my senior year did Anita Hill bring sexual harassment to the national consciousness through her brave testimony on Capitol Hill. Not that anyone listened. Concepts like "enthusiastic consent" and movements like "#MeToo" were decades away.

However bad that adolescence was at that time, in the late eighties/early nineties we weren't worried about young White men bringing assault weapons to school to commit mass violence. But as I entered a sociology PhD program at UC Berkeley in the late nineties, the nation had already witnessed horrors out of Paducah, Kentucky; Jonesboro, Arkansas; and Springfield, Oregon. A nation watched horrified as students in Littleton, Colorado, fled their school, hands over their heads, to escape the terror fellow classmates had unleashed on their school. Policy makers, parents, teachers, and politicians alike fretted over the cause of these shootings—video games, broken homes, mental illness, access to guns, bullying. But, at that time, few people were talking about the gender or race of the shooters, even though invariably at that point these mass shooters were White boys. To me, as a budding sociologist, this repeated violence waged by young White men raised this question: What was going on with adolescent boys? I thought that by understanding what sort of messages we were sending to young men about what it meant to be a man we could understand, in part, some of the violence we were witnessing.

This is the question that brought me to River High, the high school that felt, in so many ways, like mine, even though it turned out that this school was different in significant ways. At first, though, it seemed little different than the late eighties/early nineties. It even seemed *more* homophobic at River High than at my own high school, if that were possible. As I walked down the hallway it was like being in the middle of an auditory storm of homophobic epithets. Insults like "faggot" rang out followed by peals of laughter as the backing soundtrack during passing periods. The phrase "that's gay" was so ubiquitous that even I, as a fairly radical queer woman, found it echoing in my head when I thought something was stupid. However, despite the initial appearance of pervasive homophobia at River High, social dynamics had actually changed since I had attended high school. When I talked to boys at River High about why they relentlessly used this sort of homophobic language they told me it wasn't because they didn't like gay people. In fact most of them told me they supported things like gay marriage. One boy even told me he wouldn't ever call a gay person a "fag" because "that's mean."

What I came to find in talking to young men about their use of homophobic epithets was that these insults were part of two social processes through which young men came to see themselves and each other as masculine—a "fag discourse" and "compulsive heterosexuality." What young men repeatedly told me was that when they used these homophobic epithets they were trying to send the message that someone wasn't acting manly enough—they were being too emotional, too touchy, or displaying incompetence. These young men told me they monitored their behavior to avoid being on the receiving end of these homophobic labels because being called "gay or fag," as one boy put it, was "like saying you are nothing." In other words, at River High, boys' homophobia was and wasn't about sexuality. I came to call this type of homophobia a "fag discourse" or a way in which masculinity became, in part, a continual lobbing of emasculating epithets at one another paired with the constant attempt to avoid being subject to them. Importantly, the way these epithets were used was racialized, in that White boys could use these phrases with impunity in a way that Black boys could not. While, on the surface, it seemed that the homophobia I was witnessing had changed little since my own high school days, boys' explanations and behaviors suggested that it had, that rampant use of homophobic language was at least as much about masculinity as it was about not liking gay people.

While boys' homophobia seemed to have altered a bit, their sexism had shifted little. In the hallways, at school dances, and even in classrooms I watched boys and girls "flirt" in ways that looked a lot like male dominance. Boys at River High controlled girls' bodies— lifting them up, jerking them around, constraining their movements—and bragged or joked about sexual assault, talking about girls as if they were sex objects on a regular basis. Memorably, in the hallway one day, one boy even jabbed his drumstick in a girl's crotch while yelling, "get raped, get raped" as she struggled to get away. Girls, in response, laughed uncomfortably or tried to ignore the boys. Rather than accepting this behavior as some sort of natural or inevitable expression of heterosexual desire, I came to call boys' behavior a "compulsive heterosexuality" to capture the way girls' bodies and heterosexuality became a shield against emasculating homophobic epithets. By demonstrating control over girls and their bodies, boys could show others exactly how masculine they were, so that the ubiquitous homophobic insults, insults that suggest "you are nothing," would be less likely to be directed at them.

Suffice it to say, this first book, *Dude, You're a Fag: Masculinity and Sexuality in High School,* was a very hard book to write. Even as a healthy, athletic twenty-something, I came down with pneumonia during the process of researching it. I can't say for certain the illness was related to the stress of what I was documenting, but it sure felt like it. And while nothing I found there spoke *directly* to concerns over school-related violence, concerns that had led me to River High in the first place, the stories told to me by students at River High shed important insight on messages we send to boys and boys send to each other about what it means to be a man. I spent the ensuing years talking about the way homophobic harassment, bullying, and sexism shape the experience of high school, not only for queer and trans youth, but for cis gender and straight boys and girls as well. And wow did things change in the following years—Gay/Straight Alliances, once a rarity, are now in every state and most school districts; state-level laws protecting youth on the basis of sexuality and gender expression appeared even in some unlikely states (although certainly not all of them); public expressions of homophobia dropped drastically, and same-sex marriage even became the law of the land. Teens also got cell phones. Along with those cell phones came a national panic about bullying, specifically cyber bullying, a discussion that was so nonexistent during my time at River High (where young people were still accessing the internet via their home computers and talking on landlines) that even in an entire book about harassment I only mention the word "bullying" twice.

By the time I got to American High, about fifteen years after I first conducted research at River High, *everyone* was talking about bullying. The school (and the town surrounding the school) was plastered in signs encouraging people to be nice to each other and young folks readily talked about mean behavior as bullying. As I walked around the school I saw very little of the homophobic harassment and sexism that characterized my own high school experience or that of the young folks at River High. In fact, I even turned to a friend early in my time at American and commented, "I'm going to write a happy book!" wondering how my more critically minded colleagues in academia would respond to such a rarity. While the story that unfolds at American High is more complicated than that, I do think the book that follows is a happy one. It's happy because unlike at River High or in my own experience of high school, many of the folks at American are deeply engaged in working for social justice—from racial justice to celebrations of queer youth, to addressing classed and gendered inequalities. That's really the story at the heart of this book. It's a book about a school culture characterized by kindness at a time when the leadership of this country was anything but kind or even respectful. As their president regularly bullied and harassed American citizens, fellow politicians, and other world leaders, folks at American High emphasized building each other up rather than tearing each other down. As one student put it, the school is full of "violently accepting people." This book, however, is also about the limits of kindness as a strategy to reduce inequality, primarily through avoiding topics that those at American High call "political." What I found during my two years at American High is that when kindness is not paired with understandings of justice and equality, then it not only does not reduce inequality, it obfuscates the fact that inequality is being reproduced rather than reduced. This book details the way that conflicts between students, staff, and administrators over a drag show, a Black Lives Matter display, mental health concerns, and gendered rituals show the limits of just being nice.

Months after I ended my research at American High in 2019, the world changed in ways very few of us anticipated. One of the many important things we learned as the pandemic altered so many parts of our lives is exactly how important schools are. They are social service agencies—connecting students with resources that are difficult to access elsewhere like mental health care, physical health care, or intellectual support. They are social safety nets—providing food, internet, caring adults, and, for at least part of the day, shelter. They are important spaces where young folks can socialize with one another, especially given how many public places criminalize youth for simply existing in those spaces. Schools, in other words, do so much more than educate.

Perhaps because of the outsized role schools play in caring for young people, as I write this preface battles rage across the country about the nature, purpose, and content of public education. Under a banner of "parental rights," legislators are passing laws that target trans youth and their families. Arguing that they have no place in school, school boards are forbidding "political" symbols like gay pride and Black Lives Matter emblems. Claiming that learning about racism irreparably harms White children, coalitions of parents and politicians are outlawing discussions of so-called "critical race theory" (by which it seems they mean discussions of racial inequality itself). Book-banning efforts have increased at a rate never before seen in the two decades such bans have been tracked.[1] As an educator myself, I know that I'm not alone in my heartbreak as book after book containing stories of and by people marginalized because of race, gender, and/or sexuality are snatched from library shelves.

While the story of American High is not the story of those schools, I think the struggles that happen at American can tell us something about how to address these battles. What the struggles at American High tell us is that we need to develop a more robust language to talk about inequalities both in and out of school. When we locate inequality in individual effort or individual bias, it is hard to capture the way that these inequalities are built into institutions, organizations, traditions, and American culture itself. When we say that schools should be nonpolitical spaces, what we are saying is that they are spaces where we can't address these kinds of inequalities and that leaves us with little leverage to counter the sort of discriminatory practices increasingly being put into place at schools across the country. Telling the story of young folks' experiences in schools is important, whether it be my experiences from the 1980s, the experiences of the boys at River High, or those of the young folks at American, because schools embody and pass on messages about who we are as a country, messages that convey what we are contesting, what we believe, and possibilities, both hopeful and discouraging, for what we could become.

1 *No Room for Hate*

Racism: If I hear people making racist jokes, then I can ask them to stop.

Homophobia: If I hear any homophobic comments, then I will ask why does it matter to them?

Playful Joking: If I see another person physically harassing someone else, then I will speak up and protect the victim.

Sexism: If I hear a sexist comment, then I will step and in and say how would that feel if that was you?

As I enter American High School I walk past these student-generated anti-bullying posters cascading under a sign reading "No Room for Hate," and, on many mornings, I hear Craig's warm laugh echo down the hallways, well before he comes into view. Most days, Craig, a forty-something Black man, and one of two security staff at American High, greets students, staff, and me from his perch on the edge of one of two large planters in a blue-locker-lined lounge at the heart of the school.[1] His greetings reverberate through the cavernous cement-floored space, a high-ceilinged interior courtyard lit by filtered sun entering through multiple skylights. The vast majority of students pass through here several times per day as they head to their classes, grab a drink from the "coffee bar" located in a repurposed utility closet, wrangle a snack from the occasionally working vending machines, or socialize with friends at the cluster of blue metal tables bolted to the floor under red, white, and blue banners hanging from the ceiling exhorting students to display "Eagle Pride." In front of Craig sits his table, typically covered with flyers for events of interest to students, markers, snacks, and paper on which to color.

The second member of American High's security team, Little J, a forty-something man of Polynesian descent easily recognized by his trademark sun visor, so-nicknamed because he was most certainly not little, could usually be found standing next to Craig and his table. Most mornings, they welcome students by their nicknames with greetings like "Hey, Fifi!" and "Good morning, Lulu!" and "Have a good weekend, French Fry?" On this particular morning, Craig asked a set of students if they had their permission slips for the upcoming Black Leadership Conference. He hollered in a fatherly way at another student, "Get me your essay!" referring to a written reflection on the Town Hall on Institutionalized Racism he had chaperoned the previous week. As the bell rang to signal the start of class time, Little J gruffly urged students to get to class, saying, "Why you breathing my air? Get out of here and back to class!" Students laughed and rolled their eyes but also heeded his warning and began to walk toward the classroom-lined hallways that spoke off the lounge.

One of the students making her way to class was Anna, a popular Black senior with long braids and striking blue-green eyes. Craig called out to her: "You know what I'm going to ask you?" "Where's your essay?" she responded, rolling her eyes. "Yes!" Craig laughed, while Anna launched into an explanation of why she did not have the essay—she overslept and rushed to school and now her pants were wet because her bike seat was cracked and it rained the night before.

Craig called over Tilly, a soft-spoken White teacher, who suggested Anna cover her seat with a plastic bag, telling her to bring her pants to the "yoga room" where they could put the clothing in a dryer. Moments later Madison approached, a diminutive White student with shoulder-length blond hair tucked into a baseball cap, holding back tears as she explained to Craig that she had been kicked out of her house again last night. First, to ensure that Madison was fed, Craig dipped into the food stash of instant noodles and granola bars he and Little J fund with their own money. Then he spent a few minutes connecting her with staff who could help solve her housing challenges. After getting Madison settled, Craig turned to me, saying, "Students just want connection." Then motioning toward the hallway down which Madison exited, "*She* wants connection." His goal is "to connect with students," providing "wraparound services, you know, where we wrap around the students" moving his arms into a symbolic circle of care. Young folks at American, for all their eye rolling, feel this care deeply. As Cassia, a soft-spoken junior and president of the Black Student Union, told me of Craig, "He does so much more than what a security guard does. He connects with every single one of us," a sentiment echoed by many of the students at the school.

American High is just that kind of school, the kind of school where there is "no room for hate," the kind of school where care, connection, and kindness characterize school culture. At every turn I see manifestations of this kindness and care. Students, for instance, recently founded a "Be Nice Club" to promote kindness and inclusivity. On Valentine's Day, cheerleaders plastered the blue lockers with white notes dotted with black hearts reading "Have a wonderful day!" and "You are an amazing person!" In the girls' bathroom, a cacophony of student-generated affirmations fills a large yellow piece of butcher paper. Under the heading "Write Something Positive Today," students scrawled messages like "You look very nice today!" and "You are perfect just the way you are. Never change." This culture of kindness extends beyond American High to the surrounding town of Evergreen where "Be Nice" signs, part of a town-wide kindness campaign, dot front lawns of the modest ranch-style homes and duplexes surrounding the school.

Given this culture of kindness, it's little surprise that when community members talk about American High, they call it a "special place." Lauren, a White senior, describes American as full of "the sweetest people in the world." Leila, a White junior, says, "Students would burn everybody alive if they were, like, mean. American is so defensive of each other. Everyone stands up for each other. I think it's awesome. It's, like, oh, you're homophobic, that's not cool. You're a bully, that's not cool." Devin, another White student, describes American as full of "violently accepting people." As Emily, a White mom of an American High student, says, folks at American will "accept the bejeesus out of you." Many folks I talk to readily contrast this culture of kindness at American with the aggressive and competitive ethos of the more well-resourced school up the road, Timber High, where young folks are, reportedly, "bullied out." This culture of kindness and acceptance among students and staff creates the sort of school that students want to come back to even after they graduate. In fact, when meeting with the seniors to prepare them for graduation, Principal Walt, a fifty-something balding White man with an easy laugh who frequently sports jaunty multicolored bow ties as he strolls through the school, warned the students that even if they miss the staff, "you can't just come in and hang out with your teachers" after graduation. After spending two years in the classrooms, hallways, auditoriums, and bleachers at American High, it is abundantly clear to me why so many students want to return to hang out for a bit with their teachers: the sense of kindness and acceptance makes American a space that's hard to leave.

What American High may lack in terms of financial resources, it more than makes up for with this community. While something like a "yoga room" (where Anna's clothing ended up in the drier) feels quite fancy, the sort of thing one would find at a wealthy White suburban school, American High is decidedly not fancy. In fact during my time there, I saw a lot of extra classrooms that could be used creatively, because so many students "choice out" of American to attend other, more well-resourced, higher-performing high schools. Unlike these other schools, the parking lot at American is full of older, noticeably used cars, not the new SUVs or expensive electric cars of Timber High. Roughly 50 percent of the students at American High qualify for free or reduced lunch, a rate that is double that of the two other area schools—Timber and Valley High Schools.

When people say a school has heart, they mean a place like American, a place where resources are not exactly scarce, but they aren't exactly abundant either. What it does have is kindness and acceptance. As a sociologist who had spent the better part of the previous two decades documenting gender- and sexuality-based bullying and harassment, I realized with surprised relief that this kindness and acceptance extended far beyond signs at the front of the school or Craig's nicknames. It permeated classrooms, social interactions, and young people's relationships with each other. But, as I came to discover during my time at American High, this kindness and acceptance had limits, limits that became clear when students and staff took stands against systemic racism, when young folks demanded safer schools and inclusive mental health care, when girls grappled with gendered inequalities, and when long-standing rituals shifted in attempts to be more inclusive. These limits, limits that are at the heart of this book, came as a surprise given the care expressed by so many at American, care that, perhaps, helps us understand why so many students want to return for a visit after they graduate.

Take Ms. Bay's class, for instance. I spent multiple mornings each week in her cheery, light-filled biology classroom at the end of A Hall. Jars of animal specimens sit on the shelves spanning the side walls, and colorful posters of marine life paper the remaining wall space. Unlike the windowless classrooms that spoke off most hallways at American, windows line the back wall of Ms. Bay's room, allowing the sun to shine in on students who sit clustered around black lab tables. A White forty-something woman with long, brown wavy hair, a wicked sense of humor, and a penchant for sprinkling eighties pop culture references throughout her lessons, Ms. Bay is much more than a biology teacher. Hailing from a working-class background in rural Idaho, Ms. Bay is a popular mentor and role model for many of her first-generation and working-class students. Along with her lip-sync partner, Craig, she regularly wins the staff lip-sync competition at quarterly all-school assemblies. Most recently she and Craig brought down the house with an epic performance of Jay-Z and Alicia Keys's "Empire State of Mind." She teaches the UPWARD class, a class designed in a cohort model that, over the course of four years, prepares a group of mostly first-generation and underrepresented students in college readiness. Rather than focusing on a particular topic, the UPWARD class emphasizes study skills as well as peer feedback and peer tutoring.

Ms. Bay spends much of her time demystifying the journey to and through college for her students. Because I had been a university professor for a little over a decade, Ms. Bay regularly called on me in class to help explain the college-going experience regarding everything from note-taking practices to financial aid processes. Sometimes I was able to help, like when I spoke with the class about how to choose a major or the differences between liberal arts colleges and research universities. Other times, my advice highlighted a distance between university and high school classrooms. For instance, despite Ms. Bay's requirement that her students take and turn in Cornell notes, at one point I had to admit that I had no idea what those were and certainly didn't require them as a college professor, an admission that led to righteous indignation and laughter on the part of the students and a joking glare from Ms. Bay. When the young folks in class had questions about college, I did my best to point them to the correct office or find an email they could contact at the appropriate university so they might get their specific query addressed.

As part of her goal to demystify the college-going process, Ms. Bay invited back former UPWARD students Ethan, Harper, and Jaxon to share their post–high school experiences as first-generation and working-class students. As the three of them stood in front of the twenty-five current UPWARD students clustered around black lab tables, Harper, a White college sophomore wearing a trans pride shirt, said, "College is not that easy . . . ," and detailed the financial challenges they had experienced as a self-supporting student at a local public university, sharing that they were considering taking some time off to pay down college loans before finishing their degree. Ethan, a Latino student who was in the midst of transferring to a four-year state school from the local community college, laughingly reassured the UPWARD students that even though college is hard, "graduating from high school is the best."[2] Jaxon, a Filipino senior who attended a local private university on a track scholarship after losing his housing, living in his car, and dropping out of a large state university, laughingly shared with the UPWARD class that being an adult means that "you can eat all the ice cream you want but you have to buy all the ice cream." After an hour of tips and tricks about how to succeed after high school, the three concluded their advice with appreciation for Ms. Bay. Jaxon said, "Ms. Bay is amazing!" Referring to their annual trip to a local fun center, Harper laughed, "She's the Bay-inator when we played laser tag!" Ethan advised the class that after they graduate, they need to "check on Ms. Bay. Man, she's awesome. She loves you guys in a weird nonpsychotic way. You're her children." Jaxon chided them, asking, "Did you remember her birthday?" The current UPWARD students eagerly answered, clamoring over each other to be heard. Joss shouted out, "We did on Facebook!" while Rayna announced, "We got her a shark sweater!" The class members laughed proudly because those marine predators are Ms. Bay's favorite animal by far, a fact that students frequently leveraged when making jokes or getting her presents.

Teachers throughout American High demonstrated a similar, in Ethan's words, "weird nonpsychotic love" for their students, love that manifests as care around issues of class, gender, sexuality, and racial inequalities. Over in the J hallway, for instance, sits Coach Ted's Human Sexuality classroom. Coach Ted's classroom is the opposite of Ms. Bay's. Rather than vibrating with the living nature of science, it feels like a shell of a classroom, the walls bare of décor save for a hastily pinned-up football picture. So many desks and chairs crowd the room that most days I have to physically move them in order to find a seat for myself. Coach Ted, the thirty-something White football coach at American, with close-cropped blond hair, dressed as usual in oversized shorts and a T-shirt that hangs off his small frame, told me that he and his wife, also a teacher, live only a few blocks from the school because they are "work-a-holics." He bragged that he could bike to school in "two minutes" and bike home for a nap between teaching and football practice. Both he and his wife, he told me, come from "football families," sharing that she has never missed a game of his. "It's part of the deal," he said. "She's at a football game every fall Friday night of her life. The relationship wouldn't work otherwise."

According to Coach Ted, he teaches the Human Sexuality class not because he has specific training in it, but he has the "EQ" or "emotional intelligence" to do so. I frequently watch Coach Ted's "EQ" in action as I sit next to Craig on his planter. Coach Ted regularly stops young men in the hallway to ask why they missed football practice, quickly strategizing to solve whatever problem the player had encountered that prevented them from attending, whether it be financial stress, transportation problems, family issues, or academic struggles. While it might be tempting to think that his football players were the only recipients of this sort of care, Coach Ted regularly solved similar problems for non–football playing young folks at American. For instance, when he overheard a group of students in his class bemoaning the fact that once again they had been mislabeled in the local paper as Timber High students in an article covering a protest in which they had participated, Coach Ted took immediate action. He looked up the journalist's name, pulled out his cell phone, and immediately called the paper's phone number to leave a message requesting a correction. This was not the first time American students, especially those leading a protest, had been misidentified as Timber High students. This repeated misattribution was part of what led to a widely shared sentiment that Timber High students were often lauded for their work, while American students were ignored. In that sense, Coach Ted's action, though a small one, was deeply meaningful to his students.

Perhaps to make up for his little training in teaching sex education, Coach Ted brings a coach's energy and tactics to the classroom. He regularly provides mantras to help young folks understand key concepts. For instance, when the class was asked, "What is sexual orientation?" Oliver, a White junior, raised his hand to answer with one of those mantras: "Who you go to bed with!" Mario, a Black junior excitedly added the second part of this mantra: "Gender is who you go to bed *as!*" Oliver and Mario's answers echoed the "as/with" mantra Coach Ted had taught the class to help them understand the difference between sexuality and gender. Coach Ted affirmed Oliver's response saying, "Sexuality isn't a choice or a lifestyle." Students nodded knowingly as Coach Ted added, "When I was younger I didn't choose to be attracted to girls. I'm just a straight male. You like who you like. It's what attracts you!"

Coach Ted ended class with another one of his mantras, his "three things" mantra, asking, "Everyone walk out of here with three things?" Will, an Asian sophomore, responded excitedly: "Sexuality is a variable thing that isn't a choice. Asexuality exists. Being trans is not a sexuality." Coach Ted proudly cheered the class on, saying, "Look at us, we are learning!" As students packed up, Oliver asked

Coach Ted, "Are you and your wife going to do something special for Valentine's Day?," to which Coach Ted smiled and said, "Every day is Valentine's day" while students groaned and laughed. Contrary to stereotypical images of a boorish, sexist football coach, Coach Ted self-consciously tries to create a classroom environment intended to both educate as well as celebrate sexual and gender inclusivity.

Across the student lounge and down C hall sits Nella's classroom, a space that feels like how I imagine it would feel to walk into a common room at Hogwarts if that common room were dedicated to social justice and racial equity. Despite the fact that, like Coach Ted's room, it is windowless, the classroom is always bathed in a warm glow. Fairy lights drape the walls and shelves, faux candles sit on bookcases, and torchier lamps softly light dim corners. Couches and upholstered chairs cluster around the circle of desks that constitute the main part of the room. Student-generated artwork and posters fill the walls with homages to civil rights leaders, Black and Brown cultural icons, authors, artists, and musicians. Most days, quiet hip-hop music plays as we filter into the room. Nella, a slight, tattooed, and bespeckled forty-something teacher of mixed racial descent—the daughter of a Black father and White mother—leads her Daring Discussions classes with compassion, love, and care. Daring Discussions, an English class, focuses on topics of social justice with specific attention to racial inequality, awarding students credit for an ethnic studies class through the local community college. For many of her White students this class provides a critical opportunity to talk about race and learn about the persistence of racial inequalities, rather than understanding those inequalities as things that happened long ago, and to analyze whiteness as a powerful social category. For her students of color, Nella has created a space where they can speak more freely about their experiences of race and racism with a supportive, understanding, and knowledgeable adult in charge. Just as Cassia called Craig "so much more than a security guard," so too do young folks of color name Nella as someone who has quite literally changed their lives and educational experiences.

As part of her strategy to create an environment that empowers students to address topics that might be liberatory for some, challenging for others, and potentially painful for many, Nella bases her class in community-building exercises that allow students to concretely witness their commonalities and differences. One of these community-building exercises is a "community circle" that Nella facilitates each term. Moving to the front of the room with a grace and presence that reflects her years of dancing, Nella began one of these circles by inviting students to arrange their chairs in a circle as she read statements on slips of paper, some student-generated, some Nella-generated, that describe an attribute or experience. She told students to stand if the statement applied to them. For twenty minutes or so, students silently stood or sat as Nella read categories like the following, saying, "Stand if you . . ."

Like the color blue
Are a Netflix addict
Play an instrument
Have indigenous ancestry
Feel respected in school
Grew up poor
Live with one parent
Know where to get drugs

While the young folks around me laughed as I remained seated when Nella read "know where to get drugs," as most of them stood, I was struck, as perhaps some of them were, at how many of them remained standing for categories like "have a family member in prison" or sat for categories like "live with one parent." I suppose that is the point of this exercise, to reveal these often invisible commonalities and differences in ways that may humanize fellow classmates and build a sense of community.

The creation of community at American High, whether it be Craig and Little J's morning greetings, Ms. Bay's playful care, Coach Ted's mantras, or Nella's rituals, made me feel much like those graduating seniors, like this place was some kind of home that I wouldn't want to leave when it was time to be done with my research. Of course I was not an eighteen-year-old itching to be done with coursework: I was a forty-six-year-old sociology professor at a large public university who had come to American High to research my next book, this book, about young people's social worlds. This project was inspired by my students (and my own children) who were continually telling me stories about school that sounded different than the sort of adolescent homophobia and sexism I had documented over a decade before in my book *Dude, You're a Fag: Masculinity and Sexuality in High School.* That research showed that boys used homophobic epithets to remind each other to be acceptably masculine, that boys sexually harassed girls as a typical part of the school day, and that schools themselves structured these sorts of gendered and sexual inequalities. These dynamics played out in racialized ways as young men of color were punished for behavior White boys often engaged in with impunity.

But, as my students and children repeatedly told me, much had changed since I had done that research. Gay marriage had been legalized. An increasing number of states had passed laws protecting young folks' rights to be free from gender-identity-based and sexuality-based harassment in schools.[3] Social movements demanding class, sexual, and racial justice like Occupy Wall Street, marriage equality, the DREAMers, and the Black Lives Matter movements had shifted public discussions of what sort of society we lived in and provided visions of what sort of society could be possible.[4] According to my kids and my students, these sorts of discussions and visions, in addition to the possibilities offered by increased information contained in the digital devices plastered to young folks' hands (devices that had become ubiquitous after that earlier research), had radically altered what it meant to be a teenager.[5] So, with the permission of Principal Walt, whom I had met through parent networks at the local elementary school, I entered American High, a primarily White, working- and middle-class high school of about one thousand students, to document what it is like to come of age as a public school student during a time of expanding language about what sort of world could be possible, even if these possibilities were far from realized.[6]

A few months before beginning my research at American High, however, the American social and political landscape shifted dramatically as Donald Trump took the oath of office to serve as the forty-fifth president of the United States. By now we are all familiar with what came next. The most visible and powerful politician in the country used his megaphone to stoke, encourage, and approve of those with racist, nativist, transphobic, homophobic, sexist, white supremacist, and nationalist beliefs in a way that normalized and amplified hateful rhetoric, social policy, and violence. By the time I was researching at American High, then President Trump had encouraged white supremacists, calling them "very fine people," separated migrant children from their parents, forcing many of them into inhumane conditions, appointed a far right nationalist as an advisor, rolled back legal protections for trans youth in schools, withdrew from the Paris agreement on climate change, mocked sexual assault survivors, repealed gun control legislation meant to curb mass shootings, and used an epithet to describe a professional athlete who knelt during the national anthem to protest racist violence.[7] As we now know, this language, these decisions, and the ensuing policies enabled, emboldened, and reflected the worldviews of those who had opposed social, cultural, and legal shifts aimed at increasing (if only haltingly and in imperfect ways) social equality that had, in part, characterized the years leading up to this election.[8] This enabling, emboldening, and reflecting manifested in increasing numbers of hate groups and hate crimes during this presidency as well as social and legal backlash to gendered, sexual, racial, and economic equality. It was in this particular social moment, one of rising opposition to various forms of social equality, that I entered American High, a school community characterized by kindness and acceptance, a school community that was grappling with what this new political regime meant for them and for their country.

It's little wonder then that I felt like many of the students did, that I didn't want to leave American High once I found myself there given the relief I felt in encountering a community that explicitly emphasized kindness, acceptance, and care. Not only was it in some ways a respite from some of these harsh forces in the outside world, but after spending several months at American High, I did not hear or witness in the hallways the sort of homophobia or sexism I had documented in previous research. As often happens though in stories about shifting social norms and the complex currents of social inequalities, the story at American High turned out to be a little more complicated than what was happening in the hallways, a complication that became clear to me on the day of the annual "Senior Assembly."

The Senior Assembly is an annual tradition. In addition to typical assembly events such as the staff lip-synch battles and class competitions like relay races, at this end-of-the-year event seniors are "knighted," the staff performs a choreographed dance in honor of the senior class, and the soon to be graduates end the assembly with a "senior run," dashing through a tunnel made of teachers' raised arms. Like most assembly days, second period ended early as the student body headed over to the gym. Students found their way to the bleachers where they sat divided by class. Nella, Coach Ted, Craig, Little J., and Ms. Bay joined other teachers and staff by the glass doors lining the entrance to the gym, as they often do at assemblies like these. What happened next, however, set off a series of events at the school that reflected the limits of the culture of kindness and acceptance at American High.

The Show Choir took to the floor and began, as they typically did, to sing the opening lines of the national anthem. Teachers, staff, and students stood, and some removed hats and placed hands solemnly over their hearts. As the choir neared the end of the song, a slight rustling occurred in the group of staff by the glass entrance doors. Out of the corner of my eye I saw Max, a tall middle-aged White man with short-cropped brown-gray hair, and the only out trans teacher at the school, slowly drop to one knee. Several staff members turned their heads toward him. Slowly five other staff members, including Nella, silently dropped to one knee in a now recognizable movement popularized by NFL player Colin Kaepernick to protest racist police violence. Not a single student joined the teachers in their silent statement in support of Black lives and few even visibly acknowledged the ritual as their eyes remained focused forward on the Show Choir.

When the anthem ended the kneeling staff members stood and the assembly continued as if nothing happened. Officer White, the armed school resource officer and the third member of the security team, handed Principal Walt a faux sword as Principal Walt stood in front of the bleacher filled with graduating seniors. Holding the sword aloft, Principal Walt said to them: "It's been a long year, a good year, a tough year. You've got a life waiting for you. You've had a long road to now. It's time to celebrate. With the values of American being persistence, respect, honor, resolve, and excellence, carry these forward with you. We're going to miss you all!" he ended, solemnly waving the sword over them as if knighting them. The staff followed this ritual with their annual senior dance, this year dressed in full 1990s' regalia—sideways hats, overalls with one strap hooked, and colorful shirts. After performing a choreographed routine to a 90s medley, the teachers joined arms in a kick-line to raucous applause and cheers from the students. They ended the assembly by joining hands to form a tunnel through which the seniors ran laughing, cheering, and high-fiving each other.

The apparent normalcy that briefly followed the kneeling, however, belied the emotional and social weight of the brief protest. Nella told me later that the decision to kneel was so heavy that she "shook" as she knelt. While it may seem surprising that at a school full of "violently" accepting people the decision to kneel as part of, by that point, a multiyear nationwide protest against racist police violence would be fraught enough to cause a physical reaction, the ensuing community response to the act of peaceful protest provides some important context. Community members wrote letters to the editors of local news organizations. Parents weighed in. The principal expressed displeasure. The teachers who knelt received formal reprimands as letters were placed in their personnel files. According to Max, the letters served as a warning that, should this behavior continue, it would constitute a fireable offense. According to the letters, making a public statement against racist police violence constituted an "act of political expression." And acts like these were forbidden "during the workday." As Principal Walt later communicated to the student body, "Politics in the school house is not okay."

The Political

American High may be no place for hate but it's no place for politics either. At a school where folks will "accept the bejeesus out of you," kneeling to protest the murder of Black Americans becomes an issue not of hate, acceptance, or justice, but one of politics. This wasn't the only instance during my time at American where the concept of politics was invoked to quell actions related to social issues, specifically issues having to do with inequality. The messages of kindness and acceptance that blanket the school—from the cheerleaders' notes to the Be Nice Club to claims that American is "full of the sweetest people in the world"—stop short of including space for sentiments, acts, or expressions considered political. Intolerance for hate has limits, in other words. And those limits are signaled by the political.

What becomes increasingly clear when looking at how the concept of the political is used at American High is that it does not necessarily mean politics in terms of formal governing apparatuses or partisanship. Take, for instance, a discussion during a meeting of the Climate Action Club. This group meets weekly in Ms. Bay's room. When they made plans to participate in a global youth protest to demand government action on climate change, they too encountered the limits of the political. Club members had advertised the protest in the previous weeks, as clubs often did, by placing fliers around the school, fliers that were repeatedly removed. Jessa, a Latina club member, investigated their removal and shared with other club members that she was told that "Climate Action Club is promoting this walkout and so it's political." As club members protested this label, saying that trying to save the planet was a general concern, not a political one, Cameron, a White senior, made the astute point that the school authorities do allow politics, saying, "There's a Young Republicans Club! That's *actually* about politics." Cameron's point is an important one, because it raises the question of what we mean when we call something "political." His analysis suggests that it doesn't necessarily have to do with formal processes of governing or political parties.

A look at the way the word "politics" is used on the American High School's football team's social media pages can help us to understand the work that a concept like politics does, not only at American High, but perhaps in other contexts as well. The front image on one of the team's pages features a line of team members fully suited up with their hands over their hearts facing an American flag captioned with a line from the national anthem: "Over the Land of the Free and the Home of the Brave!" Below this image a description of the page reads: "We are here to have fun and focus on the athletes, not on politics or anything destructive. When you comment please be positive with your words. We will not tolerate negativity, profanity or any references to race, religion or sexual orientation." Politics, in this context, seems like it is something that, by its very nature, is destructive. Politics is not positive nor is it fun, according to these guidelines. Politics here belongs with a list of things that are negative, like profanity and the mere topics of race, religion, or sexual orientation.

When he directly addressed "destructive" and "political" topics like race, religion, and sexual orientation, a beloved White teacher, Seth, also encountered the limits of the political. Concerned with "racist, sexist, transphobic, homophobic and xenophobic rhetoric," he sent an email to a list of colleagues: "Dear beloved colleagues," he wrote. "I have shared space, meetings, hurried lunches, laughter and tears with many of you. I am writing to you all, and to myself, only to add one humble drop to the collective fountain of courage and critical faculties that we possess in order to face our current reality." Directly addressing claims like those made by Principal Walt, that "politics in the school house is not okay," Seth wrote that increasing racism and nationalism renders a "separation between education and politics" untrue, writing, "When our students of color are being terrorized, this separation is false. When we as professionals censor our voices in the face of mass deportations in order to carry on with schooling as usual this separation is false. When we maintain a professional aloofness while our families are threatened, and terrified to walk down the street, the notion of separation between enlightened knowledge and politics has to be vigorously interrogated." Rather than receiving responses that echoed concern about rising threats to already marginalized populations, instead Seth was instructed to "discontinue" using email for "political discussions." Seth's comments focused on potential and actual harm being done to vulnerable groups of students, concerns that were more related to morality, ethics, and student safety than to formal politics. But, much like the teachers who knelt in support of Black lives, Seth was told that this expression of concern for the racialized dimensions of student safety was a political expression, and, as such, one that should take place elsewhere.

After spending two years participating in the social world of American High School, I would suggest that what is going on in the schoolhouse, and schoolhouses across the country, is profoundly political and that this emphasis on kindness and acceptance is a way to avoid whatever it is we mean by the "political." This disjuncture between a focus on practices of kindness and acceptance and the limits of the political is at the heart of this book. These tensions between what is considered political and practices of taking a stand against hate and intolerance at American High reflect larger social tensions in the United States. This is a moment in which, by some measures, social equality has been increasing, organizations have been taking steps to increase diversity, and representation of a multitude of voices has come to be seen as a social good. It is also a moment of rising nationalism, of increasing numbers of hate groups, and of creeping authoritarianism. It is, in other words, a moment of reckoning with what kind of country we want and are going to be. This reckoning goes far beyond the walls of American High, but what is happening there can shed light on what is happening in many communities right now.

The story of the political is central to this reckoning. As such, it needs to be unpacked, because the work it does at American High School reflects the work it does in American culture at large. In the United States a language of politics has long been seen as a contaminant in terms of civil discourse.[9] As sociologist Andrew Perrin points out, when Americans talk about social issues, the "rules of politeness

. . . prohibit talking about politics and religion."[10] Scholar Nina Elia-soph, in her research about American civic life, suggests that our very ability to build and sustain community actually depends on our explicit avoidance of topics designated as political.[11] Echoing the sentiment shared on the American High football team's social media page, this approach suggests that the nature of what it means to be political is to be destructive. That is, the political itself threatens the ability to build and sustain community and relationships. Introducing political topics to discussions not only violates rules of politeness, but threatens our capacity to build and be in community with one another. Politics is, a priori, destructive.

However, as Cameron so aptly points out in his critique of the way the Republican Club is not considered by school authorities to be problematically political, the political is not always the same as partisan or formal politics. So what is it? What is this thing that is so powerfully destructive? Andrew Perrin's study of American's talk indicates that "political talk specifically addresses issues of power, resource distribution or public morality."[12] In other words, when we call something "political," we don't mean capital P political. We actually mean a variety of things. We mean social inequality. We mean values. We mean issues of who receives or deserves resources and what resources they should or do receive. We mean whose voices and needs count. We mean who gets to make decisions about these things. In other words, who does or does not have resources, who does or does not have the power to award or deny others those resources, and the written and unwritten moral code that contours social power and resource flows are the things of little p politics. That is, inequality and the ideologies that justify or challenge inequality are the things of politics.

More specifically, when we call something political we are suggesting that it has to do with the *systemic* nature of these inequalities. By "systemic," I mean the way that the issues of little p politics are built into our social institutions themselves. Social institutions, like economic, religious, family, educational, and political institutions, are systems of norms, roles, and organizations that make up and meet the needs of societies. While these institutions may seem neutral or unremarkable, the issues of resource distribution, power, and values that we refer to as political are a part of these institutions. Talk that addresses systemic inequalities is political talk, regardless of whether or not it is partisan talk or has anything to do with a formal governing apparatus.

Why might some folks at American High, and in the United States more generally, avoid or be told to avoid addressing social issues, specifically those relating to inequality, rendering them off-limits by designating them as political? The answer to this is complicated but part of it lies in American culture, or the general system of beliefs and values in the United States. As a culture we typically address the topics of race, class, sexuality, gender, and other types of inequality in two ways, both of which emphasize individual, rather than systemic, understandings of inequality. The first way Americans understand inequality is through what may be alternately called an "achievement ideology," a "bootstraps ideology," or the "American dream."[13] That is, if one just works hard enough, no matter what is thrown in their way, they can achieve anything they set their mind to. The idea that America is a land of opportunity where every individual has a shot at achieving their economic and social goals free from legal barriers is enshrined in our most scared documents. The logic we are left with then is that to the extent that inequality exists, it is due, in part at least, to the lack of an individual's hard work or drive. We believe, that is, that we live in a meritocracy.[14]

The second way we typically understand inequality has to do with the fact that we locate inequality in the minds, attitudes, and behaviors of individuals, rather than as something that is built into those social institutions—educational, religious, political, or economic institutions—that constitute our society. We tend to think of race, gender, class, or sexual inequalities in terms of racism, sexism, classism, or homophobia. These "phobias" and "isms" locate inequalities in individual sentiments, ideologies, or practices. An individual person *is* homophobic, sexist, racist, or classist.[15] This framing suggests that if we could just change people's minds about minoritized groups or groups with less social power, this could solve the problem of social inequality. Certainly, the popularity of anti-bias trainings to address racial, gender, and sexual inequalities suggests that an individual strategy is a preferred approach to reducing inequalities. However, this type of individual strategy only goes so far. The vast majority of Americans, for instance, report that they are not racist and approve of things like interracial marriage and friendships.[16] The data about interracial romantic relationships or friendships, however, suggest that the approval rates for these types of social connections differ greatly from the extent to which such connections exist in the real world.[17] In other words, a complicated and nonlinear relationship exists between individual sentiments about inequalities and the persistence of inequalities. Individual people can change their racist, homophobic, sexist, or classist beliefs, and data suggest that many people have changed those beliefs, but these inequalities endure. To shift these inequalities requires more than an emphasis on individual expressions of kindness or acceptance. Those individual level sentiments, while related to larger issues of resources and the distribution of power, are not the same as those things.

The persistence of these types of inequalities may be due to the fact that they occur not only because of individual effort or bias, but because they are embedded in social institutions themselves. Inequality, in this perspective, doesn't solely reside in individual belief or result from a lack of individual effort but is part of the infrastructure of our social world. This is what we mean when we talk about systemic inequality, as opposed to individual bias or prejudice. One way to think about this is by looking at organizations like schools. Organizations are not simply "self-operating entities";[18] rather they are "spaces in which individuals' efforts are coordinated to jointly accomplish a set of tasks to fulfill some goal or set of linked goals."[19] This coordination of individual effort requires maintaining shared definitions of a day-to-day reality, in and out of an organization. These shared definitions are organizational logics or the "common sense" of an organization. These logics help us communicate with one another, ensuring that we are on the "same page." These logics may also take on a life of their own in an organization, existing regardless of the individual biases or beliefs of those who are part of the organization. In other words, organizations themselves are gendered, racialized, classed, and sexualized, operating on and reproducing logics that may reflect existing social inequalities even as many folks in the organization, like the individuals we have met so far at American High, work hard to care for others in ways that are not sexist, homophobic, classist, or racist.[20] Thinking about inequality as something that lives in these organizational logics suggests that even well-meaning people who might think of themselves as people who are non-racist, non-sexist, non-classist, or non-homophobic might find themselves participating in rituals, processes, or interactions that rely on and reproduce particular forms of inequality.

When we talk about "systemic inequalities," this is what we mean—the way inequality exists and persists even when individuals may be opposed to these inequalities. Taking a systemic perspective on inequalities rather than an individual one suggests that we cannot bias-train our way out of inequality, no matter how popular that answer seems to be right now. A systemic perspective requires that we examine these organizations and institutions themselves to reveal the way that their governing logics may sustain inequalities to which many of us may be opposed, a process that may require figuring out how to integrate the uncomfortable topics of the political into polite conversation.

The dominant logic at American High is one of kindness and acceptance. The school's embrace of this sort of kindness culture exists without seriously addressing these racial, sexual, gender, or class inequalities, precisely those issues so often regarded as political. This leaves school members without a language to address many of the very inequalities that such a culture should ameliorate. This logic sustains many existing race, class, gender, and sexual inequalities even while it seems to address them. What is happening at American, in this sense, may be a version of what scholar James Thomas calls a "diversity regime," or a culture that seems to include a commitment to diversity, but that commitment may actually obscure or intensify existing inequality.[21] While Thomas specifically refers to racial inequality, this concept may also capture a set of intersecting inequalities at American High, inequalities that may be hidden by what we might think of as a regime of kindness.

That said, these organizational logics are not all powerful. While it may be difficult to argue against a regime of kindness, youth activists, often empowered by adult allies, push back against these logics, creating space and demanding possibilities for a more just and equitable society. By tracing out these logics, resistance to them, and alterative framings of inequality at American High School, I suggest that in recognizing and identifying these logics we can help to shift some of the stubborn inequalities with which we continue to be confronted in and out of schools and perhaps take steps to reduce them.

From Kindness to Care

We expect a lot of schools. We blame them for and demand that they solve inequalities that originate far outside their walls. Part of this is because we have tasked schools with socializing children into the meanings, norms, and values of a society.[22] As such, schools "occupy an awkward social position at the intersection between what we hope society will become and what we think it really is."[23] They are micro-cosms of society but are also responsible for producing citizens for the next generation of democracy (and capitalism).[24] Looking at what young folks learn in school and how they navigate its social and organizational landscape can tell us something about American val-ues and what we think these future citizens should look like. Because of their unique role in society, the social life of schools, or what soci-ologist Robert Crosnoe calls the "informal processes" of schools, can shed light on how inequality is sustained, or challenged, not just in schools but in society at large.[25] Rather than looking at inequality as a lot of educational research has done, by examining school funding, the achievement gap, or tracking, this book focuses on the social life of schools.[26] As such, it focuses more on "relational inequalities"—inequalities related to how power may be unevenly distributed among racialized, classed, gendered, and sexualized groups —than it focuses on formal educational outcomes.[27] Who counts and who doesn't, whose voice is heard and whose is not, whose needs matter and whose are unseen are all part of the social life of schools. This social life addresses the way members of the school community have a sense of belonging, a sense of citizenship, a sense of themselves as agentic and meaningful members of a community who can help shape and sustain that community. It addresses which members have the ability to have bodily integrity, have their struggles acknowl-edged, see reflections of their own experiences, and be free from har-assment or threats of harassment. This means that the social life of schools looks a bit like the social life of other organizations—churches, volunteer groups, workplaces—and as such a focus on this social life might help us understand how inequality works in Ameri-can life in general, rather than focusing more narrowly on topics like learning loss, test scores, or the achievement gap, which are the measures more often used to assess inequality in schools.

During my two years of observations at American High, including more than fifty interviews with students, staff, and parents, and the examination of school documents, I kept wondering how it was that at a school where there is "no room for hate," a school where staff went out of their way to care for students, and a school where students themselves reported that they appreciated and valued each other, some voices and some needs still mattered more than others in ways that reflected larger inequalities around race, gender, class, and sexuality.[28] What I found during my time there was that well-meaning members of this school community, like many Americans, had a limited language for dealing with inequality, such that even in a place where folks were excited to embrace diversity and reject hate, social inequalities persist systemically. When well-meaning people are participating in processes that sustain some forms of inequality, it may perhaps be time to think through the tools available to talk about inequality and to find a language to link individual experiences, beliefs, and practices to systemic processes that maintain these inequalities. Such a language may involve a shift from focusing on a regime of kindness to a culture of care.[29]

American High is the most racially diverse high school in this liberal, very White town, in a liberal and very White state. Oregon is more White than are three-quarters of other states, and Evergreen, the town in which American High is located, is even whiter, at about 78 percent to Oregon's 61 percent. American High itself is more racially diverse than both Oregon and Evergreen. Of its roughly one thousand students—1 percent are Native, 2 percent Asian, 3 percent Black, 17 percent Latina/o/x, 10 percent multiracial, 1 percent Pacific Islander, and 67 percent White. American High is known as a not particularly academic high school compared to Timber High, the school up the road attended by the children of the doctors, lawyers, and professors, where houses cost substantially more. And it's definitely not as wealthy or religious as Valley High, the football-focused school in the south part of town. It's a high school that draws mostly working- and middle-class youth, with a smattering of upper-middle-class students. It's a high school that is trying to do the right thing, filled with dedicated teachers who survive on little sleep, who go above and beyond what is required of them to support their students. It's also a high school that recently installed facial recognition technologies on its security cameras. It's a high school without a single Black man as a classroom teacher, but with two security guards of color. It's a school where the only person who has a weapon is the White school resource officer. It's a school that is struggling to be inclusive, but still sends important messages about who counts that are stratified by class, race, gender, and sexuality.

This book is a story of how these contradictions are sustained, how, in the words of education scholars Amanda Lewis and John Diamond, "despite the best intentions" of many teachers, staff, students, and parents, racial, class, gender, and sexual inequalities still persist in the social life of American High. In the two years I spent at American, poring over digital and physical documents like yearbooks and talking to staff, students, graduates, parents, and community members, what I saw again and again was a dedication to kindness and acceptance and a simultaneous undermining of race, class, gender, or sexual equality. This book documents how school practices, rituals, and common sense explanations of inequality that focused on individual kindness, equalizing difference, and avoiding the political constitute a regime of kindness that rewards already privileged groups of students while further marginalizing others.

As such, this is a story about much more than a high school. It is a story of systemic inequality in America and how kindness and good intentions will not solve it—whereas developing a language to address the political might help. It is a story about how a focus on positive emotions can elide the systemic nature of inequality, making these inequalities seem like they are individual problems of merit, hurt feelings, meanness, individual effort, or resilience. This book argues that a regime of kindness works as a logic that enables us to avoid the political, and how unpacking this logic shows the way systemic inequalities come to be understood as individual problems.

During my time at American I watched as limits to a regime of kindness were revealed in several key moments—when the students put on a drag show; during student walkouts to protest gun violence and climate change; when students and staff struggled to put on a Black Lives Matter event; during the annual Powder Puff football game; and when, for the first time in the school's history, a girl participated in the historically all-male Mr. Eagle Pageant. These liberalizing shifts revealed several tensions that tell us something about how inequality is both sustained and challenged—tensions that show us how approaches based in securitization, positive emotions, empowerment, and tolerance may obfuscate systemic inequalities by seeming to address them.

This regime of kindness at American High is part of what I came to think of as a *politics of protection,* or the way that dangers, threats, or harms to young folks are framed as external, random, and individual, not necessarily as preventable, systemic, or related to social inequalities. The rest of the book explores the various ways the politics of protection can appear—in terms of race, gender, sexuality, class, and their intersections. Students, for instance, suggest that racial inequality is "sugarcoated" at American High as part of a larger project of "benign diversity" in which love and kindness are deployed to solve the problem of racial inequality, while treating all difference as equal to all other difference. Girls are left to navigate edicts of kindness through a response of "girl-boss feminism" as they attempt to be resilient in the face of a "mundane misogyny" or the daily onslaught of symbolic, discursive, or physical gendered violence.

Raced, classed, and gendered privilege intersect in the production of what I came to think of as a "student citizen," a production in which this privilege gets disguised as merit and is obscured by an ideology of tolerance. In terms of these dynamics, the social life of American High School is a case of larger cultural, organizational, and political practices and ideologies about the existence of and solutions to social inequality. It shows how a serious challenge to any one of these systems of inequality necessarily implicates other inequalities such that none of the challenges to them are legible within the school's regime of kindness.

This book tells a story about how systemic inequalities get made to look like individual ones. But it's also a story about how to counter these inequalities, not with a politics of protection, but a *politics of care*. That is, a regime of kindness won't solve inequality, but a politics of care might make a dent. While slogans of kindness and acceptance may feel good, kindness is not care. A politics of care is an approach to issues of power, resource distribution, and public morality that centers human needs, vulnerabilities, subjectivities, and disparities in institutions and organizations themselves rather than relying on individual responses like kindness and acceptance as solutions.[30] As social critic Barbara Ehrenreich tells us, this focus on kindness may be a part of an American tradition of positive thinking, a tradition that historically ignores the problems we need to solve to actually *be* happy.[31] As such, the story of American High is a story that is bigger than this high school, because it may tell us something about America itself and the way we rely on individual solutions when systemic ones are needed. If inequality can be systemic, so can care.

So, welcome to American High. It is a school full of the sweetest people you'll ever meet. We'll get to know Craig, Little J., Ms. Bay, Cassia, Sarah, Natasha, and the young folks in the Gay/Straight Alliance, the Black Student Union, the Women's Empowerment Club, and the Eagle Pageant. We'll spend time in Nella's classroom and listen to young women tell stories of assault and resilience. We'll watch as young folks work for racial justice, safety, and climate change solutions. We'll see the importance of teachers and staff who demonstrate care for students. We'll learn that in many ways the story of American High might be the story of some of America itself, a group of folks who are working to make this world a better, more equal, more just, and caring place, even in the face of forces that mitigate against the creation of the kind of world we would like to see.

2   *The Politics of Protection*

Cops ran through the school, shooting guns at teachers. Along with other staff members, Ms. Bay crouched in the corner of a darkened classroom for safety. At one point a cop threw open the door and Ms. Bay said, patting her chest, "He shot me right here. I watched as the bullet hit my chest." The cops were real, but the bullets were not. The police were using nerf guns during an active shooter training to simulate a school shooting. Trainings like these, designed to prepare teachers and students to respond to school-based gun violence, regularly take place in schools across the country.[1] Ms. Bay told me that the first time she went through one she "went home and sobbed," enduring "nightmares for six months." When her husband asked, "What did you do today?" Ms. Bay answered, "I had to pretend I got shot at by a cop." When he asked, "Why?" she answered, "Good question." It *is* a good question. Research, in fact, suggests that the effectiveness of this type of training is, at best, debatable especially considering the emotional toll it exacts on many who participate.[2]

The notable number of students who were absent on active shooter training day may have something to do with this emotional toll. Some of these students skipped school, and Craig and Little J have a list of others they pulled from classes to shield them from the emotional impact of the trainings. Class attendance was so sparse that day that James, a Latino senior, commented after seeing all the empty seats in Ms. Bay's class, "So many people missing!" Marc, an Asian senior, asked Ms. Bay, "Are we going to be barricading the room?" as they had done in previous trainings. Tasha, a Black senior, responded, "We gotta be ready. We got to know what to do!" Then, looking at the lab table in front of her, she said, "I feel like you couldn't shoot through these." Marc checked out the table, knocking on it as if to check its durability, as Ms. Bay mused, "They're chemical proof and fire proof, but probably not bullet proof." Marc concurred, "I don't think these would stop a bullet. I'm diving head first through a window." James added, "Someone needs to get a van and park out there so everyone can hop into it and get away!" as his classmates laughed at his gallows humor.

Similar discussions took place in classrooms across the school that day as teachers led students in the training. On this particular day, the training was not a live action simulation. Instead teachers clicked through a slide show guided and timed by instructions read over the loudspeaker. Several halls away from Ms. Bay's biology classroom, students sat unusually quiet and hushed in Nella's room as they listened to a disembodied voice telling them, "You have twenty minutes to complete slides 1–20." Over the following class period, teachers and students followed the instructions on each slide, like this one:

Practice Four Drills
Lockout: 8 Minutes
Lockdown-Barricade: 9 Minutes
Lockdown-Counter: 8 Minutes
Lockdown-Evacuate: 12 Minutes
Debrief Questions

Nella, as instructed, read the "Practice Lockdown Procedures" slide aloud. "The first thing we need to do," she said, "is barricade."

In response, Colin, a White sophomore, asked, "The doors open out—how do we barricade?" Nella responded, "Let's improvise," and picked up a chair to jam the legs in the door handles. The loudspeaker voice interrupted her demonstration, abruptly ending their barricade practice, and told the class to proceed to the "lockout" slide.

As the class moved through various slides instructing them on lockdown and lockout procedures, the emotional weight in the room grew heavy. Typically, students in Nella's relaxed and welcoming classroom chatted with each other, made jokes, and occasionally shared funny social media posts. Today, however, several young folks stared off vacantly into the distance. And no one tapped out messages or scrolled through pictures on their phones, quite frankly a surprising sight at a school where young folks, like their peers across the country, treat their mobile devices like an extra appendage. Noting this, Nella broke protocol and stopped reading the slides, instead saying to the silent, subdued students, "All of you have been in lockdowns multiple times in your ten years of education. It can get uncomfortable. You get hungry or have to go to the bathroom." As she expressed these thoughts the loudspeaker voice once again interrupted: "Three minutes for discussion about the lockout." Nella pointedly ignored the voice and its instructions, and instead invited students to share their "lockout stories." Immediately the subdued students perked up, many talking over each other to share a story about seventh grade, when a lockout occurred at the end of the school day and they "had to stay in school forever" and "no one knew what was going on!" After listening to them recount this experience, Nella gently reassured them, "I'll make sure you are safe. I'm the adult in the room." She told them that if they needed to evacuate, they could go to her house across the street where she would make them "a cup of tea."

Continuing to ignore instructions about lockdowns droning from the loudspeaker, Nella opened up a discussion about gun violence, asking, "When was the last mass shooting?" Kelly, a White sopho-more, answered, "At a country bar." Together, Nella and the students counted recent mass shootings and concluded that at least three had occurred since they had last met as a class, two months prior.[3] While the loudspeaker bleated, "Please debrief about lockdown-counter," Nella asked, "What do you notice is consistent in most school shoot-ings?" Beth, a White sophomore, answered, "Usually they are com-mitted by people you know." Jason, a Latino sophomore, added, "They do it during passing periods." Finally Kelly said, "They are mostly male." This discussion of the violence that characterizes American culture and their experiences of schooling was again inter-rupted by the loudspeaker as the voice announced a "two minute warning."

Nella responded by initiating a "check-in" to see how her stu-dents were faring emotionally. She asked the class, "Using one word, how are you feeling?" One by one the students answered, most with a muted affect: Fine, Tired, Okay, Alright, Annoyed, Good, Normal. More than any other word, I heard them say "tired." The young folks in Nella's class did not seem particularly scared, just emotionally ex-hausted, as if dealing with the possibility of deadly violence via PowerPoint was simply too much to take in. This type of depleted emotional response is not limited to these young folks. Research sug-gests that these types of trainings are associated with increased anxiety, fear, and depression for those who participate in them.[4] To counter this emotional depletion, Nella suggested, "Let's end with something happy." Jason, with a burst of energy proposed excitedly, "Play the 'If Animals Were Round' video!" Nella and the rest of the class chuckled as she pulled up the video on YouTube. We all erupted in peals of laughter as dogs, birds, and giraffes rolled across the screen with impossibly round bodies and absurdly short legs.

We needed those rolling animals and that laughter, me included, after what felt like an endless morning of listening to an unemotional voice reading a script over the loudspeaker instructing us to practice what we would do should we experience the unimaginable.[5] The disjuncture between the robotic instructions and the terrifying possibilities for which it was training us left the class somber, exhausted, and, perhaps, dehumanized. It was as if the horror of the events for which these slides were preparing us could be mitigated by a bureaucratic normalization of responses to violence. Nella lovingly responded to this dehumanization with joy, laughter, and the absurdity of rolling animals, exhibiting her characteristic care and concern for young folks.

This training had taken place a few months after another deadly rampage in a high school, a type of rampage that had occurred almost annually since these young folks had been alive.[6] This sort of violence continued to cut short young lives regardless of the presence of armed police on school campuses, the sort of lockdown procedures practiced by these students, and pronouncements of thoughts and prayers about bad guys with guns.[7] Tired of these ineffectual responses to gun violence, some young folks at American worked to organize student participation in a nationwide student walkout, the March for Our Lives, to demand increased gun control measures. The March for Our Lives event was scheduled to take place on the anniversary of the shooting at Parkland High School in Florida, which, at that point, had the distinction of being the deadliest school shooting in US history. The students planned to leave class at 10 a.m. to meet at "the rock" (a large boulder surrounded by wooden benches) in the middle of the quad where they would stand in silence for seventeen minutes, the length of the Parkland violence, to honor the young lives lost. After this silent memorial, they planned to leave campus to join students from Valley and Timber High Schools to march to the courthouse to demand increased gun control in the form of more robust background checks, raising the age of gun ownership, closing legal firearm loopholes, and banning assault weapons, bump stocks, and high-capacity magazines.

These young activists, however, soon encountered pushback to their calls for safer learning environments and public spaces. Principal Walt addressed the planned protest in his weekly email to students writing, "We all know that there is a plan for a walkout on Wednesday. This is an important issue to many, but we as a school cannot take a stand on this issue," concluding with a statement that encapsulated important social and moral currents at American High: "Politics in the school house is not okay." Students were informed that "the school will be marking students unexcused if they go on the march." Additionally, teachers were told that "staff are not to leave their classrooms." Much like the staff members who encountered the limits of "the political" when they knelt in support of Black lives, so too did these young folks run into this boundary, in this case as it limited their capacity to advocate for their own safety.

This message had a chilling effect on students and staff alike, especially because the walkout was taking place during the week of final exams. Alie, a Black senior, said she wanted to participate in the walkout, but "can't because of finals." She had an exam scheduled for the exact time of the event and feared that an unexcused absence would affect her grades, because she had already missed too many classes due to her responsibilities as a member of the soccer and basketball teams. Principal Walt's message about penalties for participating in political action left some students feeling nervous to participate in any part of the walkout, from the silent memorial to the march. As he sat in Nella's class, Terrell, a Black junior, said, "I don't know what to do," shrugging his shoulders helplessly when she asked her students if they were planning to walk out. Similarly frustrated, Carrie, an Asian senior, referred to the messaging students had received, saying, "Supposedly they support us all the way but 'we can't make accommodations.'"

While staff were told to remain in their classrooms, they still found ways to signal solidarity with students. Craig, for instance, wore an orange shirt with white letters that read "I stand with students," as he sat on his planter perch. Sheets of black-and-white stickers from the Oregon Education Association reading "Safe Schools Now" covered his table. Because she was also wearing one of those orange shirts, when Terrell expressed his ambivalence, Nella responded gently to him, "I can't tell you what to do, but you can read my shirt." She also wrote a quote from Winston Churchill on her whiteboard that read "Fear is a reaction. Courage is a decision." Nella said to her class, as students shared frustrations about the lack of adult support, "There are ways to build a system that supports you." Nella is not wrong; there are ways to build systems that support young folks in their demands for safer learning conditions. Over at Valley High, for instance, the principal adjusted the bell schedule so that there was a break at the exact time of the walkout, so students like Alie would not be penalized for missing their final exams.

Regardless of the threatened sanctions, shortly before 10 a.m., multiple students slowly, silently rose out of their seats and left their classrooms, walking to join one hundred or so of their classmates at the rock. At 10:01 silence descended, cell phones tucked away, as students stood for seventeen minutes, memorializing the length of the devastating shooting. Some students held hands, others raised their faces to the sun, and others cried quietly as we honored the young lives lost. Slowly Lain, a tall Native junior with curly brown hair, raised his fist as others followed. At 10:17, he lowered his fist and students shifted, relaxing and moving slightly. A classmate handed him a megaphone and Lain asked the group, "Guys, are you ready to march?!" "YES," the assembled group yelled back. The throng filed out of the school, past the administrators who stood watching from the shadows of the surrounding hallways, to march down the busy thoroughfare toward downtown to join their peers from surrounding schools to demand increased gun control.

The students and the administration at American took two different approaches to safety. The school, following district requirements, deployed a defensive approach, one characterized by a logic of securitization. A securitization logic is one that focuses securing the material and discursive borders of an organization against external, unpredictable, often unclear, and sometimes mysterious threats.[8] Such a logic is a familiar one at this point; it's the same logic that animates those multicolored threat level warnings against terrorist activity that have been a part of our lives since the early 2000s. Securitization processes position dangers to young folks as those outside school walls, normalizes the possibility and perhaps inevitability of this external violence, and, importantly, interrupts the ability to make sense of and process gun violence by obscuring the social conditions that give rise to it.[9]

The young folks, on the other hand, are focusing precisely on some of those social conditions by calling for stricter gun control measures. They have spent years in school learning to crouch behind desks, barricade doors, and evade bullets. Instead of accepting that deadly gun violence may be a normal and inevitable part of everyday life, something to which we may all be subject, these students are demanding systemic change in terms of gun availability and type. The change they demand goes beyond accepting society as it is. Instead it is a step toward changing a violent culture, one that, as the young folks in Nella's class began to point out, is tied to gender norms, gun availability, and, as research shows, a noxious combination of social inequality, a lack of robust state support, and mental health concerns.[10]

The disjuncture between these two approaches to student safety reflects larger dynamics at American High about conceptions of student health, well-being, and safety. As with staff who took a knee against racist violence, young folks who demand action on climate change, or Mark's impassioned plea on behalf of marginalized students, the distinction between these two approaches is a boundary drawn by the concept of "the political." At the heart of this particular invocation of the political is a sense of protection—who needs it and what they need it from. Who is protected, who is not, what they are protected from, and how they are protected from it are questions that go well beyond active shooter training and calls for increased gun control. They are questions that speak to the nature of inequality and how this inequality can be obscured by a regime of kindness.

A politics of protection captures the way dangers, threats, or harms to young folks can be framed as external, random, and individual, not necessarily as preventable, systemic, or related to inequalities. At American High, the biggest dangers to students are often not understood as connected to systemic race, class, gender, or sexual inequities. Instead, issues like gun violence, gender and sexual identity, and mental health are defined and understood in ways that allow little room for connecting them to organizational, systemic, or intersectional inequalities. These understandings get built into the process of schooling itself, obscuring the way that racial, gendered, class, and sexualized concerns are sustained through school rituals, practices, curriculum, physical environments, and programs. The logic of a politics of protection can be seen across contexts at American High, from the reaction to a group of LGBTQ students putting on the first-ever drag show at American to young queer folks' calls for a school environment that isn't just interactionally tolerant, but is organizationally inclusive, to the way that mental health is dealt with such that psychological harms to some students are more readily legible than others. Questions about and answers to who need protection and from what illustrate the limits of a regime of kindness and begin to point toward the need for a politics of care rather than protection as way to address the systemic inequalities that shape the lives of young folks.

The Drag Show

On a cool January evening, the house lights dimmed as the opening beats of Selena Gomez's catchy "Love You Like a Love Song" echoed over the speakers in the American High auditorium. "Madame Music," a Latinx teenage drag queen sporting a short burgundy bob wig and wearing an ill-fitting shiny floor-length purple gown took her position in the center of the stage. As the audience cheered her on, Madame Music danced, lip-synced, and leapt in time to the music. At one point when she briefly tripped, the audience applauded, shouted encouragingly, and then she strutted her way to a big finale, dipping down to one knee and jumping dramatically up and backwards, jazz hands held high with a triumphant smile on her face.

As a rowdy crowd cheered for the American High basketball team in the packed gym across the quad, here in the auditorium, with its rows of red padded seats and black-curtained stage, Queen Quixotic, a professional drag queen of mixed racial descent, and the mother of The House of Ridiculosa, welcomed seventy-five or so friends, family, and school staff to the first-ever drag show at American High School. Statuesque and buxom, clad in a floor-length sparkling red gown with a black stole draped down her back, Queen Quixotic commanded the stage as she explained to a largely first-time drag audience how to behave at a drag show. She told them, "It will be fierce!" before teaching the mostly cisgender and straight audience how to exclaim "Yaass!" and "Work!" by raising one arm and snapping. Laughter erupted as audience members did their best to emulate her. Over the assorted giggles and murmurs, Queen Quixotic laughed along as she continued her routine saying, "I love the sound of my own voice! Applaud for me one more time!" an instruction with which the obedient, if restrained, audience complied. Queen Quixotic even hinted to the show attendees that they might want to appreciate the evening's performers with a dollar or two. She also, however, explained the more serious dimensions of drag saying that "many people think that drag is this," motioning to her outfit and makeup, "a cisgender man doing all this work. But that's not it. Drag is the performance of gender. It's the performance of our identity."[11]

Over the course of the evening, young folks in full faces of makeup and professional drag queens in high heels, sparking jewelry, and big hair entertained the audience as they danced and lip-synched to pop songs like Panic at the Disco's "High Hopes" and Broadway tunes like "A Winter's Ball" from the hit musical *Hamilton*. Two teachers even contributed their talents to the evening—Tom, a White cisgender teacher who donned a blond wig and played his ukulele, and Max, one of the staff members who had knelt during the national anthem. Perhaps not surprisingly, Max's drag performance was no less political than his decision to kneel in front of the entire school as a statement against racist police practices.

For his routine, Max emerged from behind a black curtain dressed as his drag persona, "Pious Patty." Students had wheeled a grand piano onto the stage, along with a divider topped with "stained glass," reminiscent of a church wall. A White student drag king clad in a black leather jacket and jeans sat down at the piano as Billy Joel's classic "Only the Good Die Young" began to play over the sound system. As the music played, Pious Patty walked slowly toward the front of the stage, head down, wearing a demure white dress and clasping her hands as if in prayer. As the song continued, Pious Patty grew increasingly agitated, moving back and forth across the stage as if searching for something. Eventually Patty disappeared behind the divider only to reappear having thrown off the dress and triumphantly sporting jeans and a black T-shirt. This wasn't, however, just any black T-shirt. Across the front it featured the distinctive bold white-and-red logo of the 1990s trans rights activist group, Transsexual Menace. While some of the parents in the crowd may not have recognized this reference, certainly some of the queer students did and the cheers for Max's performance were some of the loudest of the evening.

After a few more performances, the event came to an end. Queen Quixotic praised the young folks who worked hard to put on the show, thanking them for helping to create "a safe future for our gender diverse siblings out there." She commented that society had changed since she had been a teenager, saying, "We would never have had anything like this" at her California high school. Speaking directly to the assembled, beaming members of the Gay/Straight Alliance (GSA), Queen Quixotic exhorted, "Please never stop being yourself. Keeping doing you! See these people here?" motioning to the audience, "They all support you!" clapping in celebration. As she finished speaking, Lady Gaga's anthem, "Born This Way," blared over the loudspeakers as house lights rose and the young folks rushed the stage dancing and waving their arms in delight. Amid this joyful celebration, Nancy, a middle-aged White mom, turned to her son as they walked out of the auditorium and asked with a gentle smile, "Are you inspired?" The members of the GSA ended the night by taking selfies with each other and with the drag queens amid an excited, festive energy more typically exhibited by young folks at school celebrations like homecoming, prom, or football games.

From my seat in the back of the auditorium I watched their delight and joy as tears ran down my cheeks, tears that spill over even now as I write this story. On this night, the ability to bear witness to a queer celebration *in and facilitated by* a school *with* parental support felt like the joyful culmination of years of queer and ally activism by and on behalf of young folks. Not only were these students experiencing an affirming school-based event free from harm and harassment, they were also getting to participate in a specifically queer form of celebration—drag. Drag shows have long been an important part of LGBTQ life, emerging out of collective and often underground practices in marginalized communities.[12] Historically at these gatherings, shows, or balls, men would "cross dress," often an illegal practice then, and participate in a beauty pageant–like event involving dancing, humor, and competition.[13] These festive events became important gatherings, as well as locations of joy and celebration in queer communities.[14] To have a drag show at a school suggests that rather than being merely tolerated, meaningful parts of LGBTQ life and culture can actually be a part of in-school life for young people, something that is especially important in a time of rising transphobia and anti-queer sentiment in some public schools.[15] Putting on this show allowed young folks to participate in a ritual that connects queer generations, allowing them to rejoice in their identities and community in a deeply emotional way, which makes what came next even more notable.

In a regularly scheduled GSA meeting in the weeks following the show, Rose, a young White teacher with turquoise hair who served as an adult advisor to the group, let club members know she needed to share with them some feedback she had received about the show from the district's equity coordinator, Vanessa.[16] According to Rose, Vanessa expressed three specific concerns: First, she worried that the trans students would be the target of public outrage and anger if there was pushback to the drag show. Second, she suggested that the drag show may affect trans students who were not "out," asking what if "people ask to borrow a trans student's wig?" Finally, according to Rose, Vanessa proposed that the drag show itself could be offensive to trans students since drag usually consists of cisgender folks dressing like the "opposite"—here Rose gestured with air quotes—"sex."

As Rose shared these insights, club members repeatedly interrupted her narrative with "what?" and "huh?" before bursting into a group-wide protest. Storm, aka Madam Music, a genderqueer student who had been assigned male at birth and whose "pronouns depend on the day," incredulously shouted out, "BUT I'M TRANS!" Other students in the club, about half of whom identify as trans, gender-fluid, or agender, echoed this claim, while some laughed and shook their heads in confusion at Vanessa's feedback. A few pointed out how supported they felt by the teachers and staff who attended and participated in the show. Nia, a gender-fluid White junior, for instance, commented about how "powerful" it felt for a teacher who was a cisgender White man to sing while dressed in drag to show them support. Certainly, Max's pointedly political drag invoked a legacy of trans activism, something that placed their fun evening event in a larger context of inequality and resistance.

As a queer woman who grew up in the deeply homophobic 1980s and 1990s, who spent years documenting hostile experiences of LG-BTQ youth in public schools, I felt as incredulous as Nia and Storm seemed to feel. How could it be that, at a school where young folks describe each other as "violently accepting people," these students were being told that an event *they* created, an event aimed at celebrating their identities and cultural practices, was one that could *increase* their risk of being bullied or harassed? Thinking back to the joy and elation I witnessed that night among the GSA club members, not to mention my own sense of "Wow, things really have changed!" as the tears rolled down my cheeks, and hearing Queen Quixotic's claim that "we would never have had anything like this" when she was in high school echo in my head, I struggled to make sense of Vanessa's concerns.

On the one hand, Vanessa is right to be worried about gender-based bullying and harassment. This type of aggression continues to be a problem in schools across the country. In fact, almost all LGBTQ students report hearing homophobic or transphobic comments at school.[17] Additionally, over half of LGBTQ students report experiencing gender- or sexuality-based harassment at school.[18] Impassioned and equity-minded school and district staff like Vanessa have certainly made a difference in the lives of queer youth by attending to the problem of school-based gender- and sexuality-related bullying. Shifts in curriculum, programming, and policy have all played an important part in creating a positive school environment for queer youth. In part because of these shifts, during the twenty years that the Gay, Lesbian, Straight Education Network has been surveying LGBTQ youth about their school experiences, reports of gender- and sexuality-based bullying declined fairly steadily.[19] So while gender- and sexuality-related harassment still happens in schools, many school contexts, like that at American, have shifted to become more affirming ones.[20]

In fact, LGBTQ teenagers simply do not report being bullied at American High. As we heard from Leila in chapter 1, "It's, like, oh you're homophobic, that's not cool. You're a bully, that's not cool." Apart from one notoriously homophobic and racist White football player, Brad, whom students—gay and straight alike—tell me about, young folks with whom I spoke didn't report this type of interactional aggression. From straight classmates picking up "ally" stickers as Sarah, a White sophomore and GSA member, handed them out on the Day of Silence, to young folks excitedly high-fiving each other for getting answers right about gender and sexual diversity in Coach Ted's Human Sexuality class, straight and cisgender young folks at American, it seems, not only did not typically bully each other based on gender or sexual identity, they went out of their way to embrace gender and sexual diversity. In fact, early in my time at American, I watched, marveling, as Storm strolled through the school sporting painted nails, a short black dress, and tennis shoes, as well as a face full of stubble, and didn't receive a single double take from others in the bustling student lounge. Their experience was a far cry from the sort of interactional homophobia and transphobia we may often expect to see in high schools. And it wasn't just Storm or other students involved with GSA who reported being free from the sort of homophobic or transphobic harassment we may associate with school hallways; no students reported rampant homophobic or transphobic behavior, nor did I see it during my time at American.

This isn't an accident. Staff at American High have worked to respond to the needs of queer and trans students to feel interactionally included in the school, from the anti-bullying messages adorning the hallways, to the ubiquitous rainbow lanyards hanging around teachers' necks, to Nella's annual invitation to a local trans activist to speak in her class. Some teachers, like Nella, even opened their classes by asking students to share their names and pronouns. While occasionally a student balked at this practice, asking "what" or "huh?," by the end of the term, Nella's gentle corrections (such as suggesting language of "he or him" when a student would say that he used "normal" pronouns) usually resulted in a seamless set of names and pronouns during class introductions. Ms. Bay, for her part, worked purposely to ensure that Trey, a trans student of hers, was referred to by his correct pronouns at school precisely because Trey's parents refused to do so. Knowing how important this kind of affirmation is, Ms. Bay made sure it happened at school so that Trey's identity would be supported somewhere even if not at home. Max, the trans teacher who closed out the drag show, even led a memorable meeting in the GSA where he facilitated a discussion about strategies some trans men might use to urinate standing up, a discussion that elicited both giggles and gratitude from students. The care these teachers exhibited for queer and trans youth went beyond the easy display of lanyards to the everyday work of making school feel welcoming in terms of recognition, stepping in where families could or would not, and imparting embodied knowledge like how to use a bathroom in a gender-affirming way. In this sense, the experiences of youth at American mirror those of roughly half the queer and trans youth in the United States who report that they find their school to be a welcoming and affirming environment, some even more so than their home environments.[21]

This work doesn't go unnoticed by queer youth at American. When Nia, for instance, suggested that club members grade their teachers in terms of "how LGBTQIAA+ affirming" they were, the students, while eating bagged lunches and trying to avoid talking with full mouths, took turns assigning their teachers A's and B's. Not a single teacher earned less than a B from this group on their efforts, a telling sign of how supported these young folks feel at school. This sense of feeling at home at school may be why some trans youth in the GSA extended generosity to the few teachers who did struggle with correct pronoun usage. Marcel, for instance, a White trans cheerleader, said that one of his teachers, Mr. Johnson, "kept misgendering" him because, in Mr. Johnson's words, "I just know so many Marcels who are girls!" The other students in this particular GSA meeting laughed and rolled their eyes because, of course, Marcel is not a common girl's name, a fact that perhaps rendered Mr. Johnson's excuse a bit flimsy. However, the young folks don't seem particularly upset by Mr Johnson's defense, likely because his response was not typical in terms of their experiences at American.

Given this information, Vanessa's concerns about the drag show leading to bullying may seem confusing, if well intentioned. It seems perhaps ironic that fears about transphobic bullying might prevent queer youth from participating in celebrations of queerness, transness, and community. Vanessa's fears, however, echo those fears that animate school safety practices, fears that are at the heart of a politics of protection. That is, fears about bullying itself are tied up in a process of securitization. Around the school, for example, glossy blue signs read "Use SafeOregon to anonymously report bullying, violence, drugs or harm you see or hear about at school." The signs provide a web address, a text/phone contact, an email address, and the name of a downloadable app with which students could "report a tip." These tips end up at the Oregon State Police's "tip line."[22] That is, bullying itself is conceived of as a problem of securitization, one that gets routed through the police. Even the language of "tip reporting" mirrors the messaging found in anti-terrorism campaigns in public spaces and on government websites. Bullying, in other words, is treated as a threat best dealt with defensively and through external and perhaps carceral measures, not one related to inequalities that may best be responded to through education, activism, and rituals of belonging like the drag show.

Assumptions about the problem of peer-based bullying being a bigger problem for trans youth than a lack of opportunities to participate in queer rituals relies on conceptions of trans youth, what their needs are, and the sorts of things they need protection from in a way that is divorced from the lived realities of young folks at American High.[23] These assumptions about trans students and their needs flatten out the complexities of the lives of trans young folks. Though often well-intentioned, they may emerge out of research on the experiences of trans adults who came of age in a different social, medical, and mental health context, something scholar Joe Latham describes as a "trans singularity."[24] It is true that trans youth need to be protected from interactional aggression like bullying and name-calling, but they also need to be able to participate in queer culture and rituals. When listening to queer young folks at American talk about their needs, what becomes evident is that these needs have as much, if not more so, to do with organizational issues than with the sort of interactional aggression upon which adults often focus. While queer young folks at American did not report bullying, forced outing, or experiencing peer victimization, they did repeatedly express frustration with school policies and infrastructure regarding sexuality and gender identity, a frustration that suggests the limits of a politics-of-protection approach to student needs, one that positions these needs as individual and interactional, not as organizational and systemic.

Queering Schools

While queer young folks felt quite at home among their peers and supported by their teachers at American, they did not feel like the school was as organizationally inclusive as it was interactionally inclusive. That is, while these young folks expressed little concern about being bullied or harassed, they provided extensive critique of the way the curriculum, policy, and physical infrastructure of the school marginalized LGBTQ young folks. They specifically highlighted sex education, policies governing queer events and identities, and the gendered nature of bathrooms as ways that gendered and sexual inequality are physically and systemically built into the school itself.

Perhaps unsurprisingly, given that Coach Ted had little formal training in teaching sexual health, LGBTQ students did not always feel like their experiences and identities were fully reflected in the Human Sexuality curriculum. For all the enthusiasm he brought to teaching Human Sexuality, Coach Ted simply did not know enough about gender and sexual diversity to educate students sufficiently. After several missteps, such as continuing to refer to polyamory as polygamy (a misstep that generated friendly laughter from a few of his students), Coach Ted said to his class, "I was not adequately equipped to teach you about sexual orientation." To solve this problem, Sarah, a White asexual-identified student and member of the GSA, volunteered to teach a class on sexual and gender identity. On the day Sarah was slated to teach the class, she told the students, "Coach Ted was having trouble with that so that's why I'm here. I'm in GSA and I'm gay myself. I've also tried to educate myself on this."

Standing in front of the white board, with long brown hair, glasses, and wearing a purple knit sweater, Sarah had the class review the mantras they had learned so far—sexual orientation: "Who you go to bed with!" a student excitedly volunteered; and gender: "Who you go to bed as!" said another. She began to lead the class through a discussion of sexual identity in general. With a detailed PowerPoint, Sarah explained what LGBTQ stands for, saying, "In the eighties there was a movement to reclaim the word queer." In her lesson,

Sarah introduced students to a wide range of sexual identities, including pansexual, graysexual, two spirit, and demisexual. She concluded the class by having the students play a game in which each student held a slip of paper on their forehead that listed a sexual identity. They could not see the identity listed on paper but their classmates could. Each student had to ask yes or no questions of their classmates until they figured out what identity was printed on their paper. Students earnestly played the game, laughing and cheering when they guessed the correct answers. For the final fifteen minutes of class, the room was a cacophony of voices as students asked their tablemates things like "Do I like dudes?" or "Do I experience same-gender attraction?" and then cheering and saying, "Dude, I can't believe I got one right. That's so sick!" after they yelled out answers like "lesbian!" or "polysexual!"

Even though Coach Ted was not able to teach about sexual identity in a comprehensive way, queer youth at American do not seem frustrated with him personally. Instead, they credit him, as they do the teachers who struggle with pronouns, with trying. As Adell, a White bisexual junior, pointed out, Coach Ted may not be an expert in LGBTQ issues, but "he's *trying*," a sentiment followed by nods of affirmation from other students at the GSA meeting in which she made the comment. While queer youth should not bear the burden of teaching their classmates about sexual identity, when young folks sense that a teacher has given it a good-faith try, such a burden may feel like a solution to an organizational problem rather than to a personal failing on the part of a teacher.

LGBTQ youth at American point to similar sorts of systemic issues facing gender- and sexual-minority youth there. For instance, the only time queer young folks shared worries about the possibility of involuntary outing, one of the concerns expressed by Vanessa, the risk of outing was directly related to school policy. Specifically, GSA members pointed out a policy that required a signed parental permission slip to attend Pink Prom. Pink Proms (or variations of them) emerged in the early 2000s as a way to provide an affirming space where LGBTQ students could celebrate and dance free from harassment.[25] Unlike the traditional proms at area high schools—an end-of-the-year school-sponsored formal dance for juniors and seniors typically held at a nearby hotel or event center—the Pink Prom is sponsored by multiple schools. Also, unlike the typical prom, and the focus of the GSA members' grievance, is that Pink Prom requires a signed parental permission slip for attendance. GSA members pointed out that this policy could involuntarily out students to their parents and that students may not go to the prom because they fear their parents' reactions to such an event.

The Pink Prom policy wasn't the only one flagged by GSA participants as needing updating. Members of the GSA spent several meetings reviewing the twenty-five-page-long district policy document for "Gender Nonconforming Students." In each meeting they put the policy up on a doc cam, darkened the room, and annotated it with the goal of sending a set of comments on it to the district leadership. Ave, the White senior president of the GSA, led the group in an initial discussion of the policy, saying it was "oddly dated" for something that had been written only two years prior. As an example, Matt a White junior, pointed out the repeated use of "the phrase 'transgendered,'" to which Greta replied, "It's not a verb!" Club members talked over each other to laughingly recall and jokingly demonstrate how they enacted "transgenderedness." Ave, to illustrate, dangled her arm awkwardly swinging it back and forth over the small desk she was sitting at to show how she "transgendered," saying, "We decided it was this," as the group laughed. Ave asked, of the language used throughout the document, "What does 'gender nonconforming' even mean?" Marcel, imitating a teacher by speaking in a robotic stilted voice, answered, "You are wearing a men's T-shirt today—are you going by them/they pronouns?" Other group members giggled and murmured in support. Brett, in a similar imitative voice, asked, "You play sports—are you a man?" Greta chimed in, "Like, would they say a transboy is engaging in gender nonconforming behavior if he's doing 'boy' behavior?" Finally Ave claimed, "They are confusing behavior with identity."

Some of the points the students raise represent shifting understandings about gender and identity. As they point out, language around gender identity and expression has shifted rapidly in the years before and since the policy had been written, such that the phrase "transgenderedness" seems a bit incomprehensible to them. Similarly the students highlight that for them, gender is about identity, not behavior. One *claims* a gender identity; it's not something imputed by others based on someone's behavior, clothes, or habits. That is, one may appear to an observer, based on clothing or comportment, to be a girl, but clothing or comportment doesn't make one a girl. For these young folks, only that person's identification can make them a girl. This understanding of gender identity makes some of the district policy, focused as it is on behavior and presentation, a bit confusing and perhaps outdated to these students. As Ave asked, "What does 'gender nonconforming' even mean?" While this term has been used fairly widely to address trans youth, the young folks in the GSA question whether there even should exist a set of gender norms to which they should be conforming. In their analysis, to call something "gender conforming" is, in itself, a way of enforcing a problematic and stereotypical distinction between boys and girls. As both Marcel and Brett point out, T-shirt–wearing and sports-playing does not render one a particular gender. The students conclude their critique of the document with an analysis of the phrases "transboy" and "transgirl" throughout the text. For them transboys are *boys* and transgirls are *girls* and should be treated and referred to as such. The club sent their finished critique to the district administration. However, when I checked to see if the guidelines had been updated as I wrote this book, they had not.

The third concern raised by members of the GSA, in addition to the Pink Prom permission slip and conceptions of trans youth in district policy, had to do with "the bathroom problem"[26] at American High. Like other schools in the district, American has a designated gender-neutral bathroom. Brett and Marcel, however, both trans, highlight the problems they face using the only gender-neutral bathroom at the school. Brett said, "I don't use it because there's only one stall . . ." The gender-neutral restroom is a repurposed men's staff bathroom, sitting just across the hallway from the women's staff bathroom in the office at the front of the school. Unlike any other bathroom in the school, including the women's staff bathroom only several feet away, the gender-neutral bathroom sports a prominent sign on the door with words and images in vibrant colors and bold letters describing the rules for using this bathroom. A clock on the sign denotes a time limit and the words state that only one person is allowed in the bathroom at a time. Because of these regulations, the line to use this bathroom frequently stretches down the hallway between classes. The strict rules, the out-of-the-way location, and the long wait time mean that young folks often avoid using this bathroom.

Brett and Marcel both say they have used the boys' bathrooms at the school, but this practice is fraught. Brett laughed while explaining his history with using the boys' bathroom. "The only time I used the boys bathroom it was hilarious. Oh my god, they were in there hiding," laughing and making motions like the boys were trying to hide their eyes. This is as close as young folks came in terms of describing transphobic bullying at American. Marcel, the only boy on the cheerleading squad, described similar reactions to his bathroom use. "If I have to do my business during [cheerleading] practices I usually just go in the guy's bathroom." The boys' bathroom is located on the opposite side of the gym from the girls' bathroom, such that as he exited it one afternoon during practice, another cheerleader asked suspiciously, "Where were you?" to which Marcel responded, using a "no duh" tone, "The bathroom." While neither described this sort of behavior as transphobic or as harassment, such behavior did mark their gender identities in ways that seemed, perhaps, less than optimal. However, the young folks suggest not that their classmates be dealt with as bullies, but that the school respond with an organizational solution: additional and more-accessible gender-inclusive bathrooms. That is, to the extent that transphobic bullying is experienced at American High, it grows out of policy and organizational concerns, not out of the cruelty of classmates.

During these discussions students shared stories they have heard about other schools that seemed to have similar bathroom problems. They mention a middle school that has a gender-neutral bathroom, but it's usually locked, and a school where students have to request a key from a staff member to use the bathroom. Nia suggested, however, that these bathroom issues are not inevitable, referring to another middle school that has "an easily accessible bathroom. It was just in the middle of a hallway. It was nice." When the district requested students, staff, and community members provide feedback about building priorities to help focus plans for future school buildings, the GSA students offered pointed commentary about preventing these "bathroom problems" in new buildings. In their statement they suggested that gender-neutral bathrooms need to be accessible and have more than one stall, and there needs to be more than one at a school. At the end of the discussion Sarah added, "They have to have somewhere to put pads and tampons!" Brett agreed, saying, they need to have receptacles "inside the stall" because "you can't do anything with period stuff in the guy's bathroom." Marcel, however, in thinking about the administrators' responses to their suggestions, commented that "people will freak out about multiple-occupancy gender-neutral bathrooms."

While we don't know what the administration will or won't do, Marcel was picking up on something important. Some schools, and this is especially true of Oregon schools, have made great strides toward welcoming trans students, but a binary logic of gender still governs the built environment in most schools. That is, there are still boys' and girls' bathrooms, boys' and girls' locker rooms, boys' and girls' sports teams. This means that students, cis or trans, who fall neatly into the categories of boy or girl can be fairly easily incorporated and accommodated, but for students who are between or without gender or who push for a built environment that reflects something other than a binary understanding of gender, things become more complicated in a way that reveals the gendered and sexualized nature of the organization, a gendered nature that goes beyond concerns over bullying and harassment and is built into the school itself.

It is clear that most of the needs LGBTQ students have about interactional acceptance are met by the leadership, staff, and students at American High School. While these social needs of queer young folks are recognizable, the organizational claims to be included as full organizational actors are less so. The biggest challenges for these students were not those imagined by school representatives—bullying and forcible outing by peers. Rather, the students expressed concerns with formal policies and school infrastructure. During my time with them, these young folks made concrete requests of the school—to change and update their policies about gender, to make it easier for students of all genders to experience bodily integrity, and to change rules governing participation in meaningful rituals that might expose sexual- and gender-minority students to increased risk. What they did not talk about or suggest was that the school increase attention to homophobic or transphobic bullying. Apart from some awkward moments in the boys' bathroom or with girl cheerleaders, both of which trans students laughed off, they simply did not report much interactional aggression.[27] And when they did experience this aggression it was tied to school organization and policy.

This mismatch between the assumptions about what young folks need protection from and what *they* say they need protection from is based on a particular conception of who a trans student is and what their needs are, needs that are seemingly divorced from the legacy of play, celebration, and irreverence that historically characterized queer culture. An imagined trans youth is legible in this logic, but the actual queer young people who are part of this drag show, celebrating transgression and queerness, are not. In this logic a trans student is always a potential victim who lives under the threat of interactional aggression from other students. An imagined trans youth is protected against what are considered to be the biggest threats—bullying and interactional aggression—but are not easily included in the life of the organization itself.

The solution offered to protect against the presumed threats facing these students is not to fix these systemic exclusions; rather it is a form of what Joyce Bell and Douglas Hartmann call "happy talk." Happy talk is an organizational response that "appears to engage and even celebrate differences, yet does not grasp the social inequities that accompany them."[28] Rainbow lanyards and anti-bullying concerns become forms of happy talk when attendant organizational changes—like policy, curriculum, and infrastructure—are not addressed. The focus of a politics of protection on solutions like "happy talk" and securitized responses to student safety means that when things like mental health are addressed at American High, they are addressed in ways that are similarly divorced from some forms of systemic inequality.

You Are Loved

From Mental Health Awareness Month events such as lunchtime tai chi and yoga, to chalked affirmations throughout the school like "you are loved" and "see a counselor," to those notes of positive affirmations in the girls' bathroom, concern over mental health permeates everyday life at American High. Such an approach is not without cause. Certainly we have evidence that mental health challenges are on the rise among American youth.[29] Schools, in fact, are one of the primary providers of mental health resources for young people.[30] As part of this attention to mental health, during my time at American, staff, representatives from county public health, and a select group of students joined together to form a "Teen Action Committee" (TAC) to focus on mental health promotion, as well as health disparities, social justice, and equity. The story of how mental health came to be conceptualized in TAC suggests that while queer youth are framed as uniquely vulnerable to mental health challenges caused by homophobic or transphobic bullying, youth of color are framed as uniquely *invulnerable* to mental health challenges caused by systemic racism. The logic of a politics of protection, in this sense, is a racialized one, involving seemingly race-neutral notions of harm focused on gun violence, transphobia, and homophobia that obscure the way systemic racism threatens the safety of students of color.

On a foggy winter afternoon, a racially diverse group of fifteen students (give or take the few who wandered in late and left early), all members of Teen Action Committee, settled around a set of tables with Craig, Luis (an assistant principal of Chinese descent), and Carrie and Hailey (two White representatives from county public health). As folks around the table introduced themselves with their name and grade, Sarah, the GSA member who had taught the Human Sexuality class, noticed that the participants were not mentioning their pronouns. She suggested that everyone introduce themselves again, this time with pronouns. After covering the ground rules for the meeting, such as "discomfort is a part of learning," and "assume best intentions," the assembled group began to review their task for the previous month: recording microaggressions they witnessed or to which they were subject. Before they went around the room to share highlights from their microaggression diaries, Craig reminded everyone about the definition of microaggressions, saying that they are "verbal comments or behavior which is a racial insult." The goal of documenting these microaggressions was to lay the foundation for a training session for teachers about microaggressions at an upcoming teacher training day.

After Craig's reminder, the group took turns reading the stories of microaggressions they had documented. Laird, a White boy, said that as he dined at a Japanese restaurant with his grandmother, she repeatedly referred to "the orient." When Jill, another White group member, asked, "What's wrong with that?" Craig explained that the "orient" is "a thing and not a person." Laird added that the term is "super outdated" and so "we shouldn't use it." Lain, who had led the March for Our Lives walkout, flipped through several pages in his notebook, saying he took notes at a Black Student Union (BSU) meeting where "every single person shared a microaggression." Lain explained that it "was really powerful" and that "no one intervened in any of the stories they told." After Lain's comments, Isaac, a White boy, manually counted on his fingers the microaggressions he had documented over the previous month, saying, "one two three . . . ," as he moved his hand down the page, ultimately ending at "twenty-three." Isla, a Latina student, recounted her experience at a football game a few weeks prior against the neighboring hyper-white school, Crossville High. She watched as several White boys yelled at a Latino boy wearing a backpack, mocking him, saying, "Are you about to go cross the border with that backpack?!" Isla said, "But it wasn't funny at all because I'm Mexican." Terrell, a Black junior, shared that when he told a friend about his family's holiday plans, the friend responded with a microaggression. Terrell explained, "I come from a big eating family. We like to eat. We are focused on food!" When the White friend asked him what they cooked for Thanksgiving, Terrell said he listed off the "regular stuff," like sweet potatoes, turkey, cranberries, and "fried chicken." The friend responded, "Oh, you guys are known for eating that." "I know he was joking . . ." Terrell said, trailing off as gasps echoed around the room.

After several more stories, Anna, whom we met earlier in chapter 1, concluded the discussion by sharing a story about her hair. Anna said she has a "different hair style every other week," but she receives the most comments on it when it is styled like it is the day of the meeting, rising an inch or so above a wide green band that sits at her hairline. She commented, ruefully shaking her head, "The amount of people who have touched my hair when it looks like this . . ." Anna said that most days she rides the bus and chats with the regular driver on her route. Typically he comments on her hair and she says, "thanks." But on this particular day, he said, "Nice hair. Is that yours? Did you steal it?" Again, gasps echoed around the room as Anna continued, "it's not like there's anywhere in Evergreen I could steal it from in the first place!" Her comment referred to the fact that Evergreen is such a White town that Black hair products, care, and wigs are not easy to come by. At that time the town had only two salons that specialized in Black hair.

While the assignment had been to record microaggressions about race, a few group members shared examples of microaggressions that focused on sexuality or gender. Rachel, a White student, for instance, looked through her journal to read about an interaction she recorded with a teacher who repeatedly referred to her as "bossy" when she had some suggestions about an assignment. She said he called her bossy so frequently that she began to question herself, thinking, "Should I even ask this question?" Sarah shared,

"I'm asexual, which means I'm not sexually attracted to anyone." Frustratingly for her, she explained that her family members often make comments like "you have a crush, you must!" and repeatedly ask her questions about dating. Sarah reflected, "I hate it when someone asks me, are you dating someone?" Krisha, a White student, shared exasperating discussions with her family in which they insisted that "they/them" pronouns are "grammatically incorrect" even though she told them, incredulously throwing her hands up, "No, it's not—it's just transphobia!" as other students laughed and nodded in agreement.

After the club members read the stories they had recorded, the group moved to a discussion about the form the microaggression training could take. Some suggested a panel, others a video, and some a question-and-answer session. Laird commented that he "would love to have a discussion about mental health." Sarah added, "Especially right now." Jill reached into her backpack to pull out a paper she wrote on suicide, saying, "Suicide rates are high." Rachel agreed, saying, "It's even worse among trans people. They are twice as likely to commit suicide." Hailey, one of the public health representatives, explained that she had just attended a conference panel on how best to support trans students where she learned "if you're at a school where people use your preferred pronouns" that serves as a protective factor against suicide. Over the course of these comments, the panel turned from one that had been initially focused on racial microaggressions to one addressing the mental health of trans youth.

This move was part of a larger shift in TAC in which issues of racial inequality were increasingly sidelined in favor of a focus on issues facing queer youth. According to Cassia, the president of the Black Student Union and a former member of TAC, the direction that the microaggression discussion took was not unusual. At some point, she told me, most discussions would get "turned around to be like how

LGBT people are not found anywhere in the history book." When TAC started the microaggression project, this dynamic intensified. Cassia said that as the microaggression discussion continued over several weeks, "Our examples felt out of place. Like, we were talking about maybe you should teach your kids not to say the 'n-word' or touch your hair or something like that. Maybe you should teach your kids that we're not animals. You don't walk up to a person with straight hair and say, 'Hey, can I run my fingers through your hair?' You don't do that. So, teach your kids to not do that to anybody at all. Ever." But, Cassia said, when she or another student of color would raise examples of microaggressions and racial inequality, a discussion about race wouldn't ensue. Instead, the conversation would return to the topics of sexuality or gender. As a result Cassia found herself asking, "Should we go from talking about lesbian people?" Sometimes she and other students of color "would not talk for a while," because "when we were talking about slavery and stuff, it kind of felt like out of place," even though as Cassia pointed out "slavery affected people. People's kids got sold right in front of their eyes!"

Eventually, Cassia said of sexuality and gender, "that's all we started talking about." Concerns over gender and sexuality eclipsed concerns about racial inequality and became the focus of the group. As a result, Cassia declined to go on a field trip with the TAC because she felt like "the students-of-color concerns aren't being represented. It seems like all the TAC wants to focus on is sexuality." Over the course of a year, Latina/x/o, Asian, Pacific Islander, Native, and Black students gradually left the Teen Action Committee, as did the Black and Asian staff members, like Craig and Luis. As Craig told me, "We don't like the direction it's taking . . . it's different than what we thought it would be." By the end of the year, White students and leaders populated TAC meetings, which had moved fully to a "health" focus, a focus that seems to more easily encompass some social problems than others.

The story of LGBTQ youth is one that is often told through the lens of mental health. It's a story of suicide hotlines, It Gets Better campaigns, and Days of Silence. It's a story of a "love is love" approach to inequality where bullying and name-calling are seen as the problems and kindness and acceptance are the solutions. Certainly we have evidence that queer youth suffer disproportionately from mental health challenges.[31] However, as the queer youth at American suggest, the focus of this narrative on mental health can, in part, elide young people's calls for systemic organizational inclusion through policy, curriculum, and infrastructure. A focus on the mental health of queer youth is important, but such a focus needs to both include the racialized and classed dimensions of young people's lives as well as the policy and organizational context that shapes mental health.

Unlike the story of LGBTQ youth, the story of youth of color is not one that is typically told through a lens of mental health. We don't have nationwide suicide hotlines, It Gets Better campaigns, or Days of Silence dedicated to youth of color. However, plenty of evidence documents the mental health toll exacted by racism, racial inequality, and racist violence.[32] Youth of color are often not understood in mainstream mental health discussions as being at higher risk for suicide or bullying victimization, the way queer youth are, even as suicide rates for Black youth, specifically, are rising dramatically.[33] This is true even in the face of data that suggest that mental health challenges may be more common among trans youth of color than they are among White trans youth.[34] Much like the way health professionals minimize, dismiss, or do not take seriously the physical health concerns of Black folks, so too do they, like the members of the TAC, downplay their mental health concerns.[35] As such, the mental health challenges of students of color in TAC, as well as the connection of these challenges to systemic racism, are not addressed, even as research suggests that mental health itself should be seen as a racial-justice issue.[36]

Mental health concerns are tied to and shaped by social context.[37] As young people's experience in the TAC suggests, however, some aspects of social context are more readily visible as mental health issues—like the effects of transphobia, for instance. As queer students' critiques of policy and school infrastructure indicate, however, this visibility may, perhaps, cloud other more systemic issues they face, ones that are codified organizationally. Conversely, a focus on mental health as a locus of harm may also render some students' experiences of marginalization less visible if those experiences have not historically been considered mental health issues. Mental health, in this context, is treated as an individual problem, one that is divorced from larger systemic issues, like racial inequality. This approach to mental health positions some youth as in need and worthy of protection while excluding others from this protection. In this sense, the politics-of-protection logic prevents concerns from students of color about historical and contemporary racial inequality from being addressed in the Teen Action Committee in the same way that it prevents queer young folks from being heard regarding organizational inclusion. In the same way a politics-of-protection logic prevents queer young folks from being heard regarding organizational inclusion, it also prevents concerns from students of color about historical and contemporary racial inequality from being addressed.

Building Systems That Support Youth

As Nella gently said to her students who struggled to decide whether or not to demonstrate for increased gun control, "It is possible to build systems to support you." Regardless of the care demonstrated by individual staff members like Craig, Nella, Ms. Bay, and Coach Ted, the systems in place at American High do not yet fully support youth. This isn't because bad people run the school or the district; it's because of logics about where harm is located and how to respond to that harm. An approach informed by a politics of protection may reflect deep concern for students and well-being, but that concern is rooted in individualist notions of harm and not systemic inequalities in ways that exclude patterned and intersectional dimensions of harm and health. This means that students are prepared for defending against a murderous massacre, but are not allowed to engage in collective action for gun safety. It means that American High has no room for hate, but questions a drag show in the name of bullying prevention. It means that programs related to mental health will focus intently on gendered and sexualized dimensions of wellness while ignoring the racialized dimensions of mental health.

In this sense, the politics of protection involve what Sarah Ahmed calls "stranger making," a process by which "some more than others will be at home in institutions that assume certain bodies as their norm."[38] Stranger-making at American emerges out of an organizational logic that locates harm in interactional dangers rather than in systemic ones, an approach that recognizes a bullied trans student but perhaps makes strangers of trans students who advocate for organizational inclusion, or makes strangers of students of color who advocate for mental health programming that takes racial justice into account. This stranger-making isn't just about individual decisions; it's also about funding. Current conceptions of school safety are nested in decades of funding programs to make schools safer through implementing surveillance systems, security equipment, fencing, alarms, the presence of armed police officers, and militarized training.[39] Initiatives in multiple states continue to link mental health, bullying, school violence, and suicide concerns under a securitized approach to school safety, often routing them through carceral structures like the police. However, some studies suggest that securitized approaches do little to keep students safe and may, in fact, erode the sort of social trust that research indicates can make a school a safe place to be.[40]

If part of being in a community means avoiding politics to maintain the existence of the community, then solving problems through strategies of securitization, anti-bullying, and individualized notions of mental health are all ways to maintain community.[41] Participation in queer traditions, in student activism demanding policy changes, or in linking mental health to systemic racial inequalities become, in this approach, political. A securitization approach combined with an individualistic mental health approach allows some dangers to be seen and dealt with while marginalizing others. This means that things that are easily recognizable as bullying, such as transphobia, are translatable into action, whereas organizational issues like bathrooms or policy or society-wide issues like systemic racism are rendered less visible.

The politics of protection entails framing particular groups of students and their imagined needs in ways that are informed by an anti-bullying logic and focuses on individual qualities in a way that forecloses the addressing of other student needs that may challenge the organizational ordering of gendered, sexualized, raced, and classed power at the school. The rest of this book shows how this happens in terms of race, class, gender, sexuality, and their intersections. It documents the way that racism is framed as an individual issue of love and kindness, how similar expectations of kindness hinder responses to gendered inequalities, and how individual and emotional understandings of inequalities can benefit already privileged students while making that benefit look like merit. The role of emotions like love and kindness in the process of stranger-making at American High comes to the fore when students and some staff negotiate issues of racial inequality at a Martin Luther King Jr. assembly, in their classrooms, and as they attempt to put on a Black Lives Matter display, all events that highlight what happens when individual feelings are framed as solutions to inequality.

3   *Love and Justice at American High*

The annual assembly in honor of Martin Luther King Jr. Day started off like many other assemblies at American. Students and teachers filed into the auditorium, talking quietly as they made their way down the rows of red upholstered seats to sit with their classmates. Craig took his position center stage to lead the student body in a call and response, as he frequently did at all school gatherings. "A!" he boomed, as the students shouted back "H!" "S!" After a few rounds of this back and forth, Craig ended the ritual saying, "Two claps," as he clapped rhythmically until the students clapped along with him, a practice that had the effect of calming the chitchat and focusing the audience.[1]

During Craig's gathering ritual, however, something happened that roiled the school community for weeks to come. As students and teachers filed in, several students broke from their classmates and walked to the front row of auditorium seats. Each member of this breakaway group wore a bright red baseball cap sporting the now familiar white letters reading "Make America Great Again." This group of students wearing MAGA hats sat down in the middle of the row and remained there for the rest of the assembly. The message on their hats invoked a historic time, with a promise to restore an apparently broken nation by returning it to that imagined time. This promise, however, may have felt more like a threat to the mostly Black, Asian, Latina/x/o, and Pacific Islander young folks on stage honoring a civil rights leader slain in one of these prior and, according to these hats, better times.[2]

Craig continued to welcome the audience, encouraging everyone to "listen with the intent to learn" as Charity and Caitlin, two representatives from the Black Student Union, joined him on stage. After thanking him for his leadership, they announced that through "social justice and equality, the spirit of Dr. King lives in us today." The almost entirely White Show Choir performed the Black National Anthem, "Lift Every Voice and Sing," and the band played "Amazing Grace," before the other members of the BSU joined Charity and Caitlin. The members stood shoulder to shoulder facing the audience, each holding a sign completing the prompt "We need Martin Luther King Day because . . ."

Caitlin walked down the line as they read their answers into a microphone. Some of these answers, like Noriah's, highlighted historical racism, "Interracial marriages were illegal in the US until 1967." Others, like Isaac's, "Our president expresses and condones racism," called attention to the increasing visibility and expression of overt racism during the Trump presidency, the very presidency supported by the front row hat wearers. Cassia's sign called attention to the expression of overt racism in the town of Evergreen itself, "People don't want immigrant students to be educated in our district." Her sign referenced an event that had happened few weeks prior. Calling them a form of "indoctrination," a custodian had torn down posters hanging in a local elementary school that stated, "Immigrants welcome here." Joseph's sign, "People take pride in their confederate flags in our community," underscored the existence of local racism by calling attention to the fact that even in a town like Evergreen, a town with "Be Kind" signs dotting front lawns, symbols lauding a racist past are not a thing of that past. In fact when I met Charity and her mother a few weeks later for an interview at a local bubble tea shop, we all fell silent as a giant confederate flag whipped in the wind behind a white truck as it sped down the street. As Noriah, Isaac, Joseph, Cassia, and Charity read these statements into the microphone, Nella quietly moved to the center aisle of the auditorium and dropped to one knee, while she raised her right hand in a fist, and looked directly at the students on stage with a proud, fierce smile on her face.

When the BSU students exited the stage, Nella moved back to her seat and a slideshow began, with slides featuring images of mostly White staff and students holding up signs completing the same prompt. However, many of these answers had a decidedly different tenor, focusing less on historical and contemporary racism and more on feelings of love and connection. Kindra, for instance, held up a sign that read "We all have the same heart" while Jennifer held one stating, "My family and friends are my world." Kingston's sign more directly related to race, "My true colors shine from within," but still avoided referencing the racial disparities.[3] Rather than addressing legal inequality or overt expressions of racism, these signs invoked a sense of kindness and acceptance that could have been equally appropriate in an assembly on any other topic as they were in an assembly focusing on civil rights and racial inequality.

Over the following hour, student affinity groups like the Asian Club, the Pacific Islander Club, Latinos Unidos, the GSA, and the Climate Action Club gave a series of presentations that echoed the BSU's emphasis on intensified experiences of and responses to racism.[4] Students representing Latinos Unidos, for example, played a video entitled "Children From Latino Families Reveal the Sacrifices Their Parents Made," and shared stories about their own parents waking up before sunrise to put in long days of work for less than optimal pay, while still making time to teach their children a new language. Zoe described her parents as "great American role models," while Valentina said, gratefully, "They taught us how to be good

American citizens." Miranda called attention to the political context of these sacrifices, telling the audience that they watched their parents work incredibly hard, but, "Meanwhile we have a president who labels us." Presumably Miranda's comment denoted President Trump's repeated use of terms like "thugs" and "animals" to refer to people of Latina/x/o descent. After multiple presentations like this, the assembly closed with a video of Dr. King's "I Have a Dream" speech and a choral rendition of U2's anthem about civil rights, "In the Name of Love."

After the assembly, students spoke to me with anger, sadness, and outrage about the hat-wearers. Amelia, a White junior, said, "I was just stewing with anger when that happened. So much disrespect. It was just disturbing." Angelina, a Latina senior, agreed: "All four of them walked in and then sat in the front. But it's not right at all. No student should be presenting and giving something meaningful and then people just come in and make them feel like it doesn't matter. It's not right for them to do that." She told me that when she saw the hats, "I was so shook. This girl even cried in LSU [Latinos Unidos or Latino Student Union], because it should never be like that." Nicole, a Pacific Islander junior, described the hats as "a silent microaggression . . . They don't have to say anything. You can just read the words on their hat." Craig pointedly placed this racist symbolism in historical context as he said to me during one of our morning planter chats, "They used to wear white hoods, but now . . . ," gesturing toward his head, he trailed off.

In the days that follow the assembly, students, staff, and parents lamented a lack of any public response regarding the hats by the administration. Nicole worried that a lack of response would only embolden this sort of sentiment: "It just makes them know that it's okay to do it again. I just don't think that should be allowed." Angelina noted that the school's inaction might also discourage students targeted by this sort of behavior, saying, "They don't want to speak up about it anymore. They basically deal with it themselves." The public silence about the hats led some to question the shared perception of American High as a distinctly accepting place. As Amelia processed the event, she mused, "Maybe it's like we're not as open as we think we are. Maybe we have this idea that American is this great place, where kids can be who they want and express what they want to express. But maybe inside we're actually fighting the same battles as Timber High and fighting the same battles as Valley High."

This silence about the MAGA hats symbolizes a more general approach to racial inequality at American High. When talking about the assembly and the silence that followed, Lisa, a White parent of two American students, suggested that the lack of a public response had to do with conceptions of diversity itself at American. As Lisa explained, "It turns into this weird, well, you have to honor my diversity of being a MAGA person. You're the hater if you don't want me to wear this hat in your face." Diversity, in this sense, becomes less about purposeful inclusion of historically excluded groups of people and becomes quite simply about a celebration, or at least a tolerance, of difference. Difference itself becomes a valuable social goal, whether or not that difference has historically been rooted in, shaped by, or been given rise to by inequality. We might think of this type of diversity, a diversity that celebrates difference regardless of power differentials or inequality, as a benign diversity.

A benign diversity approach positions diversity as a cultural value, but limits the linking of diversity to inequality, instead framing something like racism as an individual problem of offense or hate rather than a form of systemic exclusion and domination, exclusion and domination that benefits White people and consolidates racialized power. A benign diversity approach emphasizes kindness and acceptance as solutions to racial inequality rather than justice or equity. The signs, for instance, suggesting that Martin Luther King Jr. Day is necessary because of "heart," "friends," "family," and because one's "true colors shine from within" exemplify the way positive emotions come to be a stand in for justice or equality. These emotions are ones that sociologist Eduardo Bonilla-Silva calls "racialized emotions" or those emotions that sustain racial inequality.[5]

It may be tempting to think about racialized emotions in terms of hate or rage, emotions that we associate with racist beliefs or practices, but as Bonilla-Silva points out, these emotions don't necessarily need to be negative. In fact, racialized emotions at American High suggest that a focus on love and kindness can cloud the existence and persistence of racial inequality while seeming to address it. This regime of kindness— from signs about hate, to interpersonal niceness, to positive messages on a bathroom poster, to dictates about politeness that include avoiding politics—may be something that allows White folks to feel like they are addressing racial inequality while simultaneously permitting them to avoid the hard work of actually interrupting racial inequality, interruptions that may come at a cost to them.

Benign diversity and racialized emotions are part of what scholar Sarah Mayorga-Gallo calls a "diversity ideology," an ideology that "creates space for minor acknowledgment of structural inequality in the abstract" but "psychologically and materially protects whites and white organizations from discussions of racial inequality."[6] A diversity ideology allows people to seem to address racial inequality but also avoid grappling with what it would mean to solve inequality personally, organizationally, and socially. A diversity ideology, in other words, may create room for an MLK assembly, but stop short of being able to address the effect of a symbol with racist meanings at such an assembly. Similarly, when it comes to something like the Teen Action Committee, a diversity ideology may provide space to address racialized microaggressions but stop short of being able to sufficiently address the way that systemic racism takes a toll on young folks' mental health. The inability to address systemic racism comes to a head at American when students and staff team up to put on a Black Lives Matter display, a display that, much like the staff's kneeling protest, comes to take on outsized symbolic importance about the state of racial inequality at the school.

Importantly, however, the story of benign diversity and racialized emotions are not the entirety of the story of racial inequality at American High. Examining everyday activism around racism at the school illustrates the way that positive emotions do not need to sustain racial inequality. As cultural commentator bell hooks writes, to combat social inequality we need to see "love as an action rather than a feeling" in a way that involves "accountability and responsibility."[7] By embracing and not avoiding "the political," a group of dedicated adults at American demonstrates love as an action by creating spaces and opportunities to empower young folks to call attention to the systemic nature of racial inequality, spaces and opportunities that can serve a template for an emerging politics of care.

Sugarcoating Inequality

Nicole and Angelina, both of whom had expressed outrage about the hat-wearers, spend much of their time together laughing, talking about who is dating whom at American, or processing current happenings in and out of school. The recording of my interview with them as we chatted in a bare windowless room off the library is interspersed with trenchant analysis of racial inequality and bursts of laughter from all three of us. Both of them critique the way racism is addressed at American. As Nicole said, "Everything at our school is sugarcoated. We never get to learn about slavery, because it's sugarcoated. Or, we can't learn things about racism or something because it's sugarcoated." They say that apart from two Black teachers, Nella and Ms. Taylor, who "say it as it is," most American teachers do not talk about racial inequality. Instead, Nicole said of the teachers, "They just want to keep living in this world that's like so sugarcoated. And don't ever want to say the truth." Angelina suggested that they should train students to deal with racism at least as well as they train them to deal with highly unlikely natural disasters. It's "like how we practice for tornado drills. We're not going to *not* experience racism in the world. So, you might as well teach us while we're in school and let us experience it, so we know how to deal with it." Angelina blamed this, in part, on the lack of racial diversity among the teachers, saying, "We have like how many teachers of color?" Angelina answered, "Enough to count on one hand." Nicole responded, "That's why I feel like sometimes students are not as educated as they need to be on certain things, because they're like—oh, I didn't even know that happened. Or I didn't even know that occurred. But it's just like because people don't like to tell us the truth. They just like to tell us the side that we're supposed to hear at a school." The "side that we're supposed to hear at school" captures the way in which race and racial inequality are framed as issues offense, opinion, difference, or kindness rather than issues of exclusion, power, or domination. When issues of racial inequality are "sugarcoated" this way, it leaves young folks like Nicole and Angelina with few tools to make sense of race in general, much less the inequality they continue to see and experience.

Take, for example, the issue of cultural appropriation. Cultural appropriation typically consists of more powerful groups adopting elements or symbols of other, less powerful groups. Both school and district guidelines prohibit students from engaging in cultural appropriation, but the way this is prohibited elides issues of inequality, power, or domination. During an assembly to prepare seniors for graduation, for instance, Assistant Principal Laurel, a White woman, walked students through a discussion about expectations around clothing at graduation. Reading from a PowerPoint slide, she talked them through "what's culturally appropriate." She said to the assembled group that any adornments worn during graduation "have to be culturally appropriate to the person wearing it" and gave as an example, "Stoles—we don't appropriate from other cultures. Don't borrow from another culture." Assistant Principal Laurel finished her brief discussion of cultural appropriation by saying, "We have a great reputation at the Civic Events Center for being classy. Let's keep it like that." While certainly having a policy against cultural appropriation is an institutional nod toward racial equity, the explanation of these guidelines feels, in the words of Angelina and Nicole, sugarcoated. Assistant Principal Laurel provides no language as to *why* such appropriation may be a problem, an explanation that, perhaps, would include language about the way more powerful racial groups use, deploy, or claim as their own symbols, practices, or traditions from less powerful ones. She makes this an issue of being "classy," not, say, of being equitable and justice-minded with an eye toward the history and present of power relations between groups.

In the absence of language about power or inequality, a language of "offense" often comes to frame the problem of cultural appropriation. Offense became an issue when student leadership (class presidents and representatives who are elected each year by the student body) posted a "spirit theme" for an upcoming football game on their social media accounts, as they often do. A spirit theme involves encouraging the student body to dress in a shared color or style to show school spirit at a sporting event. Themes have included "blue out," in which students dress all in blue; "USA," in which students dress in patriotic gear; or "camo," in which students dress head to toe in camouflage print. Late in the fall, student leadership announced a "safari" theme for an upcoming game against Valley High. On social media they wrote, "The theme of this Friday's game vs Valley High is Safari! Here are some ideas on what to wear for our theme tomorrow night!" and followed this announcement with suggestions in the form of four emojis: a Hawaiian print shirt, brown cargo shorts, a fanny pack, and a safari hat. The announcement caught the attention of the school administration because it violated school policies about cultural appropriation. After school staff had a conversation with student leadership members, they issued a new announcement, shifting the theme from safari to "tourist":

> The theme this week can include stereotypes. If we can all be generous and not be stereotypical that would be great! We want all our Hawaiian students to not be offended in any way! (Be cautious of grass skirts, coconut bras, etc.) We know that this is not what people of that culture wear on the daily basis! It is a stereotype and AHS stands against that! Come in your best tropical, beachy, touristy gear! Hawaiian shirts, hats, cargo shorts as well as leis are perfectly fine to wear. We will even be giving out some leis at the game!

As in the first announcement, this one concludes with a series of emojis: football, palm tree, hibiscus flower, beach umbrella, sunshine, waves, pineapple, a hand making the "hang loose" symbol, sunglasses, bikini, whale, and crab.

In this announcement wearing safari-themed clothing was framed as a problem because it could "include stereotypes" and Hawaiian students could be "offended." A language of "offense" does several things here. It centers hurt feelings rather than highlighting the historical nature of colonization that renders this sort of racialized cultural extraction a problem. Second, the message focuses on the good intentions of the presumably White students who are referred to as "we," who would not want to deploy offensive stereotypes. Third, it is difficult to see where a line may be drawn between which symbols or themes, like safari, may offend and which are (apparently) non-stereotypical fun, like tourist. Taken together, a frame of offense and stereotypes individualizes systemic and historical inequalities. By centering offense and stereotypes as the problem, this message clouds the way settler colonialism and White Western power made symbols of "exotic" far-off locales seem luxurious and fun to the West in the first place, in a way that misrepresents cultural beliefs, traditions, and symbols in the name of school spirit.[8]

A language of offensive fills in for other silences around race at American High. That is, if the problem is offense or hurt feelings, then the solution is to not be offensive, to not hurt feelings. The solution, in other words, is to be nice. When offense and kindness are divorced from discussions of power and inequality, diversity becomes a matter of difference, opinion, and perspective, an issue that goes well beyond the hat-wearers at the assembly. My discussion with Becca, a vivacious White senior involved in the Honors Academy and student government, shows what happens when, under a regime of kindness, hurt feelings, rather than inequality, becomes the problem. As we talked in a local coffee shop and I asked her about what it's like to be a teenager at this particular point in history in this particular town, Becca lowered her voice and looked around saying, "I grew up conservative," in a way that underscored exactly how unpopular it is to identify as conservative in this community. However, she pointedly said, she's not *that* kind of conservative, adding, "I wouldn't even call myself a Trump supporter."

In Becca's government class, well into Trump's presidential term, students discussed the increasingly restrictive federal mandates regulating immigration, mandates that inspired the "Immigrants Welcome" posters that were torn down at the nearby elementary school. Becca told me that one of her classmates "was telling us how her family was from Mexico, and when they were emigrating here and her dad got murdered, I think. Something like that. I don't remember, exactly. But just towards the end of the story, she was like, 'Anyone who is conservative, anyone who is Republican; it's your fault,' that her dad was dead, basically." Growing agitated as she talked, Becca said, she was "just basically yelling at us." The girl "bitched us out for like five minutes. Which is a long time, when someone is just yelling at you in a classroom full of other kids." Becca said angrily, "It was just a long time to be sitting there. We knew she was calling us out. She obviously wasn't like pointing and calling our names, but she knew who we were." The "we" Becca referred to were the few other conservative students in the class. Becca asked plaintively, "Why did my teacher allow that to go on?" throwing up her hands questioningly. Becca concluded her story by telling me, "It's okay to feel strongly one way versus the other. I am all for having your own opinion, 100 percent. I would love to hear other people's opinions. But not in that way."

Not in that way indeed. Becca's classmate was entitled to have her own "opinion" about what led to her father's death, but she was not entitled to link that death to a belief system that entailed policies that actively harmed immigrant families. Becca's analysis suggested the problem of international racialized inequality was one of "people's opinions" not systemic exclusion. Rather than attending to the global inequalities that undergird violence and access to life-sustaining resources, things that may be considered "political," Becca suggested that there may be different perspectives on topics such as these, perspectives that could all be shared dispassionately, rather than with the emotion that arises in response to racially motivated, state-sanctioned violence that cuts lives short and tears apart families.

When racial inequality becomes a problem of offense and opinion, kindness and benign diversity become the solutions. This leaves students like Tara, a White senior, concerned that she will be unkind, while she also expresses a bit of defensiveness about how "careful" she has to be to not offend. "It's kind of hard," she told me, "because we have to be super-careful. And especially me being White, I have to be even more careful. I hate offending people. Seriously. I hate offending people." As the young folks in the opening of the book suggest, people at American think of themselves and each other as kind.

But this regime of kindness can be a form of "sugarcoating" that does not link offense, diversity, or cultural appropriation to systemic, contemporary, or historical racial inequalities. This lack of connection allows White folks like Tara, Becca, or those on student leadership to see these inequalities as individual problems of hurt feelings, rather than inequalities from which they may benefit. Thus, Tara plaintively suggests as a solution, "We should all fricking love each other. Why can't it be like that?" This sort of emotion-based solution, however, relies on a carefully cultivated refusal to know or learn about racial inequality, a refusal that characterizes the experience of some White students at American High.

I Really Don't Like Talking about Race

A decade or so ago, Keegan-Michael Key and Jordan Peele performed a now famous sketch entitled "Substitute Teacher." This sketch featured a Black substitute teacher, Mr. Garvey, teaching in an almost all-White classroom. He mispronounces typical White names like Jacqueline as Jay-QUEL-inn, Blake as Bell-AWK-ay, Aaron as Ay-Ay-Ron as he calls roll. As the White students correct him, Mr. Garvey grows increasingly agitated, angrily calling students "insubordinate and churlish," and breaking his clipboard over his knee. Like much of Key and Peele's creative work, this sketch critiques racial inequality. In this instance White names are subjected to the type of mispronunciations to which non-White names are regularly subjected, especially in schools.[9]

As part of a fundraiser at American High, a group of mostly White male students recreated this sketch. The actor portraying Mr. Garvey was White. All but one of the actors playing the students were White. Their names were typically White names. And the audience at the fundraiser laughed uproariously at the mispronunciations. Ryan, a White boy sitting next to me, said between peals of laughter, "This is so good!" The skit, having dropped the racialized critique central to the conceit of the original sketch, was funny because familiar names were being mispronounced. It's not clear that the performers or any of those laughing seemed to know that the original sketch served to critique the workings of everyday racism.

This sketch, as well as the laughter at it, while not overtly racist, may be forms of what scholar Jennifer Mueller calls "white racial ignorance."[10] White racial ignorance involves White folks' intentional or unintentional lack of knowledge about racial inequality and non-White experiences. A carefully cultivated practice of not knowing can sustain the problem of racial inequality as one of offense, opinion, kindness, and benign diversity. This sort of not-knowing takes place throughout the school, in rituals, classrooms, and high-profile events like graduation.

If there is a place to get students' names right, it's the most important day of the year for many students, graduation. American High typically held a rehearsal for the graduation ceremony at a local performing arts center after a celebratory senior breakfast. During the rehearsal, seniors excitedly lined up backstage, surrounded by black walls scrawled with the names of musicals and signatures of cast members from Broadway shows like *Rent*, *Les Misérables*, and *Waitress*, to run through the graduation ceremony as a White female guidance counselor, Ethel, read their names. She had instructed the students to write out how to pronounce their names for her on index cards, saying "within reason use your legal name or a phonetic spelling." Regardless of the effort some students put into making their names easy to pronounce for her, Ethel proceeded to misread the names of multiple students of color. As Imani walked across the stage, Ethel stumbled over her name, while Imani shrugged, saying, "sure," as if resigned to this sort of thing. At another point Ethel apologized to Aliyah after fumbling her name as well, saying, as Aliyah passed her, "Sorry about your name." Aliyah looked Ethel straight in the eye and responded, "I'm used to it." As the rehearsal progressed, several Latina students repeatedly sounded out their names for Ethel, resulting in various degrees of success.

At one point, when she encountered a name she found particularly challenging, Ethel commented, "That's as bad as Barry's." Indeed, when Barry's name appeared Ethel said, with dread, "I knew that would come." Making a "time out" signal with her hands, she paused rehearsal to read and study Barry's full name, Barry Kealoha Lokela Johnson. After failing to say it right multiple times, Ethel asked in front of the entire senior class, "Barry Johnson, can you please see me after you are done so I can figure out your name here?" Barry, an outgoing, genial senior of Pacific Islander descent, dutifully met with Ethel after the rehearsal to help her learn how to pronounce his name. Later that night, however, it seemed that his efforts were for naught. At the graduation ceremony that evening, in front of a packed three-tiered auditorium filled with cheering friends and family, when Barry appeared on stage Ethel said, "I need some help with this one, I call him Barry but his name is . . ." followed by yet another mispronunciation of his name. Barry, having had his name once again misread, stepped forward to huge cheers anyway, making his way across the stage to collect his diploma.

Perhaps not coincidentally, when the seniors had their chance to write their names on the white brick wall on the side of the school, an annual tradition, Barry staged a small bit of activism. Typically, graduating seniors write their name or a nickname in the middle of a single brick, sometimes accompanied by a flower, a saying, a list of programs they participated in, the college they were going to, or their team number. Rather than taking up one brick as most graduating students did, however, Barry wrote his full name in red marker, all in capital letters and underlined, across *four* bricks smack in the center of the wall. Though I do not know if he meant it this way, it seems to me that the size and placement of his name was a way for him to fight back against the repeated racism he experienced. Names are bearers of cultural meanings, so these White mispronunciations are not simple mistakes. Rather they are a demonstration of White racial ignorance that sends a message to students of color about their value, worth, and the level of respect they and their heritage are due.[11]

This type of White racial ignorance goes far beyond names. It takes sustained work, effort, and cultivation.[12] During my two years sitting in Nella's Daring Discussions class, one of the few places in the school that provided an environment and language for young folks to discuss racial inequality, I watched as primarily White groups of students actively avoided discussions of race, even in situations where it seemed impossible to do so. One day in the early fall we all settled into our seats as Nella reminded the class that their homework was to watch the new Nike Colin Kaepernick ad for that week's "decode your feed" discussion. Nella designs these lessons to help students understand, talk about, and process the messages they receive via social media, especially around issues of race, gender, and sexuality. The specific ad she had assigned them to watch was one that Nike produced after multiple years of protests against racist police violence led by Kaepernick and adopted by athletes in the NFL and beyond, protests that led to Kaepernick losing his position in the NFL (and the form of protest that resulted in discipline for Nella and her fellow teachers).[13] As Nella played the ad for the students she asked them what idea, statement, or meaning in it spoke to them. The majority of the students (all White except for two) made comments like:

"The message was motivational."
"Look outside your expectations."
"You can accomplish anything you set your mind to."

None of their comments referred to race, racism, or social change, even as the ad itself focused on social change and drew heavily on

Black power iconography. After hearing their responses, Nella, as she often did, tried to suggest an analysis that centered a racialized reading of the commercial, commenting on the fact that Kaepernick's hair is styled in an afro, he is wearing a military-style jacket, and, in her words, he is "all but raising a fist." Not a single student, however, referenced the importance of Kaepernick's society-shaping protest against anti-Black police violence, racial inequality, or activism in general. These are teens, of course, and keeping up with and commenting on larger social issues isn't always at the forefront of their minds. However, when paired with other discussions of race *in a class about race,* a class where they had spent the previous months learning about racial inequality, their reluctance suggests that some young White folks may be actively working to avoid discussions of racial inequality.

This wasn't the only time White students in Daring Discussions avoided talking about race in a class about race. Angie, a White student with shoulder-length brown hair in Nella's afternoon class, exemplified this avoidance as she completed a "Six Words About Race" assignment. This assignment, based on National Public Radio's "Race Card" project, required that students write six words about race as the title of a short essay in which they expand on that phrase and its meaning to them. After working on her essay for a while, Angie brought it over to me for editing help. Like Ms. Bay, Nella often directed students to me for additional classroom support. Angie settled into a chair across from me as she waited for my feedback. I read through the essay, entitled "All You Can Rely on Is Yourself," noting sentences like "This is a lesson that has to be learned by each person," and "everyone will let you down," expecting, at some point, to discover how these claims relate to race. That point never came. After editing the essay for style, I commented to Angie, "I think this is supposed to have to do with race. Angie responded, "I really don't like talking about race. It makes me really uncomfortable."

Nella faced this sort of resistance daily.[14] Some White students in Daring Discussions, like Angie, tried to avoid talking about or even addressing race while others excused racist behavior with explanations that emphasized either intentions or poor decision-making. In a discussion about pictures that had recently surfaced of a governor attending parties wearing blackface in his college days, for instance, Lucas and Hunter, two White boys in the class, emphasized that the governor's intentions were key to evaluating whether or not his behavior was racist.[15] Lucas said blackface would be understandable if you were dressing up as "someone you look up to," while Hunter explained, "The expression is pretty gross, but if the pretense was good, I don't think that's a huge problem. I think it depends on *how* you dress up. The intentions behind something matter. We shouldn't impart malice on someone when stupidity would do." Hunter continued: "He was in college. Do you understand how stupid you are in college? College is a time to party."[16] In other words, doing something racist is okay if someone meant it in a positive way or if one was young and lacked judgment. Eden, one of the few non-White students in the class, countered their claims that ignorance or good intentions were an excuse for racist behavior, saying, "If you aren't educated it's your responsibility to get educated. Just because you say you are not racist doesn't mean you are not racist." Students of color, like Eden, were typically the ones who pushed back on these claims that excused racist behavior.

Part of the way White racial ignorance is sustained, even in classes where race and racial inequality are the subjects at hand, is through a sort of racialized (and often gendered) "checking-out." That is, when topics about inequality would come up in a class or assembly, some students, typically boys, typically White, would simply exit the discussion. Some of them physically "checked out." When a video of blackface played in class, for instance, Hunter got up from his seat and walked to the pencil sharpener, repeatedly sharpening a series of pencils. During the same video, Lucas put in earbuds, took them out, and put them back in, repeatedly adjusting them. During the ensuing conversation, Chet kept his head down, scrolling through his phone. Curley, another White boy in class, simply walked out when the conversation started. Such behavior was not limited to Daring Discussions. I saw this throughout the school in different settings, as young folks pulled out phones, put in ear buds, or suddenly found something that needed doing outside the classroom when inequality, especially racial inequality, became the topic of discussion or instruction.

Such behavior doesn't go unnoticed, especially by girls of color, who sometimes called my attention to these practices. Cassia did so when giving her end-of-term presentation in Daring Discussions on the history of policing in the United States. Cassia's project powerfully drew connections between the origins of the United States police force in slave patrols and the goals of the contemporary Black Lives Matter movement. Before she began her formal presentation, she turned to me, showing me her clammy hands, saying, "I'm SO nervous." Nevertheless she stood bravely in front of the class teaching them about social movements against racist police violence. "I take this issue very personally," she said, "because my brother is darker than me. Like half my family is Black and when the Trayvon thing happened, he's the same age and wears the same kind of clothes." After describing the Black Lives Matter movement and placing it in historical context, Cassia concluded with a video juxtaposing two White men jumping on police cars free of consequence and a young Black boy being screamed at by a White cop while other White police officers arrest his father. Angie, Curly, and Chet chatted with each other and laughed quietly between the juxtaposed videos. When, at the end of the presentation, Cassia instructed the students to visit posters about the Black Lives Matter movement at the back of the classroom, Angie and Chet remained seated as the rest of the class moved to read them. Angie and Chet's refusal to participate was so noticeable that Cassia looked at me and mouthed, "He's not moving," as Chet continued to joke and laugh with Angie and Curly. When Angie finally arose to go look at the display, Cassia firmly reminded Curly and Chet, "Well, not if you would *like* to, you *need* to. It's part of the activity," motioning them back toward the display as they grudgingly moved.

This resistance to learning about racial inequality includes a refusal to meaningfully engage with solutions to racism. What I heard again and again from some young White folks was a fatalistic acceptance of racial inequality as an inevitable part of life. When Cassia asked, for instance, at the end of her presentation, "What is a possible solution?," Jerry, a White senior, responded, "That's a big question; how do you change something that's been ingrained into us?" Even though Cassia's presentation had clearly covered the demands of the Black Lives Matter movement, some White students instead focused on the futility of trying to change racist patterns. Kai, a White junior, commented, "I don't think the world will be able to get rid of racism. Because that's just a personal thing between officers. This is something that's just a part of our country. The main way to get rid of it is to bring light to it. There isn't a real way to get rid of it because it's how it is and how it will be." Kai's comment suggests not only that racial inequality is inevitable, it's individual as well, because it is a "personal thing between officers." Undaunted by their fatalism, Cassia asked her classmates a more pointed question about BLM itself: "Do you think BLM has been productive or counterproductive and why?" Alyssa, a White junior, answered, "Both but also counterproductive because it's a lot of negative representations of people being shot by police and being victims." Jerry added, "I have to agree because it's highlighting the problem but it's not really presenting too many solutions." Jerry made this comment after a thirty-minute-long presentation by Cassia about BLM, much of which centered on a list of ways the movement suggests Americans can combat racial inequality through things like policing reform, criminal justice reform, housing equity, and anti-poverty programs.[17]

Again and again in Daring Discussions, students were presented with contemporary and historical facts about racial inequality, and again and again some White students checked out or excused or minimized it. Chet and his friends excused blackface as poor, youthful decision-making, not racism. Chet, Curly, and Lucas all checked out in various ways so they did not have to hear about racism—from leaving the room to putting in earbuds to laughing through Cassia's presentation. Kai and Jerry, who actually did pay attention to the presentation, still resisted systemic solutions to racial inequality, suggesting that this sort of inequality is just the way things are, even if it's regrettable. Like Ethel who refused to learn students' names no matter how many times they explained them to her, these young White folks develop strategies to actively resist learning about race and racial inequality. These varied practices of White racial ignorance sustain an understanding of racial inequality that is individual and not systemic, as a problem that is best solved through benign diversity and individual kindness, a perspective that was challenged when a Black Lives Matter event came to American High.

Black Lives Matter in High School

When teachers like Nella and Max took a knee at the senior assembly, they engaged in an anti-racist gesture, a gesture that has come to symbolize a critique of systemic racism and racist police violence, a symbol that is widely associated with the Black Lives Matter movement, a movement about which Cassia had worked to educate her classmates. Given that the staff who participated in this quiet anti-racist statement were disciplined for engaging in "political expression" during the workday, it is perhaps little surprise that when a collection of students and staff tried to bring a Black Lives Matter display to American High, they too encountered resistance. The attempt to display it at American resulted in a multi-month struggle that exemplified the limits of benign diversity as a solution to racial inequality, a solution that stood in contrast to the systemically oriented solutions of the Black Lives Matter movement.[18]

The display itself was a series of red, black, white, and yellow memorial posters. Each poster featured the name, image, and story of a specific Black victim of police murder, like Philando Castile's memorial:

Philando Castile

32 years old

Falcon Heights, Minnesota—July 6th, 2016

An officer pulled over Philando for a broken tail light with his girlfriend passenger, Diamond Reynolds, and four-year old daughter in the back seat. Philando was fatally shot four times as he was reaching for his license after informing the officer he had possession of a legal handgun. Aftermath: both officers involved with the case were put on paid administrative leave. The officers are still under trial for possible criminal charges.

Philando's Life Matters.

While this display had been hanging in the hallway of a neighboring school without incident, when the BSU and staff teamed up to bring this display to American, the resistance to it illustrated processes of sugarcoating, the "bothsidesism" of benign diversity, and the workings of White racial ignorance.

Lilith, a tall White librarian with long brown hair and glasses, was told that in order to bring the display to American High they needed to present the "police perspective" along with the memorial posters. Principal Walt had sent an email home to parents promising that this perspective would be included. Lilith expressed concern about this promise, saying that it made her feel "boxed in." Lilith said, even if she wanted to, she actually didn't have a way to comply with this request, saying "the school has virtually no books on cops" except one entitled *So You Want to Be a Cop* about jobs in law enforcement. Nella shared her frustration about the requirement, suggesting that a central tenet of BLM was to critique policing because "there is something wrong and broken about the policing of our communities." Nella underscored her point by making the analogy that "addressing the police perspective" was akin to trying to plan for Pink Prom and "inviting people from organizations that oppose homosexuality." Much like Becca's focus on "opinion" or the perception that the hat-wearers were simply expressing a form of diversity, the requirement to share the police perspective became one in which racial inequality is an issue of perspective, not one of systemic harm rooted in a racist history of slave patrols.[19]

Principal Walt also expressed concern that some parents might be upset because students "don't have the context to push back against the display." This concern suggests that students do not know enough about issues of racial inequality to take in or evaluate the messages about systemic racism and police violence in the display. Nella, however, like a few other teachers at American, said that she "tried to lay the groundwork" for students and teachers, but her offers to partner with other teachers to coordinate preparing students for the display received little response. This lack of response suggests that the "checking out" strategy deployed by some White students at American to avoid discussions of racial inequality was not limited to them but extended to some staff members as well.

Because of these concerns about whose perspective would be represented and worries about students' preparedness, Principal Walt suggested altering the event. He floated, for a time, the idea of displaying the posters at an optional evening event (rather than in the auditorium during the school day), and framing it as a "healing circle" that students could "opt in" to. While certainly racial healing is an important part of moving a society to a more just and equitable one, as Beverly Daniel Tatum suggests in her book *Why Are All the Black Kids Sitting Together in the Cafeteria?*, this sort of racial healing can't just be about feelings; it needs to be grounded in principles of restorative justice. It needs to include accountability and repair, not just emotional expression. It seems that the sort of healing circle Principal Walt was proposing, while well intentioned, was being proposed *because* White students or parents may be upset about the display, not because such a circle would serve as a restorative justice event that would involve acknowledging systemic harm and taking steps toward repair.

As staff members debated the form, timing, and context for the display, Cassia told me that the students in the BSU had a "very good sense of what is going on." Frustrated with inaction and delay, they decided to "demand" that the Black Lives Matter memorial posters be displayed. Cassia said the resistance to the display felt like an ex tension of the "two-faced" racism she had experienced at American, where they say, "we support you but we don't want to show this." In the end, the groundwork laid by staff like Nella, Lilith, and Craig, student demand, and, perhaps most pivotally in this instance, the vocal and assertive support of two White staff members, Aaron and Seth, allowed the display to go up. However, the morning the display was slated to open, it had been delayed for so long that Craig and Little J were joking about whether or not it would actually happen, ruefully laughing and saying, "There's only three days left in Black History Month!" I wasn't sure it was going to show up either. But, to our surprise that morning in late February, the same month the cheerleaders had plastered lockers in notes of love and kindness, a description of the display, location, and timing came over the daily announcements. Echoing the concerns that had slowed the advent of the display, the announcement contained a disclaimer stating that visiting the display was optional for all students.

After the announcements, I walked into the reception area of the auditorium, an area lined with glass display cases that held student artwork, trophies, and old yearbooks. I could hear strains of quiet gospel music filtering out from the set of double blue doors leading into the auditorium. As my eyes moved from the yearbooks to the sign reading "Black Lives Matter," displayed on an easel in front of the door, I couldn't help but think about the content of those old yearbooks. A few days before, Cassia had shared with me, horrified, that one yearbook contained photos of a student "slave auction" and another documented a prom with the theme of "oriental." These yearbooks contain racist ghosts that haunt the current display and the battle over it, making the past seem very present. These ghosts haunted me as I read the words on the sign itself:

Thank you for visiting the Black Lives Matter in Schools presentation. This presentation is one part of American High School's effort to meaningfully engage in Black History Month, to honor the contributions of African American people and acknowledge real issues affecting Black communities. American has a commitment to honoring diversity and creating a safe learning environment for all students, and this presentation is a part of that commitment.

The Black Lives Matter movement has been cast in many ways. Student and staff organizers want to be clear that the poster presentation at American is not intended to be anti-police, anti-white, anti-unity, or anti-anything. Instead, the poster presentation is meant to raise awareness of difficult facts in our world and to remember the humanity of African American individuals who have been killed.

American High School unconditionally values and honors police officers who put themselves in danger every day to help keep communities safe. We believe that police officers act in overwhelmingly moral ways to serve and protect, and we are so thankful for their work. At the same time, we want to offer a sustained focus on the disproportional level of violence confronting African Americans in the context of altercations with police. While this exhibit focuses on individuals who were killed by police, we believe violence involving African American people is not limited to issues of policing but is the result of systemic conditions that impact a vast range of issues including education, health care, secure housing and access to safety and prosperity for Black Americans

To address the concerns about the "police perspective," this statement focused less on racist police violence than it did on assuring attendees that the display is not "anti-White" or "anti-police" and that the efforts of police are greatly appreciated. The sign, while reflecting the focus of the Black Lives Matter movement regarding systemic racial inequality, also reflected the language of benign diversity in its claims that the display is not "anti-anything."

Beyond the doorway, black-and-white posters lined the center aisle leading to the stage. One set of posters listed the "Guiding Principles" of the Black Lives Matter Movement: Restorative Justice, Empathy, Loving Engagement, Diversity, Globalism, Queer Affirming, Trans Affirming, Collective Value, Intergenerational, Black Families, Black Villages, Unapologetically Black, and Black Women. Posters on the other side titled "Institutional Racism" provided data drawn primarily from the *Washington Post* and *US News and World Report* detailing systemic racial inequality in schools, housing, incarceration, employment, income, and home ownership. The line of posters ended at the stage, upon which sat a series of tables topped with red trifolds displaying the memorial posters.

A music list curated by Noriah, Joseph, and Caitlin, all members of the BSU, played songs by artists ranging from Solange to Billie Holiday to J. Cole as visitors walked into the auditorium. Caitlin danced through the morning, her ponytail bouncing as she explained the exhibit to entering students. She told them, "The flow starts at that end . . . the guiding principles are up there, the statistics are down there," directing visitors where to go, the best way to enter the stage, and reminding them to write their reactions afterward on the white butcher paper covering two tables in front of the memorial posters.

In front of the stage, students milled around talking quietly as they wrote on the butcher paper. By the end of the day, the paper was covered in colorful student comments that reflected the varied ways race and racial inequality were addressed at American High. Some framed race as a systemic problem, calling for education and awareness: "Awareness is power. Education is power. Please let this movement create a platform for our country to realize how much of an issue this is." Others simply stated, "Black Lives Matter."

About half the comments on these large sheets of paper, however, reflected what Bonilla-Silva calls a color-blind racism, or an analysis of racial inequality that emphasizes the similarity and one-ness of humanity.[20] Over the course of the day students wrote comments like "Skin color does not matter," or "We are all human," or, reminiscent of the poster in the MLK assembly, "Underneath the skin we are all the same," which reflected this color-blind approach. A distinct subset of these color-blind responses emphasized the racialized emotions that shape understandings of and responses to racial inequality at American. Much like Tara's plea that "we should all fricking love each other," these comments emphasized inequality as a problem of hate while positioning kindness and love as a solution. The language of love and kindness filled the large white paper as young folks wrote:

- Kindness matters!
- Why must we *hate*
- Please be kind to each other. It breaks my heart to see all this hate and inequality!

- Why can't we all JUST love each other, no matter what we look like, who we love or how we identify ??
- PEACE, LOVE, AND POSITIVITY ??
- Everyone deserves love no matter color of skin

Of course, there is no indication that meanness, a lack of kindness, or dearth of love for fellow humans is the reason why Black women and men are more likely to be killed by police than are White people.[21] But as with other social problems at American High, kindness, love, and positivity are lauded as solutions to systemic problems.

Not surprisingly, given young folks' descriptions of the American High community, only a small minority of comments expressed more clearly racist perspectives. Those that did were quickly countered by other attendees. When Elsa, a White junior, read over the comments across the butcher paper she paused when she got to the comment "all lives matter" and read it out loud to her friends. Her jaw dropped and she raised and shook her hand angrily. Then she picked up a pen and covered up the comment with a giant heart. While statements like "all lives matter" are now fairly recognizable as a way to counter a message about valuing Black lives and opposing racist police violence, the roots of such a sentiment seem to be related to the understandings of color-blind kindness that inspire messages about loving each other "no matter what we look like" or because "everyone deserves love no matter color of skin."

Some young folks responded to this sort of message by unpacking the way that a logic of kindness and sameness erases systemic racial inequalities. When Noriah noticed another "all lives matter" comment, she exclaimed, "Someone wrote 'all lives matter' here! I just think it needs to be erased." As the day went on, students scrawled responses to it. One, for instance, drew a red arrow to another comment that read, "But until people of color have the same opportunities and the same/equal chance to thrive as white people 'all lives matter' won't be true. While all lives do matter, Black people and people of color aren't being treated as though their lives matter." By the end of the day the three small words "all lives matter" were surrounded with responses refuting the statement.

This type of racism was rare at this event and at American in general. But, at this event, much like in their classrooms, some young White folks checked out and resisted information about racial inequality presented in the display. One senior, Tony, the child of Vietnamese immigrant parents, made it a point to come over to me at the display to say that he "noticed something weird. A bunch of kids from my class didn't want to come. It's weird." The "weirdness" Tony commented on is a version of the checking-out strategy used by Chet and his friends in the Daring Discussions class, in which young folks simply refused to attend the display. Some young folks also challenged the information in the display itself. Repeatedly, over the course of the display small groups of two to three White boys would pause at one of the posters with a fact about systemic racism on it, whip out their cell phones, and start a whispered conversation. One such group, Jake, Connor, and Cody, all three clad in jeans and hoodies, gathered around the posters about institutional racism that lined the aisle. Their phones were out as they pointed at the posters and talked in low voices while they tapped away. Eventually the three walked over to Assistant Principal Laurel. Cody said he found "facts that contradict facts on the posters." Specifically he challenged the employment rate information, saying that the *Washington Post* provided "different information" about the levels of Black unemployment, commenting, "It's lower than the posters make it seem." Cody said he found "other statistics" about salary information as well. Assistant Principal Laurel responded by saying, "It's always a good idea to know where you are getting your statistics from," and that "the point of school is to have these discussions. It's part of being in a democratic society. I appreciate you saying that 'this doesn't make sense to me.'" However, the discussion ended there, with an "agree to disagree" sentiment as the contradiction lingered, a sentiment that may, itself, be a way that White racial ignorance operates in which data matter less than making sure all perspectives are valued.

The Black Lives Matter exhibit and the controversy around it illustrate the way race and racial inequality are constructed, reproduced, and challenged at American High. From the messages of kindness and positivity on the butcher paper, to White boys' resistance to learning facts about racial inequality, to the principal's suggestion that an optional "healing" event was a suitable replacement for the display, the story of the Black Lives Matter display is a story of the limits of a benign diversity approach to racial inequality. In this instance, though, a logic of benign diversity did not prevent the display from going up. Students did have the opportunity to learn about systemic racial inequality and racist police violence. That is important to note. So how did this happen? It happened because of an alliance between dedicated student activists and the staff who supported them by creating the organizational space necessary for the display. That story is not a story of benign diversity. It is a story of the transformative power of love as an action rather than just a feeling. It's a way we might begin to think about a politics of care rather than a regime of kindness.

Love in Action

Kindness and love are not, in and of themselves, problems. They are problems when they become primary ways of understanding the causes of and solutions to racial inequality. They become problems because they can individualize the systemic nature of inequality, suggesting that if we just love each other, are positive, and accept each other for who we are, these inequalities will no longer be systematically built into our institutions. In other words, these positive emotions are problems when they are racialized emotions or those that sustain white supremacy and racial inequality. However, positive emotions like love, say, do not need to sustain racial inequality. In fact, they may be an important part of countering it.

As anti-racist scholar bell hooks suggests, a love ethic can be central to racial justice.[22] A love ethic is not just about being kind; it's not just being sad about "hate," or saying, "everyone deserves love no matter color of skin." A love ethic entails action, action that for White people may be costly in terms of their own privilege. A love ethic is the sort of love that led to the BLM display and the sort of love that the staff of color demonstrate throughout the school, often at a cost to themselves. A love ethic is not just a feeling, but a set of actions and commitments. From serving as role models to putting their own careers on the line, a small group of staff at American High repeatedly exemplified love as an action through the variety of ways they stood in solidarity with and cleared organizational space for students. When the handful of teachers knelt in front of the student body as the national anthem played, risking their jobs and, for some, mental health, they not only signaled to students solidarity; they represented a love ethic, something dedicated staff of color practice throughout the school.

Little J and his wife Jackie exemplify this ethic through their tireless work to build a Pacific Islander community among students, family, staff, and community members. They advise the Pacific Islander club at American and at several other area high schools, take students to statewide Pacific Islander gatherings and luaus, sponsor hula classes, hold "Ohana Nights"—events that bring together Pacific Islander students and mentors—run a business where they "bring in talent from the islands for a TGIF," and give talks in classes to inform non–Pacific Islander students about Pacific Islander history and culture. Little J says they do this because he wants to make sure that "young people from the islands don't lose their culture when they are growing up on the mainland," because it's something he sees happening "a lot." They regularly guest lecture in classes, at universities, in community colleges, and at community groups, fitting it all in between their regular jobs and course work for their respective master's degrees. People tell me that Little J sleeps only a few hours a night to keep up this busy schedule.

When Little J and Jackie talk to classes, they connect with the primarily White students by drawing on (and critiquing pop culture representations of) elements of Pacific Islander culture with which these young folks may be familiar. For instance, Jackie often opens their class lecture by asking, "Ohana, what does that mean?" The class typically answers together, "Family!" Jackie says, "Good how do you know that?" And students laughingly answer, "Lilo and Stitch!" to which Jackie replies wryly, "Disney did one thing right." In these class presentations, they teach students about Pacific Islander culture, practices, history, and Western colonization.

Rather than using equalizing language concerned with offense, culture, or diversity, Little J and Jackie actively discuss racism and racial inequality. Jackie says, "Our children look different. Our students experience racism and discrimination because of the way they look and speak." They discuss their son's experience as an example: "He was going to middle school and there was a crowd of boys at the bus stop that crowded around him. 'Wow,' his reaction was 'this is cool.' But then they started whispering. He said, 'Hi guys,' and they jumped back saying, 'Oh he speaks English!' He was asked that day if he arrived in a canoe or if he lived in a grass shack back on Hawai'i." Their son's educational experiences shed light on the sort of racism Pacific Islanders experience in this community, from staff members mispronouncing names to the symbols used in service of school spirit at football games. His experiences are central to how and why they deploy a love ethic through their Ohana nights and class presentations.

Nella in her pedagogy, humanity, and activism exemplifies a quiet and powerful love ethic. Every year, for example, the staff at American theme their Halloween costumes. One year they chose "superheroes and villains" as their theme. That year, Nella showed up to teach class wearing a Colin Kaepernick jersey with her typical black leggings. She smiled at me as I walked into the classroom, saying, "This is my superhero outfit." For Nella, a superhero wasn't a creature with mythical powers—it's a human who risked his career and public condemnation to take a stand for racial justice. Nella's expressions of love include continually supporting youth of color and expressing superhuman patience in the face of White resistance. When Lucas, Hunter, and Curley, for instance, remain outside a circle of students that Nella has invited the class to form for a discussion of racial inequality, rather than disciplining them or acting annoyed, she looked at them with a smile and said gently, "Come into the circle—join us." With a similar gentleness, Nella provided language for Cassia around racial identity. In advance of the MLK assembly, Cassia had created a banner for Craig to let him know "how much we appreciate what he does." As Nella and I listened, Cassia mused out loud about what she wanted to write on the banner, suggesting, "Thank you. You helped us reach our dreams. From the Black kids. Or the diversity kids. Or the ethnic kids." Nella, as she often did, gently helped Cassia strategize more specific language, saying, "Well, we all have an ethnicity." Certainly, even her classroom—with its posters of Black and Brown poets, artists, authors, and activists lining the walls and soft hip-hop playing quietly—mirrored the identities, music, images, and culture of students who may not see themselves reflected elsewhere in the school.

Like Nella, Craig continually carved out organizational space for students of color, inviting speakers, arranging field trips, and providing support for events focused on racial equality. From bugging the students for their essays on the Town Hall on Institutionalized

Racism, to arranging field trips to colleges, to advising many of the affinity clubs, Craig endeavored to reduce the sort of sugarcoating to which Angelina and Nicole repeatedly referred. These efforts were sometimes shut down, such as the time that he tried to hold a Kwanzaa spirit week (a weeklong event typically sponsored by the school administration or members of the student leadership) focusing on the seven core principles of the holiday and was told that he could not do this because Kwanzaa was "a religion."[23]

When dealing directly with students, Craig continually responded with patience and education, even in situations where racism was directed at him. At a school where some White staff regularly mispronounced the names of students of color, Craig instead went out of his way to help students understand the racialized dimensions of names. Tammy, a Laotian sophomore, for instance, said she was thinking about changing her middle name because she's embarrassed by it. Craig encouraged her to keep her middle name—her mother's maiden name—because doing so is an act of "cultural pride" and she's the "last person in the family to have that name," so it is her responsibility to carry on its history and lineage. Craig ruefully joked about the fact that he didn't have that opportunity to carry on his family name because "Master Johnson—that's where my name came from. I can't even carry something on!" When Jessa, a White girl sitting next to us, asked, regarding the name "Master Johnson," "Is that your rap name?" Craig and Little J chuckled and looked at each other. Craig then explained his "joke," telling her that when White people enslaved Black people, White people sometimes forced them to take the name of the White family, a practice that had the effect of erasing the heritage, history, and humanity of enslaved Americans and their descendants.[24] Craig exhibited this patience with White students regularly. When Heart, a White student who often skipped class just to hang out and say "hi" to Craig, once drew a picture for him on Halloween and titled it "to the best spook at American," he took the opportunity to educate her on racial epithets. He gently explained to her that "spook" is a "demeaning term for African Americans." Heart apologized and went on to make another picture for him.

These teachers create what education scholar Angela Valenzuela calls a "landscape of caring."[25] From Craig being "so much more than a security guard," in Cassia's words, to the empowerment-oriented space of Nella's classroom, to the community building and education done by Jackie and Little J, this landscape of caring is a central part of what makes American High such a special place. These teachers, and others like them, make organizational space for students. They work to educate some while making sure others see themselves reflected in the life of the school. It is clear, however, that this work takes a toll on some of them. Research suggests that continually confronting racism and racial inequality at predominantly White schools results in attrition for staff members of color.[26] Indeed, not a single one of these staff members is now in the position they were in when I was researching this book.

Schools as Racialized Organizations

Schools, like other organizations, are not just neutral bundles of people, rules, traditions, and buildings. They are what sociologist Victor Ray calls "racialized organizations"—that is, these rules, traditions, buildings, and people shape and are shaped by racialized practices, beliefs, and policies.[27] As in other White organizations, racial inequality at American gets framed, discussed, and understood as an individual problem, not as a systemic one. American High may be a place where there is "no room for hate," but such an approach belies the way that hate may not be the problem—systemic inequality is.[28] That is, racism doesn't just manifest in interactional aggression or name-calling; it is woven into an organizational structure itself, in this instance through a logic of benign diversity and racialized emotions.

A benign diversity approach shapes discussions of race and racial inequality at American High. Topics regarding race and racial inequality are "sugarcoated," reduced to issues of offense and opinion as racialized emotions of kindness and hate fill in for systemic understandings of inequality. In this sense, racialized emotions are, as Bonilla-Silva puts it, "more significant for the reproduction of the racial order than the actions and behavior of 'racist' actors."[29] Direct, intentional racist behavior is relatively rare at American High—limited to more veiled expressions like the MAGA hats and the "all lives matter" comments. But a culture of kindness allows a certain kind of racism to thrive, the sort of racism that sugarcoats the horrors of racial inequality, suggests that this inequality is a problem of hate—and the past, and allows White students to passively (and sometimes actively) not know about racial inequality at all. It is in this context that some staff exemplify a love ethic that supports youth of color and provides a language for racial inequality.

In her book *The Good High School*, Sarah Lawrence Lightfoot exhorts us to look for the good in schools. By the good in schools, she means places, practices, people, and systems that support, love, and encourage students. As a sociologist, too often I fall into the trap of pointing out what is going wrong. And much, to be clear, much is going wrong regarding race and racial inequality at American, but what is going wrong is not unique to American. What is going right, what is good, might be unique. The staff who exemplify a love ethic, who clear organizational space for students, they are the good at American. But individual staff members bear the burden of this work. While their behavior exemplifies a politics of care, they, as individuals, cannot *be* a politics of care because such a politics needs to be built into the nature of organizations and institutions themselves. A politics of care is a systemic solution, not an individual one. When individuals move on (or are moved on), as most of these staff members have, that love ethic may go with them. A politics of care would systemize the information, opportunities, knowledge, resources, and cultural representations these staff members work so hard to make present in these young people's lives, rather than letting it move on with them. A politics of care, in other words, entails an organization built around the love ethic they exemplify, rather than around a regime of kindness. For, as bell hooks writes, "there can be no love without justice."[30]

4   *When Powder Puff Becomes Power Tough*

"Folks, we are here for the Powder Puff game!" Jack, a White American staff member, announced over the loudspeaker as a cheer rose from the spectators settling into the mostly full stands under blue skies and puffy white clouds on a warm Oregon spring day. The Powder Puff game is American High's annual charity fundraiser in which junior and senior girls compete against each other in a flag football game. Students in the stands waved signs and flags. Some wore face paint and Hawaiian print shirts. Seven White shirtless senior boys cheered wildly from the front row, faces painted red with letters spelling S E N-I-O-R-S on their chests. In the next section over sat the members of the band, as they usually did during football games. However, their typical trumpets, drums, and tubas were absent, having been replaced by kazoos that band members played enthusiastically throughout the game, punctuating plays with buzzing versions of popular songs like "Killing in the Name Of" and "Confident." Jack repeatedly encouraged the crowd to cheer for the band, exhorting, "Let's hear it for our kazoo band! Take a breath guys!"

On the football field, junior and senior girls dressed in blue-and-white jerseys warmed up as the crowd continued to filter in, donating two cans or giving five dollars for Feeding the Hungry, the charity the game benefited. The Powder Puff "coaches," actually members of the American High football team, had dressed for the role, sporting red-and-white collared shirts tucked into belted khaki dress shorts with clipboards, visors, and whistles. Referees in full black-and-white uniforms stood on the edge of the field waiting to make their calls as Jack continued to commentate: "Welcome to Powder Puff, representing one of the great rivalries!" He compared the rivalry to competitions between the Red Sox and the Yankees and, more humorously, a "driver with test dummies in their cars using the carpool lane versus the department of transportation!" Members of Team Senior concluded their warm-up by placing their hands over each other's shoulders, and jumping back and forth in a circle while chanting "PUFF PUFF PUFF!" Then Jack introduced the players, "in no apparent order except from top to bottom!" He read a list of comical names like "Catch 'Em All" or "Little Mama," concluding his introduction by thanking the equally comically named referees—"Checka da Markson," "No Idea What Da Call Is," and "Sir Where's My Ballat"—all of whom, Jack shared, hailed from the "Powder Puff Unionization Federation."

As the game play got underway, the student coaches ran up and down the field yelling, "Let's go guys! We got this!" high-fiving and jumping up and down and punching the air in excitement as the crowd cheered for particularly good plays. Because Powder Puff is a flag football game, competitors wear no protective padding, like they would in a traditional game. However, as the girls jumped, threw, body-blocked, rolled on the ground, crashed into and occasionally tackled one another, I cringed at some of the more painful plays. I even let out a loud gasp as one player intercepted a long pass, fell to the ground, and rolled onto her head before limping back to the huddle. Judging from the noises and body shifts around me, some other members of the crowd reacted similarly.

Powder Puff games, like this one, are a fixture at high schools across the country. While the specific sport and gender swap may occasionally vary (some schools, for instance, feature boys playing softball), typically Powder Puff refers to a flag football game played by girl students to raise money for charity. The important part of the ritual is the "gender reversal" at the heart of the game in which girls, usually sans padding or meaningful training, play a physically challenging sport typically played by boys, football. This particular use of the phrase "powder puff" dates back to the early twentieth century when it was used to refer to men thought of as feminine—men, that is, who may be so feminine as to actually use a powder puff. The term eventually became associated with gender-reversed football games as women took the field to replace men who were off at war, with at least one documented report of women entertainingly pulling out powder puffs at halftime.[1]

A similar gendered humor often characterizes the modern iteration of these games, a humor that infused Jack's commentary throughout the game as he announced plays like, "She does it for the gram! Touchdown juniors!!!" His comedy extended to the halftime show as he said to the laughing crowd, "I just got word that the flying Wolindas will be our halftime performers. Kids you don't know who that is but your parents are laughing so hard right now. No word on whether or not insurance will clear them." A little later in the game he announced, "Folks: this just in! Insurance did not clear the Flying Wolindas. We've got about fifteen minutes to figure out your halftime performers." Finally Jack concluded his humorous halftime commentary by saying, "In lieu of the Flying Wolindas we have the next best thing available. It is the American Flying Kazoo Band!" The laughter continued throughout the night, laughter at girls playing a "boys'" game, laughter at the kazoo band, laughter at the mocking commentary provided by Jack, laughter that echoed through the stadium even as these young women played earnestly and sustained several notable injuries.

I have to be honest here: I was surprised that American High sponsored a Powder Puff game like this one. A fundraiser that relies on finding a "gender swap" humorous seemed to contradict the concern expressed by Vanessa about gender-based bullying, albeit in this instance young women were the butt of the joke, not trans youth. Such an event also seemed out of line with other steps taken at American High to de-emphasize gender difference, such as a shift in preceding years to gender-neutral ballots for homecoming and prom courts rather than one divided by votes for "kings" and "queens." I was surprised that the school would allow for this type of, to my mind at least, outdated gender ritual that encouraged people to laugh at girls playing sports typically played by boys. As the spring of my second year of research rolled around, I listened to the morning announcements with a little dread as I waited for the annual call for Powder Puff participants. I was not looking forward to once again sitting through an event in which talented girl athletes were collectively laughed at for charity. Given this dread, I was startled when the morning announcements featured something . . . different. What came over the loudspeaker was not a call for a Powder Puff Football Game, but for a "*Power Tough* Football Game." Confused, but with a little hope that, perhaps, like some other events at American, this one would shift toward a more egalitarian one rather than one that emphasized outdated (and quite frankly dangerous) notions of masculinity and femininity, I went in search of Coach Ted for explanation. When I found him, he told me, "I changed the name to Power Tough! Are you okay with that? I hate the name Powder Puff." I didn't answer whether or not I was "okay with that" because, honestly, I didn't understand what the name change meant.

To make sense of the new name and his reasoning, I headed over to the gym later that day to attend the meeting he led with members of the football team who were interested in serving as Power Tough coaches. During the meeting, Coach Ted outlined some of the changes he had in mind. Handing each of the boys—and the attendees were all boys—a list of guidelines and a practice schedule, Coach

Ted said, "We are going to have actual coaching staff this year. We'll have lights on Friday night to try to make it real and get as many people there as possible. You are responsible for the organization and the practice. You are going to need line coaches and running back coaches." It was clear, as he led the meeting, that Coach Ted was attempting to create a different, less humorous, and more serious atmosphere for the game. As part of this shift in tone, Coach Ted provided the boys a series of coaching tips. He told them that the girls "are gonna be quick learners. I promise they are smarter than we are," adding, however, that "no girl will be able to throw very far." He suggested some game play strategies to make up for their presumed gender deficiencies. He also warned the boys to "Keep your hands to yourself. No touching. No touching at all. You can give high five and fist bumps. Use your words to coach." He punctuated these statements by demonstrating fist bumps and high fives. In closing, Ted told them, "Your job is to prove that you are ready and prepared to lead. Your job is to provide the best possible experience. You need to make it so that they feel successful and valued and part of the team. You are not setting up dates. This is not a dating opportunity. These girls are not signing up for a dating opportunity. They are signing up to have a meaningful experience."

Coach Ted, it turned out, was quite earnest about the name change. He was attempting to shift the culture of the game by treating it less as a joke and more like an actual sporting event. He encouraged the student coaches to take their leadership roles seriously, to put together a coaching staff, and to work on plays. He warned the boys to refrain from treating the girls like potential dating partners. While he did not directly critique the humorous way the game had been run in years past, his tone and affect left little room for comedy as he exhorted his players to lead. Coach Ted's shift in tone, however, stopped short of challenging the gendered nature of the event. Rather, his comments reflected what we might think of as "benevolent sexism," a type of sexism that involves both praising and patronizing women for traditionally feminine traits like kindness, domestic labor, or attention to appearance. This type of sexism often suggests that because of these traits women are better than men, a suggestion that can seem less than sincere because of the way the praise reaffirms traditional gender stereotypes, even as those who express such sexism do not think of themselves as sexist.[2] When Coach Ted tells the boys, "they are smarter than we are," he's drawing on a tradition of benevolent sexism in which women are talked about as "better" than men because they are smarter, more capable, and more in control. They are more in control than, perhaps, the young men who have to be reminded not to let their hormones get the better of them and treat the players like potential dating partners instead of athletes.

This message of benevolent sexism framed the Power Tough game that occurred several weeks later, where, instead of Jack's voice coming over the loudspeaker, it was Coach Ted's voice welcoming attendees. "Welcome to the Power Tough football game!" he said as the players tossed balls back and forth on the field to a soundtrack of AC/DC's "Thunderstruck." While the attendees made their way to the stands, Coach Ted introduced the new recipient of the money raised at the game: "It is a fundraiser for the football program at American." Instead of benefiting a local nonprofit as the Powder Puff game had done in years past, the proceeds from the Power Tough game aided the American High football program. While the proceeds benefited the team, Coach Ted said of the actual football players, "They are not the stars of the game. The stars of the game are the participants." With this introduction, the junior and senior girls came onto the field flexing their muscles or waving at the crowd as Coach Ted announced their names, without any of the joking or humor of the previous year. After covering the rules of flag football, Coach Ted asked the audience to stand and remove their hats as the national anthem played. For the rest of the evening, Coach Ted earnestly narrated the game without Jack's mocking humor, replacing that humor with the benevolent sexism of repeated comments like, "We don't need to introduce the boys. They are not the stars of tonight."

As with the newly gender-neutral homecoming and prom courts, the move from Powder Puff to Power Tough was one of several changes shortly before or during my time at American High in which gendered rituals were shifted to be more inclusive. This type of gendered social change, however, is often halting and uneven, as the shift from Powder Puff to Power Tough illustrates.[3] Changes like this one may soften the overt mocking of girls who participate, but altering the name and humorous commentary does little to shift the gendered assumptions that undergird the ritual. While it seems like Coach Ted was trying to transform this charity event in which girls have historically been the butt of an extended joke, the underlying gendered nature of the event remains unchanged: the conceit is still that girls are playing a boys' sport, are potential sex objects, and aren't really capable of playing the game. While shifts like this may, in some ways, reduce particular forms of inequality, they also instantiate other forms while obscuring the fact that they are doing so.

Coach Ted, as he typically seemed to, appeared to mean well. He loves football. His dad was a football coach. He is a football coach. His wife's dad was a football coach. He and his wife even purchased a house near to the school so that they could orient their lives around students, sports, and coaching. He made it clear that he did not like the way the Powder Puff game was run before he took over. However, Coach Ted's approach does not really challenge the gendered humor at the heart of the game. The fact remains that it's not any non-football playing students playing flag football for a charity event; it's *girls* playing football for a charity event. Not only that, these girls are out there playing hard and getting injured *to raise money for a boys' sport.*[4] These young women, many of whom are talented athletes in their own right, are expected to tough it out, laugh at being the butt of the joke (and possibly the target of sexual desire), and keep playing for the benefit of the boys.

In this sense, the story of the Power Tough game is the story of many girls' experiences in high school. It is the story of what it means to be a girl in high school when the kind of feminism and gendered analysis that is available to you is a "girl-boss feminism," a feminism that is not about challenging systemic gendered inequalities but is about being individually empowered to navigate sexist interactions and systems that seem unchanging. A girl-boss feminism focuses less on shifting systemic inequalities, and more on empowering women to be resilient in the face of enduring gender inequality.[5] Things like the name of a football game may change, but girls are still expected to grin and bear it, laugh at jokes made at their expense, and work hard for the benefit of others. The young women I spoke with at American High suggest that this dynamic goes far beyond a once-a-year fundraiser. Their daily lives are characterized by figuring out how to deal with gender inequality with the same sort of girl-boss strategies: by getting up, brushing themselves off, and going on.

This chapter details girls' stories about gender inequality in high school and the sort of sexism that they experience. Gender inequality is so normalized in these young women's everyday lives that it's almost unremarkable, constituting a sort of mundane misogyny, even as it profoundly shapes their experiences and ability to participate in the public sphere. While many of the young women I spoke with at American High identify as feminist, they rarely name the gendered harassment, stalking, and sexual violence they experience as such. Instead they label it "weird," "creepy," or "gross."[6] When girls grapple with this sort of everyday gendered harassment, they normalize it by drawing on a language of kindness and bullying.[7] That is, the regime of kindness that characterizes the social world of American High also serves to curtail a patterned understanding of these experiences. Instead, girls rely on, and the school as an organization itself encourages, strategies of individual empowerment and resilience to deal with this everyday sexism. School programming around sexual violence does little to help flesh out this language, instead framing violence and harassment as both exceptional and divorced from gendered (as well as raced, classed, and sexual) inequality.

Weird, Creepy, Annoying, and Gross

The Women's/Human Empowerment and Crafting Club meets most Thursdays in an empty classroom in K Hall, the hall that houses the Honors Academy classes. I was struck by the name, which seemed to cover more territory—women, all humans, *and* crafting—than the other affinity groups at American like the Black Student Union, the Gay/Straight Alliance, or Latinos Unidos. The leaders of the club, all White and one Latina, junior and senior girls involved in the Honors Academy, told me that they wanted to name the club "Human Empowerment Club" so that everyone would feel welcome and included. But they also wanted to address women's concerns. And they wanted to craft. So this lengthy name was the solution. Katherine, a White senior and one of the founders, explained that their crafting, however, isn't without a purpose. It is often donated to nonprofits that help women, children, and families:

> We craft for the community. It's like community outreach through crafts. We did baby blankets for the children who are in the Safe-Women program for women who have been sexually or physically abused. And then we did crafts for the Evergreen Community Center's Thanksgiving dinner. And then we did Christmas or Hanukkah or Kwanzaa ornaments, to give to someone who affected your life positively. Right now, we're doing cards for hospitalized children.

The focus on crafting emphasizes a practice associated with a traditional, domestic femininity. It's as if this sort of focus could mitigate the potential of a club like this to actually address gendered inequalities by softening its purpose with crafting. When combined with a bit of equivocating regarding who the club is actually for—humans or women—this suggests some possible discomfort or apprehension when it comes to organizing a club that focuses on gendered concerns. It may be that the unwieldy name itself echoes the other ways in which some in the American High community work to avoid topics that could be seen as political, topics like systemic gender inequalities perhaps (and the ornament crafting for holidays that do not involve ornaments might illustrate the White racial ignorance documented in the previous chapter).

While it's true that plenty of meetings focused on crafting, despite the unclear name, this club also occasionally provides a space for young folks to talk about gender inequality and specifically sexual violence. Katherine, for instance, told me that sometimes they would discuss questions like, "What should you do if your friend has been sexually assaulted? Should you tell someone? Should you let them deal with it? How can you support them?" Part of the goal of the club, Katherine said, was to connect those who need help with support around these issues: "We have people who we know through Laura's House,[8] who have the sexual assault help line and stuff like that. So, we will try to provide resources."

On one of these discussion days, Katherine posed the following questions to the club members in attendance: "How should we deal with someone who's famous in the media? Should we try them as a regular person for sexual assault?" Katherine said, "We definitely had one guy say that he thinks that women should be put in jail if they fake rape claims, and that it happens a lot. I was like, 'yeah, that's definitely a good point.' So, guys definitely have different views on it." Of course, research suggests that these sorts of false accusations do not, in fact, happen a lot.[9] While some people may believe that false accusations are common, there is little evidence to suggest that false accusations are any more common with sexual assault than with other crime. This type of "all opinions count" approach sounded like Assistant Principal Laurel's response at the Black Lives Matter exhibit. When a group of White boys challenged the facts presented on the posters, her reaction was to validate everyone's perspectives, as if the actual facts of racial inequality, or in this case, gender inequality, were inconsequential or unknowable.

Katherine's affirmation of this perspective is especially striking given the experiences of sexual harassment young women at American report, experiences about which Katherine and her friends (with whom she runs the club), Natasha, Monica, and Hazel, text regularly. Katherine said that recently, "A guy we know DM'd me something weird, so I shared that in the group chat and I was like, 'what the heck?'" She told me, it's a "really strange story," saying this guy, who attends a neighboring school, "would consistently DM Natasha and I asking if he could buy used Nike shorts from us. Which is something very weird, and so creepy and gross. We are both underage girls. It was really strange. It was weird, because he would DM Natasha and I photos *of us together*," photos he really only could have gotten if he had been at their soccer practice. Katherine said that in an attempt to get him to stop, she tried to follow him back on social media "and be like, who is this? This is so creepy." But "he didn't let me follow him. He's just so strange." Disturbed by this young man's behavior, Katherine attempted to handle the situation on her own, trying to follow him to figure out who he was. While his behavior is quite clearly at least borderline harassment, Katherine doesn't call it that, instead describing the experience as creepy, gross, strange, and weird, a language other girls also use when talking about this sort of everyday harassment.

Katherine's experience was not a particularly unusual one among young women with whom I spoke at American High. Natasha, a

White senior, the friend who had been photographed with Katherine at soccer practice, told me that via social media, "Someone tried to buy me. Like, 'I will give you $20,000.'" Rolling her eyes, she said, "It happens to me a lot, where guys are really super-gross." Natasha told me that "one of my friends sent me a picture of how a person has used my photo on a website. It's crazy. It's kind of scary." Natasha said that she thinks the person took the image from her Twitter profile, "Which is really weird. But, I mean, I'm trying to confront it as a compliment rather than identity theft. So funny. Yeah." Like Katherine, she did not define this behavior as harassment, instead calling it scary, crazy, weird, and gross. Perhaps to soften the emotional impact of the loss of control over her own likeness, Natasha tried to reframe this harassment as "a compliment" or "funny," something we might think of as a strategy of resilience in the face of harm.

When I asked her what she does "when guys are super-gross," like this guy, Natasha answered, "You've got to block it. You have to remember, it's social media. You have the power to do that, so why not use it? I'm not going to tolerate someone sending me pictures of their naked body. No. You can't do that. I have to remember that people are stupid. It's appalling." Of course, a blocking strategy only goes so far in terms of ending this sort of harassment. Social media companies and, as we'll see in a bit, schools themselves, largely abandon girls to their own devices when it comes to staying safe from this sort of harassment.[10] What young women have left as a strategy is to minimize this behavior, curtail it the best they can, and move on. So it's not a huge surprise that young women like Natasha and Katherine develop approaches that are individual in nature—blocking and not tolerating bad behavior—because they don't live in a society where vulnerable people can reliably turn to technology companies, schools, the courts, or law enforcement for support.

This behavior is more than weird, creepy, annoying, or gross. It's a digital form of what scholar Carol Gardner calls "public harassment." Public harassment is a set of "abuses, harryings, and annoy-ances," behavior that used to take place on the street and now also occurs online.[11] Public harassment has long been a way that powerful groups maintain control of shared environments, environments that used to be physical and now are also digital.[12] Research suggests that this sort of harassment is quite effective at maintaining and enforc-ing social inequality. Even if a young woman hasn't actually experi-enced this kind of public harassment, she is likely to shape her behav-ior in response to knowledge of this sort of harassment.[13]

Madison's experience with social media illustrates the power that witnessing this sort of harassment has in shaping behavior. She has a deeply ambivalent relationship with social media not because she has had negative experiences, but because her friends have. While she tells me that "there is definitely social pressure" to have social media ac-counts, she dreads having them. Madison dreads them "because a lot of people get surprise dick picks. It's kind of disgusting. It's really tragic. They don't even ask. Guys just think that we would enjoy them sending a random picture of . . ." and she then trails off motioning with her hands. While this hasn't happened to her, stories from her friends, and one of a "a kid who picked like thirty girls just randomly" to send pic-tures of his genitalia to, lead her to feel ambivalent about this sort of digital presence. According to other young women I spoke with, Madi-son's fear is not unfounded. Tara for instance told me, as she laughed cynically, that getting requests for naked pictures is such a "common one" that "if I could count the amount of guys and I got money for it, I would be a kazillionaire." The vast majority of teenagers have social media accounts and well over half of them use these accounts daily.[14] So when young women express ambivalence about these technologies, it becomes clear that public harassment constrains their ability to par-ticipate meaningfully in public life and shared spaces.[15]

For teens at American High, these online environments reflect their offline experiences with public harassment.[16] Still laughing ruefully, Tara described her time on social media, drawing connections between harassment there and in offline spaces: "What I love looking at is my Facebook message requests. They're hilarious. You get some creepy guy that's like forty, with kids and married, and he's like—'hey, babe.' Then there's obviously walking down the street; you get the catcalls . . . It's very common for girls." Tara's comments painfully capture the way gendered harassment pervades different spheres of social life for young women.[17] As Leila, a White junior, said, "I mean, just being a female in general is kind of difficult. I don't know. I went downtown to Doughnut Divas because I wanted some donuts. There's a bunch of guys, and they're yelling—and I run to my car and lock the doors." As Morgan, a White junior, told me, one time she had to rush her mom to the hospital for an anxiety attack and "when we were there, this one nurse who was checking us in, he just kept looking at me and winking at me. I was like you're disgusting, I'm sixteen years old. What is wrong with you? It was so weird." Brooke, a White senior, said, "I was in Walmart last year, getting cereal and milk, because we wanted cereal for breakfast. My family loves cereal." As she was searching for the cereal, a man in his mid-forties hit on her. She said, "I was like, why are you flirting with me? It's so weird . . . I just want some Honey Bunches of Oats."

If these stories make it seem like sexual harassment is ubiquitous, that's because it is for these young women. As Holly, a White junior, told me, "Every girl that I know has a story of being sexually harassed, or abused, or something. I don't hear that with boys. I mean, abuse can happen to boys—I'm not saying that abuse doesn't happen . . . But I'm saying that it's more likely to happen to girls." Holly is right. Studies show that sexual harassment is a common experience for young women.[18] It's not that young men are not sexually harassed, but it is not as widespread nor does it tend to be an expression of gendered power in the same way.[19] Young women shared stories about everyday gendered harassment in a way that dramatically highlights not only how pervasive it is, but also how it happens across in-person and digital contexts. The language young women use to describe this behavior is striking: strange, creepy, gross, super-gross, stupid, appalling, annoying, sad, disgusting, tragic, and most commonly, weird. They repeatedly avoid terms involving power and inequality like sexism, harassment, or misogyny to capture their experiences.

These girls' stories and the language they use to describe them illustrates not only the everydayness of the sexism but also their girl-power responses to it—blocking people, laughing uneasily, or calling the behavior weird. I began my research at American High as the nation was undergoing a reckoning with sexual harassment and violence via the #MeToo movement and Women's Marches, a reckoning that I thought may be reflected in shifting gendered dynamics in adolescence. So I was surprised to the extent that, even at a school like American High, a school where, in Leila's words, "students would burn everybody alive if they were, like mean," this gendered harassment continued. Part of this dynamic may have to do with the school's treatment and framing of dating, violence, and gendered harassment, a treatment and framing that had little to do with inequality or power and much to do with individual responses and empowerment.

Your Body, Your Choice

On a sunny spring day, the student body convened in the auditorium to learn about dating and sexual violence. Like schools in thirty-seven other states, American High puts on programming to conform with a mandate known as Erin's Law, a law that requires that public schools provide prevention-oriented sexual abuse programming. At American High this programming took the form of an assembly—co-led by Ethel, the guidance counselor who repeatedly mispronounced students' names, and Vice Principal Aaron, a White middle-aged man with short-cropped curly brown hair—that focused on consent and sexual interactions, an assembly that sounded an awful lot like the girl-boss approaches that young women use to deal with online and offline harassment.

As roughly four hundred students settled in their seats, the auditorium darkened, except for the text-heavy slides lighting up the screen at the front of the room.[20] After Vice Principal Aaron and Ethel welcomed the students, Ethel talked through a slide entitled "Abuse and Sexual Violence Prevention." She encouraged students to "have respect" for their peers because "you never know what has happened in their life" and she exhorted them to "overcome" bad things that have happened to them in their own lives. While emphasizing the message that sexual violence can "have a lasting effect," she affirmed that "people could have happy productive lives if they get counseling," reminding them that should they need counseling, they could seek it from the school health center or on-campus counselors.

As if to impress upon her audience the importance of this assembly, Ethel emphasized the widespread nature of sexual assault, saying that she was "amazed at the frequency of sexual violence among students and families at American." She warned students that such violence can happen to anyone, by anyone, from "girl to girl, boy to boy, in families." Reviewing statistics that indicate that 1 million women and girls have been sexually assaulted in the state of Oregon, Ethel warned them that "young men and boys are not immune" to victimization. She provided no more information about boys as victims or as perpetrators of this type of violence, though she did emphasize the risk of being a girl, saying, "Teen girls are more vulnerable than any other age group." This sort of awkward inclusion of the gendered dynamics of sexual assault characterized much of Ethel's presentation. She suggested, for instance, that "Boy-girl relationships are more significant" once young folks enter high school. "When you turn into teenagers you get more interested in the other sex," she said. "This can take all sorts of forms. From male to male, female to female, or heterosexuality." While it seemed that Ethel was trying to make sure that students of all sexual identities felt included in this training, she stumbled over anything more than a surface inclusion of sexual diversity here. Like Coach Ted, Ethel has little formal training as a sex educator, a gap that is reflected in these clumsy, though seemingly well-intentioned, attempts to address same-sex relationships.[21]

Not surprisingly, given the stories shared by Katherine, Natasha, and Tara about social media, Ethel focused on technology use as a particular risk factor for victimization. She warned the students that "non-mutual contact has been exploding because of the cell phones," telling them that "pictures on their phones can be used for nefarious purposes." She exhorted them to "watch what you are doing with your cell phones and what people are doing with theirs so you don't end up on theirs." Ethel placed responsibility on young folks for monitoring what others were doing on their phones in order to avoid having a picture taken of them by someone else, something that stories like Natasha's make clear is pretty impossible to do. Regardless, Ethel told them, "This is where phones have gotten people into a lot of trouble. Once it is there you have no control over where it goes. You don't want to find that your picture is on a pornographic website. It happens." Unfortunately, as girls' stories indicate, many of them don't actually have a lot of control over what happens to their pictures or who takes pictures of them in the first place. As Katherine and Natasha's stories suggest, they are well aware that strangers can take pictures of them, but there isn't a lot they can do to prevent it. These young women receive little in the way of solutions to this problem, apart from Ethel's warning to "watch what people are doing" with their cell phones. This discussion of the dangers of social media seem far removed from the girls' experiences of everyday harassment, harassment they continually navigate in order to participate in the social life of adolescence.

After Ethel's warnings about, and lack of solutions to, the dangers of social media, Vice Principal Aaron took over the presentation to discuss consent. Telling them that consent is "when you actually say yes," Vice Principal Aaron emphasized that "consent must be freely given. It's reversible and it's informed." He provided several examples of what is not considered consent, like "if you agree to sex and then the guy removes a condom partway through that's not okay; you did not consent to that." Reminding them that "consent must be enthusiastic," he warned, "if you aren't willing to have a conversation about what's going to happen . . . if you aren't in a space to have that conversation with your partner, you are not ready to have sex. You just think you're ready to have sex." In this discussion Vice Principal Aaron echoed "sex positive" approaches to sex, or approaches that position sexuality and desire as a normal and natural and enjoyable part of being human. However, at no point in his talk did he provide a model of what a successful sexual interaction involving affirmative consent might look like.[22] Young folks were given examples of what is *not* consent, but not what is. They were told, "If you aren't in a space to have that conversation with your partner you are not ready to have sex," but were left with no words with which to communicate their desire in an affirmative manner.

Instead of providing ways to say "yes," Vice Principal Aaron followed this discussion by elaborating how to say "no." He provided the following scenario for students to discuss: "Imagine you've been talking for a while and your partner is pressuring you to have sex and you aren't ready." After instructing the students to turn to talk to their neighbor about possible responses, he asked for answers, which students enthusiastically provided. One said, to cheers from his classmates, "Can you slow down? I'm not ready for this." Students were similarly supportive when someone responded to Vice Principal Aaron's request that they imagine they are bystanders "drinking at a party and you see someone put an arm around someone who is too drunk to consent and they are going upstairs . . ."[23] After talking to each other, students volunteered answers like, "When you see something say something," or "I'd ask if I could help out," or "Force yourself into the conversation. Don't them let out of your sight." Their extensive and enthusiastic answers suggest that while the students have few examples of how to say yes, they certainly know how to say no and how to take care of vulnerable others. Their cheers in response to the setting of sexual boundaries signals a cultural shift. It is a shift that may not be playing out in individual relationships, but it is a shift nonetheless, a shift that suggests that it is customary to consent to sexual activity and that bystanders have a responsibility to intervene, if possible, when someone cannot or does not consent.

Vice Principal Aaron concluded his portion of the presentation with a slide entitled "Your Body, Your Choice," a riff on the popular reproductive rights slogan "my body, my choice." He explained to the assembled group that this slogan "means you have the responsibility to have an exit plan." As he concluded his talk, Vice Principal Aaron reminded them, "Remember, it's your body, your choice! Help prevent abuse!" At first glance, it seems fitting that a presentation on sexual safety ends with an invocation of a feminist slogan designed to underscore a woman's right to bodily autonomy and integrity. However, rather than affirming women's right to reproductive control, in this context the slogan was deployed to place the responsibility for the prevention of sexual violence on those who may be at risk of experiencing it.[24] In other words, a feminist phrase designed to critique state control becomes transformed into a sort of girl-boss motto in which young women are responsible for preventing the sort of harassment to which they are regularly subjected. As Katherine, Natasha, and Tara's stories indicate, this approach is shockingly distant from their lived realities in which harassment is normal, not exceptional. Their stories suggest that they could do little to prevent much of the behavior they are experiencing, exit plan or not.

Most of the girls I spoke with report that they learn little helpful information in these assemblies. Tara, who had said she'd be a "kazillionaire" if she received money every time a guy asked her for naked pictures, told me, "I never sit in those. I literally go and get food. I think that they're stupid. They don't help. I hate sexual assault things at school. They're not helpful to anyone."[25] One of the reasons the assemblies aren't helpful is that while young women get told, "Well, you can always talk to the counselor. The likelihood that a counselor is going to believe you is pretty . . ." Tara trailed off and shook her head. Tara echoed other girls' sentiments here. Rarely do they tell me they turn to school authorities—because they've learned through experience that authorities are less than helpful. Natasha, for instance, said that when one friend of hers reported harassment to school representatives, "They found out about her second Instagram and they tried shutting it down because people post nudes on there. They talked to her about having child pornography on her phone. Even though it was pictures of herself. Which is ridiculous. But the thing is, I have a picture of myself in a bikini on my first account—which is not a big deal to me, because that's my body. She got in trouble for that." In other words, when young women appeal to adult authorities for help in these situations, they might find themselves in trouble instead. Stories like these that circulate among the young women at American High result in such a chilling effect that not a single young woman I spoke with told me they went to school authorities to get help with online harassment.

This lack of response, or anticipated lack of response, to young women seeking help around sexual victimization or exploitation is a form of what scholar Jennifer Freyd calls "institutional betrayal," or the way that organizations like schools, universities, churches, or workplaces may betray their members' trust.[26] This type of betrayal may entail organizational representatives doing things like making it seem that a particular incident is no big deal, making it difficult to report an experience of assault, covering up a problem, or responding inadequately to an issue. The young women at American have a sense that a response from those in charge will be inadequate, that they won't be believed, or, even worse, they will blamed for their own exploitation. All of these fears are examples of what institutional betrayal might look like. Even as the school holds assemblies like those mandated by Erin's Law, aimed at preventing sexual assault, the young women have little confidence that their reports of victimization or harassment will be responded to in fair or meaningful ways.

In fact, the muddled message sent by assemblies like this one may be a form of institutional betrayal itself. The examples provided in the assembly, for instance, seem far removed from the mundane misogyny experienced by young women—the street harassment, the stolen pictures, the sexual comments from classmates. The solutions provided—bystander intervention, monitoring other people's social media use, turning to school officials, and having an exit plan—don't speak to girls' experiences. Very few of those responses would solve the problems young women shared with me in our discussions. Perhaps the fact that the assembly is, after all, being put on by the same institution that supports an event like the Powder Puff game, an event that depends on sexist laughter, adds to this sense of institutional betrayal. As such, it is little wonder that young women might not feel safe reporting gendered harassment or violence to school representatives.

Additionally, these discussions about how to respond to harassment are devoid of reference to gendered, sexual, racial, or class inequality. While plenty of evidence suggests that sexual violence has gendered, classed, raced, and sexualized components, those dynamics are ignored in favor of positioning such violence as exceptional, not typical, experiences for girls at American High.[27] That is, the problem of sexual violence is not presented as a systemic one, so neither are the possible responses to it.[28] As such, the responsibility for solving the problem of or preventing harassment is placed on those who suffer from it.

I Never Want to Be a Bully

If these young women don't feel comfortable going to the school administration, how do they deal with the mundane misogyny to which they are subject? Not surprisingly, they tend to draw on logics of kindness and anti-bullying language in an attempt to set boundaries around harassment, violence, and sexism. That is, these young women try to respond to and prevent harassment while at the same time avoiding being mean to the boys who are treating them badly.

Natasha's story about trying to manage dating violence this way stuck with me long after our conversation. Natasha, whose pictures had been posted on the internet without her consent, told me this story about a boy she briefly dated and what happened when she set boundaries with him, deploying the sort of "your body your choice" boundaries girls had been encouraged to set in the Erin's Law assembly. She shook her head, laughing a little as she began the story: "So, this is a whole story. You want to hear this? It's so ridiculous. Please put this in your book. It's the worst." Like some other young folks with whom I spoke, Natasha encouraged me to put what she told me in the book in the hopes that it could make lives better for other teens.

Over warm drinks at a local coffee shop, Natasha told me, "We went on a date to a movie. Evan picked me up from my friend's party, and we went to the movies together. My personality is kind of energetic. I mean, some would call it annoying. Bubbly?" she said, laughing easily, demonstrating the bubbliness to which she referred. "I was talking with him. I was flirting with him." She followed this with a slight qualifier, saying, "It shouldn't matter," whether or not she was flirting. However, the date took a turn once they were in the movie theater. "He kissed me, and then he like"—she paused here, then continued, "this is gross, he choked me. Tried to be kinky about it, too." Shaking her head again, Natasha said, "He kept whispering things in my ear and being super-gross. Referring to himself as like 'daddy.' Super-gross." When they left the movie theater and got in his car, "he tried to kiss me again." She described what happened next as "one of the situations in my life where I completely regretted what I did. I kind of just would just push it away. But it was a weird situation, because I thought he was cute. But I thought, 'This is over the top.' So, I kind of just tried to push it away." Natasha seemed uncomfortable at this point and did not elaborate on exactly what "it" was or how she pushed "it" away. She made it clear, however, that she was uncomfortable with what happened and was a little frustrated with herself for not setting firmer limits with Evan. Natasha went so far as to blame herself a little for that evening, "I should have been more against it, and stopped it from getting anywhere."

Natasha attempted to avoid Evan after this, saying, "I kind of just ghosted him." Natasha did, however, turn to her friends to make sense of the experience, telling them, "You guys need to know what happened; this is so weird." However, "it somehow got back to Evan that I had said he had physically assaulted me" or that "I was spreading rumors about him, or something like that." In response Evan blocked Natasha on his social media accounts and proceeded to post a series of public statements on his account entitled, "'Exposing Natasha, part one. Exposing Natasha, part two.'" Natasha said that these posts were "just paragraphs on why I'm the worst person, ever." Tears came to her eyes as she described what he wrote: "That when he picks me up from a party, I was drunk and high. That I was being flirtatious and trying to do sexual things with him in the movie theater. And that I asked him to choke me, and that I called him 'daddy.' It's just so ridiculous. It's so, so ridiculous." When she asked Evan to delete his posts he said, "'If you're going to make up lies about me, I'm going to make up lies against you.' He was so mad I had ruined his reputation. Reputation?!" Natasha said, "You could have texted me. You could have Snapchatted me. You could have Twitter messaged me. There are so many other avenues that you could have explored, rather than trying to expose me."

Reflecting on this experience and her attempts to manage it, Natasha said, "I feel bad about this, but he tries to hang out with our group of friends. I never want to be a bully or anything like that, but I have had to disinvite him from things and kind of be like, 'You can't come.' Like, to a party or something like that, be like—he can't come." Even though Evan behaved in ways Natasha found deeply uncomfortable on their date, harassed her on social media, and refused her requests to stop writing publicly about her, Natasha felt the need to conform to certain interactional norms regarding kindness and bullying when it came to interacting with Evan in social settings. Though she tried to ignore him, and requested that he stop when he harassed her, she is still left wondering if she is a bully when she sets a boundary around her own social life by saying he cannot hang out with her and her friends.

Unfortunately, Natasha's experience with Evan is less unusual that one would hope. Lisa, a White junior, described navigating similar behavior following a breakup with a boyfriend. She told me partway into our discussion at a local Starbucks, "I had been ready to break up with him for probably two months, but he was in Florida visiting family for a month or two. I didn't really want to break up there. That seemed kind of harsh, and so I waited until he got back." Much like Natasha, Lisa centered kindness in her limit-setting with an intimate partner, not wanting to be too "harsh." A few weeks after Lisa broke up with Dylan, they attended the same music festival. She told me, "I didn't really know he was going. But I really like country music, so it was a thing for me to go to. He was just super-super-drunk. Super-drunk. And he was following me around. And he wouldn't stop texting me, and calling me. I had like thirty-seven missed calls. I had to turn my phone off." Lisa said, "He got very stalker-ey after that. He would come into my work," and though he had graduated, "he would be at school during school time. That was super-weird." Lisa continued: "He won't leave me alone. He's texting me, calling me. I still have him blocked on everything. All the social media platforms. Phone numbers. Everything." When I ask Lisa if she got some help, she answered, "No, not really. It was more like I almost felt bad. I didn't feel bad that I broke up with him, but I felt bad that this was his reaction to it." Even though Lisa had tried to be kind when breaking up with him, Dylan responded with predatory behavior and Lisa is left feeling bad, not about her behavior, but about his inability to respond appropriately.

Because she felt bad for him and because she feared his response, Lisa declined to set legal boundaries around Dylan's behavior. She told me that she and her mother considered securing a restraining order against Dylan, but "eventually we kind of decided against it, just because we thought it might bring up things that could be worse than we wanted them to be. Since I was under eighteen. Just like, since he was older than me, just that kind of stuff. I didn't want him to get in trouble. I just wanted him to leave me alone." Like Natasha, Lisa navigated not only norms of kindness, but focused on her ex-boyfriend's needs rather than on her own even though she felt like he was stalking her. Her decision to not obtain a restraining order against Dylan was based on both her fear about getting him in trouble, and, it seems, fear of his response to the legal boundary itself.

The fears expressed by Lisa are not unfounded. When she stood up to sexism, Leila experienced a dramatic reaction. A year previously, when she attended a different high school, Valley High, a boy at her school, Kyle, posted "something really mean about women in general" on social media. She told me he had written, "When guys are depressed, they just play videogames and when girls are depressed, they text 100 guys and want to sleep with them." Leila responded to his post, asking, "Why do you have to be like that? That's literally not okay." She said she was upset about the post because "girls are already stereotyped enough. We're stereotyped to have a perfect body, a perfect everything." In response to her comment Kyle "posted a picture for everyone to see, with a gun in his hand and was like, 'Talk shit, get shot.'" Fearing for her safety, Leila's mom reported the post to the police. But once "people started finding out that the police were involved, it became a #itwasn'thisfault, #kylealltheway, bla-bla-bla. And I had to look at that. I had some girl in the bathroom say they wanted to fight me, because of this happening. I just wouldn't even go to school. I've never missed that much school before. It was really stressful. I didn't feel comfortable in the school. I had my guard up twenty times more than I've ever had it up." Even though Kyle had "done that to other girls before. The school didn't really do much about it." Feeling unsafe at Valley, Leila transferred schools to American, saying, "You're going to sacrifice me? That's fine. I'll go somewhere else." Leila's experience illustrates the sort of individual strategy girls are typically left with when it comes to gendered harassment. While she sought help from the school and the police, she still had to solve the problem on her own, by switching schools, so that she could feel safe.

To deal with these experiences, some young women develop a set of preventative strategies to keep themselves safe, both physically and emotionally, from the threats of everyday sexual and dating violence. Nicole and Angelina, the outgoing Latina and Pacific Islander students who talked about how racism is "sugarcoated" at American, had a lot to say about how they strategize to keep themselves safe. Angelina said, "I get really paranoid. Like, when I'm leaving out of work and going into my car it gets me paranoid. Because I'm super-afraid of getting kidnapped or raped. I'm terrified of it." She said that this fear extends to dating apps: "I think about Tinder, I'm just like—what if I set up a date with somebody and then they literally kill me?"

Both of them said when they go to the mall they park close and typically walk with a friend. Nicole shared, "Like, just two girls walking . . . I don't know; I just feel like it's too dangerous nowadays." Angelina asserted that friendships are a key strategy to staying safe: "I feel like that's why most girls are in clubs, because they like making relationships with somebody. They feel like they trust each other. If I'm in a group and it's like, half-and-half female and males, I would be more comfortable making a relationship with the females. It's kind of sketchy with all males. But I know my limits. I'll still be friendly, or whatever. But I'll sit more with the girls." Rather than finding themselves in a situation where they may be vulnerable to harassment or violence, Nicole and Angelina develop safety strategies to avoid those very situations. They make sure they are not alone in public and they join clubs at school (which they rightly point out are disproportionately filled with and led by girls) so that they can be in groups of girls as safety strategies.

Other girls shared similar tactics they use to ensure their safety. Lauren said that she avoids parties to stay safe. "I'm very small, and I'm a girl. If I get drunk at a party, I have no idea what's going to happen to me. I don't really want anything in particular to happen to me." Her friend "who is a guy" had offered to support her, saying, "'The first time you go to a party, you'll be with me.' He's like, 'because I can make sure nobody touches you.' That's nice of him. But on the other hand, I don't know, it's always somebody you know that rapes you or something. I don't know. I trust him more than any guy I've ever met. But people . . . you never can know, really." From carrying pepper spray when they run, as Reagan, a White junior, did, to making sure that a boy walks them to their car, to creating secondary social media accounts so they don't get targeted online, these young women's lives are characterized by deploying a set of tactics to manage the threats of sexual and gendered violence. As Reagan described it so succinctly, "It's scary, in a way, to be a woman."

Given the management strategies required to exist safely as a young woman in the world, it is perhaps not surprising that some girls at American High simply opt out of heterosexual relationships, describing them akin to another item on a "to do" list. As Reagan said of her now ex-boyfriend, "He asked me to be, like, his girlfriend. I told him I don't think that's a good idea, because I am so busy and I didn't think that I would have enough time to put in the energy to actually make a relationship work with someone, especially someone who doesn't do as many things as me. And my life only gets busier as the year gets on, with like Mr. Eagle happening and lacrosse, and everything." She told me that her now ex would complain about how she didn't pay enough attention to him: "He would be like, 'Reagan, I feel like you're not making enough time for me.'" She responded to his complaint by saying, "That's so understandable, but at the same time I feel like I'm stretching myself thin just hanging out with you one night of the week. I'm constantly stressed because of honors and pageant, and I'm in student government. I play two sports. I have a lot going on." Like a certain group of girls at the school, particularly White and upper-middle-class girls, Reagan is involved in a wide variety of school-based activities like the Honors Academy, student government, and the Mr. Eagle philanthropy. Her comments reflect a level of girls' involvement that often leads to exhaustion and disconnect between their lives and boys' lives. Similarly, Angelina shared that she was "glad" she didn't have a boyfriend. When I asked her why, she said, "I feel like being in a relationship is like a job." Nicole added, "It is a job. You literally have like a full-time job. That's like being a mom; a mom, you never stop working. You're always working. It's a job."

The relationships are a job. Keeping oneself safe in daily life is a job. Navigating an emotional minefield of not hurting boys' feelings or provoking them to anger is a job. The continual management of mundane misogyny is, indeed, a job. Research suggests that this sort of management is not limited to the developmental phase of adolescence; rather, adult women continue to engage in this emotional and safety management, something scholar Chloe Hart calls "trajectory guarding" or the way that women shape interactions in order to avoid being sexually harassed.[29] School messages about gendered violence that position it as something that happens "out there" and not in the everyday lives of these young women, paired with logics that frame inequality in terms of individual emotions and bullying, leaves these young women without easy solutions to the misogyny that shapes their lives.[30] As Leila put it: "What that guy posted made a huge impact on my life, and I will never forget that." We can't just think of what goes on in high schools with a sort of "kids these days" attitude. What happens during this life period can shape young folks' experience of the world, of themselves, and of their sense of possibilities for the future.[31]

Boys and Bystanders

While Leila may "never forget that," discussions about sexual harassment and gendered violence at American High suggest that some boys don't seem to take girls' experiences as seriously as girls do. Instead, in discussions of gender inequality, sexual harassment, or assault, some young men deny, blame girls for, or minimize these problems. Or, occasionally, like some White students do in discussions of racial inequality, they simply "check out" of these discussions. While young folks, including young men, cheered each other's answers about bystander intervention and boundary-setting in the Erin's Law assembly, these cheers did not translate into visible action outside of that darkened auditorium.

The limits of a regime of kindness when it comes to dealing with things like gendered harassment become clear when multiple girls tell me about their experiences with the founder of an anti-bullying club at American, the Be Nice Club. The founder of the club, Steven, had received extensive local attention the year prior, when he founded the club in response to the suicide of a close friend. Lauren, a White junior, told me that one day Steven had asked her friend Monica, "'Do you like my outfit?'" to which Monica responded, "Yeah, I do." When Monica asked Steven if he liked her outfit, an outfit featuring leggings (a popular clothing item for young women at American), he said, according to Lauren, "No, I feel like you just wore leggings just so I'll stare at your ass." Lauren said, "He's like, 'You're practically asking for it.'" According to Lauren, the leaders of the Women's Empowerment Club, as well as their friends, widely condemned his behavior. As a result, Katherine said, Steven kept herself, Natasha, Hazel, and Monica out of the Be Nice Club. "He wouldn't let them come. Because they had burned bridges with him last year, after all the stuff he had done. And he didn't want them to expose him. So, he wouldn't let them come." Steven's behavior symbolizes the limits of niceness as an antidote to inequality. While he created a club to promote kindness, this kindness stops short of systematically addressing harassment or gendered inequalities, much like the benign diversity of American High elides systemic racial inequalities in favor of simply being kind across racial categories. When young women confronted him based on his sexist behavior, he shifted the blame to them and prevented them from participating fully in the social life of the school by excluding them from his club.

In general, young men's refusal to meaningfully engage with gendered concerns persists even in the face of teachers who focus on these topics in the classroom. One sunny spring afternoon, for instance, Coach Ted played a documentary highlighting the ways boys are socialized to be tough, strong, and, sometimes, sexist. After a particularly moving portion about the role bullying and homophobia play in boys' lives, Coach Ted paused the video for a discussion, asking, "Does the first part of this documentary resonate with your experience?" As someone who spent the better part of two decades documenting the messages young men receive about what it means to be masculine, often through aggressive, homophobic teasing, I expected to hear a litany of stories, as I often do, about these experiences. Instead, however, Tanner, a White junior with short blond hair, who often spent the class scrolling social media and liking pictures of trucks and American flags, said, "I've never seen that kind of stuff happen." Brett, also a White junior, chimed in, saying of the men in the documentary, "I feel like those guys are just really sensitive." Lucas, a Latino sophomore, added, "It didn't really resonate with me." The three of them immediately begin making jokes about bullying that actually reflect the point made about bullying in the documentary. Brett mocked in a high-pitched voice, "In first grade I was bullied," as the other two laughed. Lucas added jokingly, "I'm being bullied again!" and Brett joined in, "I've been bullied!" It seems that admitting to being bullied itself may reveal a sort of gendered vulnerability that could lead to the sort of bullying that the documentary was addressing. That is, the boys were mocking getting bullied in order to prevent being bullied themselves.[32]

Perhaps thinking that a break and a change of scenery would help students like Brett, Lucas, and Tanner take the lessons of the documentary more seriously, Coach Ted suggested the class move outside to continue the conversation in the sunshine. In a sunny patch outside of J Hall the students splayed across the grass in small groups leaning or lying down on each other's laps or backpacks. Some pulled out and applied sunscreen to protect them from the rare Oregon sunshine. Instead of continuing to ask if they had been bullied, Coach Ted changed tack, telling them to think "of a time when you or someone else was a 'bystander' in a conversation that involved disrespectful language toward women." He asked, "What do you wish you or someone else had said?" Xavier, a Pacific Islander junior, answered, "I've been a bystander. One time I was on the bus going somewhere with a team. A bunch of people were talking and they were talking about a girl in a bad way." Tanner asked, "What they say?" Xavier answered, "They said this one girl was ugly. And then another guy says that a girl smells. And if you know what that means, you can figure it out," referring to sexist ways that vaginas are often discussed in terms of unpleasant smells. Coach Ted asked, "Did you feel something when those comments happened?" Xavier responded, "I feel weird about it." Coach Ted said that feelings like this are "a signal. It's your unconscious knowing what is right and wrong. Anyone else feel it and it doesn't feel good?" In response, about three-quarters of the class raised their hands. Coach Ted asked them, "What is something that Xavier could have said at that time?" After a prolonged moment of silence, Tasha, a Black senior, said, "It can feel not socially acceptable to say something in the moment." Derrick, a White junior, suggested it could feel "not cool" to say something, but then suggested, "I feel like you could be like, hey dude, that's rude." The students in this moment were significantly more silent than they had been during the Erin's Law assembly, perhaps because Coach Ted began with a real example, one that Xavier had actually experienced, rather than a "what if" example used by Vice Principal Aaron. Unlike the fictional scenarios in the Erin's Law assembly, this actual example came with real, not imagined, social pressures.

Encouraging more boys to talk, Coach Ted asked, "Any male students want to speak about what these societal pressures feel like? Someone who has been through it?" Shayne, a Black junior, like several of the boys in the class, wasn't paying attention, so he looked up and asked, "Can you repeat the question, Coach Ted?" After Coach Ted repeated his question, Shayne answered with a generic statement, "I know who I am and I know my worth so I don't have to prove myself and fit in because I know my worth." After Coach Ted prodded the group a few more times, Derrick finally responded, "Maybe I should start speaking up, but that's one thing when you are watching a video; when you are in the moment I don't know if I'd do that or not." Derrick's comment highlights precisely how much harder it is for some young men to confront sexism or gendered harassment in an actual situation, a situation in which confronting that sort of behavior might then make one subject to harassment or at risk of losing social status. Intervening as a bystander comes with a social cost, a social cost that is often not addressed in trainings like the Erin's Law assembly. As Derrick pointed out earlier, it can feel "not cool." Research suggests that pointing out or condemning sexist behavior can actually make boys more vulnerable to being on the receiving end of sexist or homophobic epithets themselves.[33]

Jerry, the young man who had expressed resigned responses to solving racism in Nella's class, questioned whether or not it might be rude to say something in a situation like this: "Depending on the person I don't know if you have the right to say anything to anyone. If it's some person you have never met before and you are trying to call them out on their bullshit. It's like aggressive or something." Jerry's comment indicates that the very nature of confronting sexist language may itself be "aggressive." In other words, confronting sexist behavior may be seen as just as aggressive as the sexist behavior itself. Jerry's response echoes the messages of kindness that shape American High: sexist behavior is unkind but so is confronting it, which makes both of them bad. When kindness is presented as a solution to social problems, it can cloud the inequality, in this case the gendered inequality, that is at the heart of the problem, leaving the problem, in essence, unsolved.

In response to Jerry, Xavier further explained the experience on the bus: "We were going to the state championship. I could have said something but they also could have just not said it. They were like arguing and stuff and I didn't want to jump into it. Like everyone has a different point of view." Xavier's analysis echoes the equal weight given to differing opinions on systemic racism or sexual assault heard elsewhere at American High. In his approach, gendered harassment becomes not an issue of inequality, but one of perspective, that "everyone has a different point of view." This, of course, is not Xavier's problem; we have heard similar analyses from Vice Principal Laurel regarding systemic racial inequality. It's another example of the bothsidesism of a regime of kindness that results when social problems are seen as divorced from social inequality.

Responding to Xavier's reluctance to confront this sort of language, Alicia commented, "What you *don't* do has as much of an impact on the situation as what you *do* do." Coach Ted agreed with her analysis, responding, "You're enabling them." Nomi, a Latina junior, said that by not stepping in, "You're condoning it." When no one else followed Nomi's comment, Coach Ted asked, "Anyone have any thoughts on the foot-in-the-door theory that Alicia just talked about?" Malik just put his head down in response and closed his eyes. Xavier said, "I was thinking about this but to be honest I wasn't really listening." Around the grassy area, Xavier and some of the other boys present continued to check out of the conversation as girls started to share their stories of sexist experiences.

Alicia, for instance, said, "Maybe this is true for other girls: if I say something to something a guy said, it makes me look stupid." She used as an example a time in class when a boy said, "All women just don't understand me." She'd critiqued what he said as sexist, "but the more that I talked, the more guys were just laughing." Alicia imitated them by using a deep voice, "Oh, you're like a girl." Alicia said that it felt like "as a girl everything you say just further puts you in that box they have already put you in. All the guys were like laughing." She concluded by again using a deep voice to imitate the boys saying, "Girls get so heated" and "You're such a girl." Many with their heads down or eyes closed, not a single boy in the class meaningfully responded to Alicia's experience of gendered dismissal. Jerry, instead, shifted the discussion from one about gender to one of individual experiences and qualities. He said, of Alicia's experience, "That's not just boys or girls either—it's like who you present yourself as. Look at me. I look like I smoke weed; it's just . . . people just disregard your thoughts because you look a certain way." The class laughed at Jerry's invocation of weed as Jerry continued, musing about speech in general, "Where's the line between freedom of speech and hate speech?" The conversation trailed off as Jerry moved the discussion from one of sexism to one of presentation of self and free speech, eliding gendered inequality and effectively ending the discussion.

These boys' responses to girls' stories of sexism echo the gendered dynamics of stories girls tell about boundary-setting and illustrate the way boys are socialized out of being empathetic, both with girls and each other.[34] Much like the girls report that boys ignore their limits in terms of dating and sexuality, so too do the boys in Coach Ted's class simply tune out when girls share stories of sexism. This refusal to hear girls' stories reflects research that suggests both boys and girls have a harder time recognizing the way gender inequality takes a higher toll on girls than on boys.[35] That is, young people, both boys and girls, have difficulty seeing how sexism affects young women. Part of this difficulty results from boys' avoidance strategies, strategies that look a lot like those that young White folks use to avoid discussions of racial inequality. These avoidance strategies involve not only checking out and not listening to girls, but also denying the effect that some boys' behaviors have on girls' lives. When his girlfriends share with him stories of sexist treatment, for instance, Brett downplays their impact, saying, "Come on, if a guy looks at you or says, 'Hey, I like your bottom' . . . 'I like your breasts,' those are words. Those are words that they're saying. They haven't touched you . . . When a guy says, 'Hey, your boobs are nice,' that shouldn't be something that you cry about."[36]

Girl-Boss Feminism

Frankly, it seems that these young women did a lot of work to not "cry about" the sorts of messages and requests they received from boys. As Natasha put it, she even tried to see some of this behavior as a compliment, rather than as harassing or problematic. Though I have researched gendered experiences in high schools for more than two decades, I struggled during my time at American High as I repeatedly witnessed examples of sexism that mirrored not only those I heard and experienced as a high schooler in the 1990s, but also those that I documented when researching high schoolers in Northern California in the early 2000s. While, to be sure, some important things had changed since those previous eras—the emphasis on consent, students collectively cheering examples of bystander intervention, and a football coach openly discussing how to be less homophobic—girls' experiences of everyday harassment really had not changed.[37]

It may be that those positive changes around consent and bystander intervention actually cloud the extent to which mundane misogyny exists and shapes these young women's lives. Young women detail this misogyny and their attempts to manage it in story after story. However, the focus at American on empowerment, gendered change, and sexual consent seem to crowd out space for these young women's experiences. When a shift from "Powder Puff" to "Power Tough" is framed as a progressive one, when the principal emphasizes consent but girls get in trouble for their social media content, when the founder of a "Be Nice" club is sexist, when one tries to see harassment as a compliment, it makes it hard to name what is happening as gender inequality.

It is notable that many of the experiences the girls describe take place in intimate contexts, either in relationships or in digital exchanges. This means that school hallways are not as filled with rampant, loud, joking harassment as had perhaps been the case historically.[38] Instead the harassment seems quieter, more subtle, more personal. No longer, for instance, does the school yearbook feature senior superlatives like "Biggest Groper," a category that last appeared in an American High yearbook from the 1990s. Instead, boys jokingly evade adult authority by including cleverly disguised sexism in senior quotes like "If the red river is flowing, take the dirt road home" (a reference to periods and anal sex) or "Fluorine uranium carbon potassium bismuth technetium helium sulfur germanium thulium oxygen neon yttrium" (abbreviations of elements that spell out "Fuck bitches get money")—much of which goes unnoticed by authorities. As a result, some of this sexism may be less visible to adults. In many ways this means that girls are more on their own to make sense of, grapple with, and, in the end, manage the everyday sexism, harassment, and violence they experience.[39]

This type of organizational ordering of gender and sexuality may shed some light on why, even though Title IX prohibits harassment based on sex and, as such, should be a resource for those who experience this sort of victimization, such harassment is rarely reported in K-12 schools.[40] A lack of organizational language or support around gendered harassment leaves young women to develop individual response and prevention strategies. In many ways, girls' analyses reflect the girl-boss feminism messages they've been given for years, messages that tell them girls can do anything and that real sexism is a problem of the past.[41] The few times young women actually name the gendered nature of these experiences, it seems that their calls are ignored or misheard in a way that insists upon the random and individual nature of these sorts of experiences. As such, gendered harassment and violence largely gets dealt with in ways that avoid "political" content or explanations that have to do with power and inequality. But, as their experiences indicate, these young women cannot girl-boss their way out of sexist harassment and assault.

That said, this girl-boss feminism is a feminism that is raced, classed, and sexualized, an approach deployed by upper-middle-class, straight White women. In that sense, this girl-boss model is related to other statuses and privileges these young women hold. Many, though not all, of the stories in this chapter are those of straight, White, high-status girls. The way these young women benefit from racial, class, and even gender inequality becomes clear when we take a closer look at the long-running philanthropy in the school, the Mr. Eagle Pageant, a philanthropy that depends on a gendered division of labor and privileges those who already benefit from classed, raced, gendered, and sexual privilege. The pageant process itself is one that makes these racial, classed, and sexual privileges look like merit. Part of the inability to recognize the systemic nature of gendered inequality in the experiences of these young women may have to do with the way this inequality is built into the organization itself and in the way young men refuse to hear the girls' stories—but it may also have to do with the way that some high-status White girls benefit from racial, class, and sexual inequality at American High.

5   *The Philanthropic Class*

Excitedly "oohing" and "ahhing" over neatly folded pink, black, and white sweatshirts lining a conference table, the eight coordinators of the Mr. Eagle Pageant trickled into the bland windowless room where they hold their weekly meetings. Betsy, a White junior, cried, "They look so good!" as she picked up a sweatshirt featuring the phrase "Eagle Pageant." The words were written in the bubbled script of the title of the 1980s movie *Grease,* a movie that served as the theme of the pageant. Hannah, a senior of Native and White descent with long brown hair, fashionable clothes, sophisticated makeup, and impeccable nails, explained that she was able to purchase the sweatshirts at TJ Maxx. "They're all small," she said and paused for a moment before adding, "except for one," looking pointedly at a set of clothing on the corner of the table. Shortly after Hannah said this, Macy a White senior with shoulder-length wavy brown hair, who, along with Hannah, served as the lead pageant coordinator—walked into the room. Making her way over to the far corner of the table where her not-size-small sweatshirt sat, Macy looked for a chair. The other coordinators had already claimed the open seats around the table, settling in with their sticker-covered water bottles, paper planners, and to-do lists. Macy stood awkwardly for a moment, shifting her weight back and forth, as she waited for someone to move. When no one did,

Macy grabbed a chair far from the table and wheeled it over. Meekly interrupting a conversation between Betsy and Addison, she asked, "Can I sit here?" Betsy and Addison mutely and almost imperceptibly moved their chairs while not making eye contact with Macy, as she tried to squeeze her chair into a small space between them.

The rest of the meeting ran as these meetings typically did, in a flurry of paper planners and rapid-fire discussion as the group of young women organized events for that year's Mr. Eagle Pageant, a long-running philanthropy that benefits a local hospital pediatric unit through a charity called Kids Aid. "Mr. Pageants," featuring the catchphrase "Save the Babies," are held annually at high schools throughout the state. As the origin lore has it, decades prior a student at Valley High had gotten himself in trouble, though the misdeed itself remains a mystery to the participants, none of whom could tell me what it was. He was assigned community service as penance and proposed a fundraiser in the form of a "reverse beauty pageant," one in which boys were the contestants instead of girls. The pageant evolved into a tradition that expanded to schools across the state and now spans the course of several months, a time period participants refer to as "pageant season."

While the "Save the Babies" motto suggests the primary beneficiaries of the pageant are infants, the proceeds can actually help hospital patients up until their early twenties—the point at which they age out of the hospital's pediatric wing. The philanthropy raises around $300,000 every year, about $25,000 of which comes from American High alone. These funds have helped to pay for everything from specialized medical equipment for the pediatric wing, such as infant-specific crash carts, to an ambulance specifically designed to transport medically fragile infants from rural areas to more well-resourced hospitals.

Unlike the pageant contestants, for whom "pageant season" is a several-months-long commitment that they apply for in the fall of their senior year, these eight coordinators go through an application process early in their freshman year. Those who are chosen are told by the White mother–daughter team who advise the Mr. Eagle Pageant, Janet and Jennifer, that they "cannot procrastinate in this program at all. Pageant needs to be part of your nightly routine. It's not just sports and homework." This team of eight young women cannot procrastinate or put other work in front of this commitment because they are in charge of the entire pageant. Each year they run monthly fundraisers, solicit sponsors, select the theme, choreograph the dances, interface with the Kids Aid charity representatives, manage the contestants, advertise the event, and sell the tickets. Their four years of participation in this program serves as an education in philanthropy. They learn about philanthropic etiquette, the nature of fundraising, the use of social media, and the leveraging of social networks—all lessons I watched in real time as I attended their weekly meetings.

It's hard to convey the amount of activity that occurs simultaneously at these meetings as the coordinators organize multiple fundraisers, thank donors, wrangle contestants, and collect money raised by them. The soundtrack of the room is a quiet buzz of flipping paper while coordinators discuss to-do lists, write in planners, input events into phones, and confirm and ask questions about dates and divisions of labor. I could barely keep up with writing my own notes about their activity as they rapid-fired questions, comments, and answers back and forth, jumping from a discussion about upcoming fundraisers at fast food restaurants like Panda Express and Carl's Jr.:

GRACIE: "We need to get the Panda Posters done."
ADDISON: "By when."
GRACIE: "Next week."
ADDISON: "Carl's Jr. will get back to me by the end of the week. They need to check what their budget is."
RACHEL: "What's the percentage?"
HANNAH: "100 percent!"

To dates for decorating meetings and flash mobs:

> GRACIE: "Is the decorating meeting tomorrow?"
> RACHEL: "What meeting?"
> GRACIE: "The senior decorating meeting for the pageant."
> HANNAH: "Next Wednesday."
> REAGAN: "We have a flash mob next Wednesday."
> ADDISON: "You could do it Thursday or Friday."
> REAGAN: "Thursday is the decoration meeting lunch."

To the specific issues with an upcoming fundraiser:

> HANNAH: "I have four Carl's Jr. posters but I won't be able to be here before school or after school for a while."
> MACY: "You can advertise on Instagram that they will give out sunglasses for the first hour."
> HANNAH: "They want us there at 4:30."
> RACHEL: "We need two people carrying orders out on trays."
> ADDISON: "They should say things like 'Guest number 56 do you need anything else?'"
> MACY: "There needs to be one person cleaning off tables."

To doling out specific responsibilities:

> HANNAH: "If you see contestants around, I've only received five skits."
> BETSY: "I've only heard back from five of them about the parent meeting."
> HANNAH: "And only five of them have turned in donations."
> ADDISON: "I have a couple of contestants who have not turned in any donations."

HANNAH: "I remind them every meeting and I reminded them this morning."

ADDISON: "Who is doing thank-you cards?"

BETSY: "Tell your mom to watch out for a box from the Hallmark store."

The rapidity with and shorthand in which the coordinators speak suggest that these young women have learned these skills so well that they could deploy a sort of insider language to ask questions, solve problems, and make plans almost simultaneously.

As this particular meeting began to wind down, the discussion turned to concerns about student enthusiasm for these events. Jennifer, the blond twenty-something daughter of the mother–daughter pair of advisors, and a former pageant coordinator herself, lamented, "It's really sad what's going on here lately with no school pride. You are in an unfortunate year because American school spirit is really depressing." She told the coordinators, "You have the opportunity and the challenge to *be* American school spirit." While I hadn't noticed much in the way of a lack of school pride, with students and staff alike regularly sporting American Eagle symbols on their clothes, hats, bags, and cars, this lament was regularly reiterated throughout the pageant season by the advisors, coordinators, and contestants. In response to Jennifer's claim, Hannah excitedly suggested, "We could do our own spirit week in the lead-up to the pageant!" Building on Hannah's suggestion, Lila added, "We could do beach themes!" She paused and looked around before asking, echoing the language of "offense" used by student leadership when putting together spirit themes for football games, "We can say beach because that won't offend anyone. Right?" Hannah responded shaking her head, "Someone's always going to be offended." Lila said, moving on from concerns over offense, "How cool would it be to decorate the school with *Grease*-themed things?!" Excitedly the coordinators started shouting out ideas:

LILA: "Greaser day!"

REAGAN: "Jean jacket?"

HANNAH: "Pink on Wednesday for Pink Ladies."

LILA: "Red for Rydell."

BETSY: "We can have a little photo thing!"

REAGAN: "Mr. Eagle Pageant as a hashtag and then we post it on social media!"

GRACIE: "We are going to transform the school!"

HANNAH: "That's the spirit, Gracie!"

LILA: "I'm really excited!"

ADDISON: "I'm really excited too!"

HANNAH: "We are going to change the world!"

These young women do indeed have a sense that they can change the world. Unlike the queer young folks who worked for organizational inclusion, or those who struggled to put on the BLM display, or those who risked school discipline to stage a walkout demanding gun control, these mostly White, mostly straight, mostly upper-middle-class young women easily take advantage of school resources. With little concern about pushback from authorities, they make decisions more typically reserved for official institutional actors, like establishing a spirit week simply because they want to.

Sitting with the coordinators at their weekly meetings, attending fundraisers, and watching the pageant itself, I began to understand the Mr. Eagle Pageant as much more than a fundraiser. Instead I saw how the pageant relies on and reproduces a classed division of gendered labor in which these mostly young White women spearhead philanthropic efforts and develop a skill set suitable for possible future roles as wives and mothers. This is a program that functions as both a reflection and a generator of intersectional privilege. By intersectional privilege, I mean the way that organizational ordering of race, class, gender, and sexuality come together to enable these young women, and the young men who are chosen to compete, to be student citizens. Student citizens are members of the school community whose identities, knowledge, and skill sets are rewarded by the school and who can, in turn, harness the power of the school and its resources for their own ends. They can, for example, declare spirit weeks (something not all members of the school community, like, say, Craig, can do), leave class for non-curricular activities without punishment (something many students feared when they participated in the gun control walkout), and, as we'll see later in this chapter, take over the auditorium while dressed in drag without administrative comment (unlike the young folks in the drag show). This citizenship extends beyond the school walls, as these young folks are being prepared for upper-middle-class philanthropic endeavors through the development of a particular form of cultural capital, or set of common sense knowledge, as well as the development of well-resourced social networks.[1] During their years of participation in this program they learn how to make the school as an organization work for them, going into young adulthood bolstered by the sense that they can, indeed, "change the world."[2]

The student citizen is produced through processes of intersectional privilege, processes that are obscured by logics of individual merit that naturalize the overwhelming Whiteness, middle-classness, and gender- and sexual normativity of the pageant itself. The pageant process, in other words, is a way that inequality masquerades as merit, a process that can help to shed light more generally on the way gendered, raced, classed, sexualized power is produced, maintained, and, importantly, justified. While none of the pageant guidelines formally excludes particular types of young folks from participating, the ideologies of worthiness upon which participation is based lead to a systematic exclusion of young folks who inhabit less socially advantaged positions.

From the (mostly) White coordinators to a racially homogeneous group of contestants, to the way the school supports this philanthropic endeavor but doesn't support "political" ones, to the way working-class students are functionally but not formally excluded from participation, the Eagle Pageant is a story of who benefits from a regime of kindness at American High. This sort of philanthropic endeavor relies on kindness in the form of financial generosity, a sort of feel-good response to social problems that requires little, if any, systematic change. This chapter details the way the gendered, raced, and classed inclusion and exclusion of the pageant is thrown into relief as the pageant undergoes a name change in an effort to be more gender inclusive: from the Mr. Eagle Pageant to the Eagle Pageant. As part of this shift, for the first time ever a girl, Kat, becomes a contestant. However, rather than signaling a new, more inclusive era, Kat's multiple lines of class, sexual, and gender difference make even more clear the way in which intersectional privilege shapes the ability to participate in this high-status activity at American High. Like beauty pageants in general, the Mr. Eagle Pageant reflects a set of values and moral commitments—in this case, values and moral commitments that highlight the limits of addressing social problems with a culture of kindness.[3]

The Ladies Auxiliary

Late in the fall term, the eight pageant coordinators—Hannah, Betsy, Macy, Addison, Lila, Reagan, Gracie, and Rachel—stood in the same conference room in which they hold their weekly meetings to welcome potential contestants for that year's pageant. Standing at the front of the room, they sported the pink-and-black clothing of the Pink Ladies, the cigarette-smoking group of cool girls from *Grease*. Boys, and at this meeting it was all boys, tumbled through the door high-fiving and loudly greeting one another. Phil, a White senior, strutted in, announcing to the already boisterous group, "I'm the horniest man alive," while Chris, another White senior, yelled excitedly, "Don't you love a good pageant? I love a good pageant!" When Tony entered the room, boys collectively yelled "HEEEEEYYY TONY!" Ryan, a White senior, laughingly chided him, saying, "He called me like five minutes ago and says, 'What does it take to be Mr. Eagle?'" Tony, wearing his trademark red Coke sweatshirt, laughed at himself in response. James, a Latino senior, confidently strode in and commented, "Dude, we got a crowd here!" as friends yelled his name in greeting. As the group began to settle down James announced, "Dude, there are not snacks here. I brought ramen," and, laughing, sat down to eat and listen.

To introduce these possible future contestants to the Kids Aid philanthropy, Addison started a video about a family who benefited from some of the items purchased by the funds raised through the Mr. Eagle Pageant while Betsy darkened the room. Some of the coordinators softly sang along to the Coldplay song backing the video. On screen we watched the story of a couple in which the pregnant wife was admitted to a local hospital with a high fever, followed by a diagnosis of the flu, which led to a monthlong coma during which her baby was born by C-section. The tiny baby spent months in the neonatal intensive care unit (NICU). The video concluded with photos of a happy, healthy baby and family in the years following these health struggles and hospital stays.

After the video ended, Janet and Jennifer facilitated a meeting about the requirements and process of the Mr. Eagle Pageant. They told the assembled hopefuls that they need to "see if it fits into your lifestyle," because if they are elected as a contestant, they are committing to "three months' worth of activities and practices," including "dance practices 2–4 days a week after school, evenings, and some weekends." Jennifer reminded them that "you need to think about your other commitments—church, college planning, family, jobs, academics, sports, and your social life." To get the boisterous group to take the commitment seriously, Janet told them, "We've had guys cry. It does get stressful." Allaying fears that often come up about the dance portion, Janet explained, "You do not need to know how to dance" because "the girls will teach you." In fact, as Jennifer added, highlighting the often ambivalent relationship between White men and dancing, "The best part is when you don't know how to dance."[4] She said that the contestants don't even need to "have a true talent" for the talent portion: "That's a rare occasion. It's mostly all SNL skits and YouTube viral videos. The funniest ones are the less talented ones. Zero talent." As Kent—a White, upper-middle-class, straight graduate of American who won the title of Mr. Eagle several years before—told me, "My talent was apparently good enough to make them laugh. I got a pie in the face, and I got hit in the head with a fork. Ran into a door. It was great. They laughed." While each year one or two contestants earnestly play the piano or sing, most opt for humor, like Kent did.

As the meeting continued, Jennifer let the potential contestants know what they needed to do to qualify. Applicants needed to have a 3.0 GPA, "exemplify Eagle pride," and turn in a filled-out two-page application by the deadline. Applicants who met these requirements would have their names listed on a ballot on which the senior class would vote. Those who did not meet the GPA requirement could "get recommendations from a teacher that says that your GPA doesn't reflect your character." In terms of exemplifying "Eagle Pride," the potential contestants were reminded that they serve as role models for the American High community. Hannah said, "If you are chosen you are going to be a role model for this school. You are going to be asking for donations and representing our local hospital. This is very serious." Janet echoed Hannah's comment, telling the assembled group, "You are representing our school in the community. You are the face of American." As such there is "zero tolerance if it is found out you are at a party or drinking or doing anything that's not school appropriate."

As they went over the expectations for contestants, Janet, Jennifer, and the coordinators repeatedly stumbled over the name of the pageant. When Janet reminded the group to be careful with their social media accounts, for instance, she commented, "If there is a picture going around and you are chugging something or smoking something . . . you will be off Mr. Eagle—or the Eagle pageant." Similarly when Jennifer welcomed potential contestants to a meeting, she asked, "Who has been to a Mr. Eagle, or any Mr. Pageant? Or, they are not Mr. anymore—they are Mr. and Mrs.?" Hannah did something similar when explaining the fundraising goal, saying, "Everyone sets a fundraising goal for themselves but it doesn't have anything to do with who ends up becoming Mr. Eagle or Mrs. . . . at the end of it if guys . . . or girls . . . contestants don't hit the goal." Up until this year, the pageant had been titled "Mr. Eagle Pageant," but, like other activities at American—the homecoming court, prom court, and Power Tough, for example—it had recently shifted to a gender-neutral name, "Eagle Pageant," a shift that resulted in coordinators and advisors continually correcting themselves.

These stumbles, however, were about more than just a name change; they were about the gendered nature of the pageant itself. The idea animating the pageant is, as Janet put it, "a beauty pageant that has gone kind of sideways." Much like the humor that animates the Powder Puff football game, a gender reversal played for laughs is at the heart of the Eagle Pageant's philanthropic endeavor. The centrality of this gender reversal to the fundraiser is made clear by some of the skits that drew the largest laughs from audiences on the night of the pageant itself. One skit, for example, featured contestants reenacting the famous scene from the movie *Mean Girls* in which four high school girls dance seductively to the song "Jingle Bell Rock." At the dress rehearsal for the pageant contestants, Austin, Bruce, Liam, and Will, all White seniors, strutted down the auditorium aisles wearing Santa hats, tight tank tops, and white-trimmed red skirts.

"OH MY GOD!" Kyle, another contestant, yelled, while Chris exclaimed, "Oh my god is this allowed? Is this allowed?" Austin, Bruce, Liam, and Will took the stage as a screen descended behind them, upon which the iconic scene from *Mean Girls* began to play. Leo stood and yelled, "YES YES!" as he tossed his hat at the performers as if they were strippers on stage. The assembled contestants continued to laugh as the boys danced seductively and Hannah laughingly filmed it on her phone. Contestants shouted out comments like "shave your pits!" and "no, wax!" and "no, dye them extra black!" as laughter echoed through the auditorium.

Later, during the actual pageant, when the emcee, George, introduced this skit, he emphasized the hilarity of straight White cisgender boys dressing in drag and dancing seductively, asking, "How many of you miss Christmas? Well our next skit might ruin it for you." After the boys danced, the music ended, and audience laughter subsided, George again commented on the performance, "Merry Christmas . . . I guess. I dunno. You can't unsee that." You can't, that is, unsee a group of young White cisgender men dressed in skirts and tank tops dancing seductively. George's comments reflect a way of thinking that suggests that there is something horrifying, distasteful, or inappropriate about men who act and dress in a manner we associate with women.[5] In other words, according to George and, if the amount of laughter is any clue, for many audience members as well, there is something distasteful about drag itself. However, unlike the drag show put on by the GSA, a drag show that celebrated queer identity, transgression, play, and belonging, these boys and the emcee treat drag and those who do it as something to be laughed *at*, not with. This laughter is not about the joy of subverting stereotypical gender norms, but about the horror of subverting these expectations, a horror that is so powerful that, as George warned, it might ruin a beloved holiday. Austin, Bruce, Liam, and Will were not unusual in dressing like women for laughs. This practice is so common during pageant season that another contestant's mom even said to me, throwing her hands up in confusion, "They just like to dress up as girls. I have no idea why!"

The "why" is that this pageant is more than just a popularity contest. It is a way that privilege looks like merit, and rewarding adherence to particular gender norms while mocking those who transgress those norms is a way to reinforce that privilege. For instance, research suggests that one of the ways that young men come to think of themselves as masculine is through distancing themselves from things that are considered to be feminine, often by mocking symbols, practices, or attributes perceived as belonging to women.[6] By making a joke out of dressing like women, these young men reinforce their own sense of masculinity *and* send a message to others about how to be appropriately masculine. A look through school yearbooks and pageant documents indicated that most pageants feature at least two contestants who dress up as female characters as part of the pageant process—from the year that the theme was Disney Princesses (in which all contestants dressed in princess dresses), to the year when the theme was Mario Kart (in which two of the contestants dressed as Princesses Peach and Daisy), to this year (in which two contestants dressed as Sandy and Rizzo)—providing plenty of opportunities to make jokes about womanhood, femininity, and drag. It is worth noting that, unlike the aftermath of the drag show, no school or district officials expressed concerns about the use of drag during the pageant. Even though dressing in drag as a joke seems designed to provoke laughter at those who dress as the "opposite" gender, laughter that we may think of as a form of bullying, never was it addressed as such by school authorities or participants. Instead, this type of drag manifests year after year in the Eagle Pageant, a manifestation that serves to reinforce gendered norms and works to exclude those for whom ritualized drag may be an important practice in terms of cultural membership and identity.

The gendered underpinnings of the pageant go beyond making fun of feminine men, girls, and women through drag. The Eagle Pageant also relies on a gendered division of labor in which girls do the vast majority of the work for the philanthropy. While this charity project seems to have been started by a boy as penance for his crimes, over the years it has evolved into a four-year commitment for girls who plan and run the program. Janet summed up this dynamic when she talked to the contestants saying, "You get the fun of it all, while for these girls it's a four-year commitment. They are working to plan everything for you and make your lives easy so you can show up and have fun and raise money. So remember that." Jennifer echoed this sentiment in other meetings, saying, "You guys get to be the face and the fun of everything. But you are representing them as well and their four years of hard work. So don't mess that up for them. You guys only have to do this for three months."

From the fundraising, to creating the actual pageant, to managing contestants, this is a lot of work for the coordinators. At more than one meeting, coordinators came in talking about how late they had been up trying to make fliers for a fundraiser, writing thank-you notes for donations, or planning out precisely the right dance routine. At one point during the pageant dress rehearsal, Hannah walked in and plopped down exhausted into a chair next to me, asking, "Is this what a wedding is like?" Having put together a wedding two decades prior, I told her that yes, it does seem quite similar, with slightly more "people to wrangle and less family to manage"—an answer that caused Hannah to laugh in commiseration. But Hannah's question revealed an important insight. Much like a wedding, pageant labor is deeply feminized. It is a public ritual in which women are in charge of the decisions, the aesthetics, and human management of the event. Raising tens of thousands of dollars during their four years as coordinators requires that this group of eight young women hone and develop organizational skills, perform emotion work, and dedicate a massive amount of time to running errands, decorating, and herding contestants. In other words, throughout the pageant process coordinators learn the gendered skills of adulthood, well before they move into family and career roles that often demand similar gendered abilities in terms of emotional, personal, and social management.[7]

The amount of work the pageant requires during their entire high school career, but especially during pageant season, shapes coordinators' lives and relationships. As Mackenna reflected, "The girls do most of the work. They have to schedule all the fundraisers and lead all the meetings." Macy agreed that the pageant takes a toll: "I kind of stopped talking to a lot of people because of the pageant. I just didn't have that time. But then, pageant just ended and I feel like I'm disconnected." At one point Hannah broke down in tears saying, "It's my senior year and it's all just so much!" sharing with the assembled group of coordinators that the other day she "had one of those moments where I just bawled! Pageant and college and work and taxes and pageant!" This exhaustion is a gendered exhaustion. Reagan, a member of the Women's Empowerment club, whose water bottle sports a large sticker reading "feminist," had shared that her boyfriend broke up with her because she didn't have enough time for him, in part because of the time she spent doing pageant work. She said, "It's so funny. God. It's the most blatant example of girls doing all of the work and guys getting all of the credit. And I'm a part of that." Shrugging, Reagan didn't really reconcile this contradiction, as if it's simply part of life about which nothing could really be done. From keeping their grades up, to managing jobs, to organizing fundraisers, to worrying about "the boys'" sports schedules and whether or not they were going to show up for fundraising events, the coordinators' participation in this philanthropy seems to be a high-school version of a ladies auxiliary. This group of eight essentially runs a small civic organization to raise money for health-care needs, fundraising to fill gaps left by state failure to provide the necessary support for comprehensive medical care. They do the gendered "behind the scenes" work—keeping track of schedules, plans, details, and to-do lists, so "the guys" can simply show up and be told what to do. In other words, these primarily White, primarily upper-middle-class, gender-normative young women were able to leverage the girl-boss feminism strategies they use to respond to everyday sexism to move into powerful high-status positions in the school, positions that both reflect and generate intersectional privilege.

This gendered division of labor and the gendered humor upon which the pageant rests were called into question as the pageant name shifted from Mr. Eagle to the Eagle Pageant and, for the first time ever, a girl—Kat, a tall, blond, UPWARD student with short-cropped hair who typically sported jeans and a sweatshirt—became a contestant. Kat was not normatively gendered in her comportment, dress, haircut, or affect. She was not wealthy. She was not from an "intact" family. She was not straight. Lauren commented that some participants in the pageant thought that Kat's participation may be a problem because "people find it funny when guys dress up as girls. So, a lot of the guys' dance is very, like, sexual, like girls. And she's a girl, so she's probably going to get some stuff for that. If the girls are going to do that, people are going to be really angry. If a girl just went up there and they were doing what the guys were doing, people would just be so angry with them." Indeed, throughout pageant season, Kat often sat out of the choreographed dance performances. Specifically, she often did not participate in the contestants' most popular dance, a routine to the Brittany Spears song "Toxic," in which the young men swiveled their hips, crawled suggestively on the ground, and jumped into each other's arms. It was, as Lauren's comment suggests, very sexual, and, according to audience laughter, humorously so. Kat's presence in the dance may have disrupted the latent homophobia (straight boys dancing suggestively and jumping into each other's arms) upon which this humor depends.

The dances were just one way in which Kat's multiple lines of difference challenged the gendered, classed, and sexual underpinnings of the pageant. The coordinators, for instance, struggled with dressing her for the pageant. The contestants typically wear tuxedos for the final portion of the pageant, but the coordinators weren't sure what Kat should wear, as Lila asked, "Are we getting one for Kat?" noting that "Kat wore a tux for homecoming." In the end the coordinators did get her a tux, but this discussion reflects the way that the pageant itself—even as it moved to "Eagle Pageant" from "Mr. Eagle," much like the football game moved from Powder Puff to Power Tough—depends on and reinforces gendered norms, practices, and ideologies. However, the pageant isn't just shaped by gender; it is also shaped by and depends on particular classed processes as well, classed processes that work to exclude Kat and students like her.

High School Philanthropists

On a cool winter morning the contestants, along with senior coordinators Hannah and Macy, gathered in the entryway of Mountain Hospital, a hospital entryway that, save for the gift shop off to the side, felt more like a ski lodge than it did a hospital, with its giant stone fireplace, double staircase, and overstuffed chairs. The contestants (though not the freshman, sophomore, or junior coordinators, who do not get to join this tour until their senior year) show up wearing matching outfits—gray sweatshirts reading "Eagle Pageant" and jeans—as they had been instructed to do by Hannah, who typically dictated what outfits the group wore at events like these. Kids Aid personnel, Kindra and Tiff, took the contestants and two coordinators through the pediatric unit and the NICU so that the participants can see where the proceeds from their charity work go. Every so often Kindra paused and asked them how much they thought a piece of equipment cost, whether it be a crash cart, equipment that lets doctors diagnose kids from a distance, or a new piece of infant-specific technology. Partway through the tour, Tiff handed Ryan a small stuffed bear with a pair of diapers on it. Tiff said that this stuffed animal is "the size of the smallest baby delivered here." As the Eagle Pageant participants responded with quiet "wow" or gasps, Tiff continued to explain about the smallest baby, that her "mom was told that she would not be able to deliver a live baby and was encouraged to terminate the pregnancy." The mother refused to do so and "was able to deliver this baby who is now four years old."

After scrubbing their hands, donning protective gear, and touring the NICU, the group filed into a windowless meeting room and settled in padded chairs around a dark wood table. NICU- and hospital-related swag was scattered across the table, including stickers featuring the Kids Aid logo next to print of impossibly small infant feet, small feet that look an awful lot like the ones on the "pro-life" pins worn by activists who oppose comprehensive reproductive health care. Dr. Frank, a White pediatrician, greeted them, congratulating the group on their work. He told them they should all "walk a little taller" because they make "THE difference, not A difference," in the lives of these babies. To close out the tour, Kindra asked the assembled group to go around the table and share one thing "you learned and one thing you are taking with you" from the day's activities. Henry commented that he had developed "a lot of empathy for how much pain the families must be in and going through." Tiff responded, "You are going to make a very supportive husband someday." Ryan contributed that the thing that "strikes me the most is that the money we are raising is going to help that little girl go to prom." Hannah commented that seeing the hospital unit inspires her so "even when I'm so tired and I don't want to do one more thing, this reminds me that it's worth it." She compared the Eagle Pageant process to other clubs at the school, saying, "How do you take it too seriously? It's saving babies! It's not like a silly club!" Given the support and positive feedback these young folks receive about the importance of their work, it's little wonder that they feel this work is not "silly" like other clubs.

Unlike other young people at American who are participating in civic engagement work—putting on the Black Lives Matter display, organizing against gun violence, or celebrating queer culture—the participants of the Eagle Pageant were continually praised, thanked, and rewarded for their work. These young folks think of what they are doing as lifesaving work—"saving babies"—rather than just participating in "a silly club." Their efforts were typically, if informally, supported by the school, even though the Eagle Pageant is not a school sponsored program. The participants were released from their classes to decorate the auditorium for the pageant, for instance, without problem, unlike the young folks who felt that their grades would be at risk should they walk out to demand to be safe from gun violence. Pageant participants were able to use the auditorium to do drag, unlike the GSA students. They were also able to use school resources—get on the announcements, call spirit weeks, and use the gym all while being praised and told they are role models, something that I never once recorded being said of young folks engaging in other civic activities.

Part of the reason these young folks receive this sort of praise and support is because the goal of their civic engagement isn't to highlight, much less challenge, the systemic nature of social problems, but instead to address these problems by drawing on a logic of individual financial generosity. These young folks are participating in a legacy of charity work that focuses on using private resources and gendered labor to address social problems rather than focusing on the social inequalities that give rise to premature births in the first place or that result in the lack of adequate medical equipment to care for medically fragile infants.[8] Rather than working to actively change society such that adequate and prevention-focused health care is available to everyone, these students are engaging in the sort of philanthropic fundraising typically associated with the wealthy. The pageant process teaches them about the practices of charity work. It allows them to more deeply embed in local social networks geared toward philanthropic work, learn about fundraising, practice how to ask people and businesses for money, develop events that draw in community members, and practice the ability to graciously accept praise for these practices. The lessons they learn about how to engage in these practices do not challenge social norms, but instead underscore a sort of "feel good" activist work that in the end may do little to change society.[9] Even the way participants are praised for being a good future husband, or see their work as enabling a little girl to attend her future prom, demonstrates how this event folds neatly into existing social norms about gender. As journalist Anand Giridharadas notes, while this type of philanthropy can look like it is "changing the world," it may change little and instead can work to preserve the status quo.[10]

The class-based nature of the pageant process is central to sustaining this status quo. While officially this philanthropy welcomes applicants regardless of class background, in practice the program relies upon a particular classed family form and educational experience.[11] As Macy pointed out, "It's really heavy with Honors Academy kids. Like, the contestants are mostly Honors kids." At one scantly attended recruitment meeting, for instance, Hannah kept repeating that there was "an honors society meeting" at the same time, so no one should worry about a lack of applicants because the next meeting, which did not have similar conflicts, would be better attended. It was. The Honors Academy is heavily stocked with the wealthier and whiter students in the school, students whose parents have attended college and seem to expect their children to do the same. According to students (and confirmed by my analysis of a decade of yearbook photos of the pageant), the final contestant roster of the pageant is typically populated by mostly White Honors Academy seniors who participate in high-status athletics such as baseball, football, and basketball.

As a teacher who hails from a working-class, rural background, Ms. Bay made it a point to encourage her UPWARD students, who are significantly less wealthy and whose parents may not have gone to college, to participate in the pageant. On the day of the Eagle Pageant information meeting, she spent the morning walking around and talking to students clustered around the groups of tables in her classroom. She paused at each table as she walked, saying, "You going to the Eagle Pageant meeting?" as a question that was really more like a statement. In his typical fashion, the class jokester, James, who was alternately unhoused, living in a group home, or crashing on friends' couches because of his unstable home life, replied, "It's so much stress!" Without missing a beat, Ms. Bay responded, "Go to the meeting!" James argued back, "I want to go to lunch today!" Undaunted, Ms. Bay countered, "Go to the meeting." Typical of the solidarity among UPWARD students, another student volunteered, "I'll walk his ass to it!" while another said, "I'll bring your lunch!" Seemingly resigned, James asked, "What's the theme this year?" to which Ms. Bay responded, "*Grease*."[12] She told them, "I'd love it if we could have four or five people go the meeting." She even read the class a text from the one UPWARD student she had taught who had participated as a contestant:

> The Mr. Eagle Pageant is a life changing experience. You get to give back to the community. You get to meet new people. You get to see your hard work come to fruition. You get to go out of high school on a high note. I mean who wouldn't want to raise money for babies in need. It's a chance to make a world of difference for a baby, but also a chance to make a difference for a mother and a father and grandparents.

Ms. Bay's exhortations challenge the gendered and classed patterns that historically characterized the pageant. She reminded her class that "people think that you have to be a dude to do it. Just because it says Mr. Eagle doesn't mean that if you aren't a guy you can't do it." She added, "I don't mean this in a bad way but I don't want it to all be Honors Academy people."

It seems her talk had an effect, as Anna looked at Kat after Ms. Bay was done and asked, "Are you going to do pageant with me?" Kat agreed to go, saying, "I'll do it with you." They hand-clasped and fist-bumped to seal the deal. James also conceded, sort of, by saying, "I'm going to the meeting but I'm not going to do it." Even Nicole and Angelina showed up to the meeting later. Notably, the only girls to show up at the interest meetings are girls from Ms. Bay's UPWARD class. And only one of these girls, Kat, was White. Through the application process that year, all non-White students were weeded out, girls and boys alike.

What none of Ms. Bay's exhortations can effectively counter is the way that classed resources structure who is able to participate in the pageant in the first place. At one of the interest meetings for the coordinators, Karon, a White working-class freshman who regularly attended GSA, sat with her typical lunch: a paper plate piled high with dill pickle slices that she slowly ate throughout the course of the meeting. As Jennifer and Janet opened up the meeting to questions, she asked, "Will you accept 504 students because I have Asperger's and sometimes I struggle to organize things. But I'm working on it and my parents are helping me." Unlike the other girls in the room who sport fashionable clothes or hip track suits, most of whom have long straight hair, Karon was wearing an unremarkable jeans and T-shirt combination and sported unkept curly blond hair and big glasses. In response to her question, both Janet and Jennifer echoed the sentiment shared by Ms. Bay by smilingly saying, "Of course! All are welcome to apply!" However, Karon's multiple levels of gendered, classed, and neurological difference, while theoretically fine, because "all are welcome," functionally work to exclude her from participation and her name does not appear on the final roster of coordinators.

When working-class students attempt to join in this philanthropic endeavor, the myriad classed resources needed to do so become abundantly clear. Tony, who jubilantly joined one of the interest meetings for contestants in his red Coke sweatshirt, encountered these classed challenges as he enthusiastically applied to be a contestant. Tony is probably one of the most organized young people I have ever met. He is deeply attached to American High and his teachers (and to me, texting me regularly just to see if I'm around so we can talk, even well after I left the school). However, he was also regularly in trouble with administrators or mad at his teachers. Typically this trouble had to do with his practices of self-medication (he regularly smoked pot), responses to slights from other young folks (he was put on a "behavioral contract" after he threatened to punch another boy who called him a "bitch"), difficulties relating to finances (he couldn't afford a parking pass so he kept getting parking tickets), or school attendance (his dad suffered from a medical disorder that required Tony to drive him up to Portland regularly for treatment). Like me, school staff seemed extremely fond of Tony. He was given the "Most Improved Student Award" at Senior Awards Night from the Science Academy learning community of which he was a part, for instance. Even Craig, who continually scolded Tony about wearing his favorite black hoodie, the one with a scientific diagram of the antidepressant Zoloft on it, often just rolled his eyes and laughed when Tony came around. Tony had been eagerly anticipating the chance to participate in the Eagle Pageant. He would have been, from what I could tell, one of the first, if not the first, Asian American contestant in the history of the program.

Shortly before one of the Thursday coordinator meetings, however, Janet pulled me aside asking, "Do you have a few minutes after the meeting? I'd love to talk." When we sat down to talk in the bare conference room, she shared that she was struggling with Tony's application, asking as she showed it to me, "So what do you know about Tony?" Her first concern was his GPA, a GPA that was, not surprisingly given the challenges he navigated, lower than the required 3.0. But, as Janet said to him and the other applicants, "If you don't quite meet it, come talk to us." Tony did exactly that. He called Janet before the contestant interest meeting to double-check the requirements and to make sure he could meet them. Tony then stayed after the meeting to talk to both Janet and Jennifer about his GPA. To make up for and contextualize his grades, he asked two teachers to vouch for him. Ms. Crane from the Science Academy wrote in support of his application that Tony had "really turned his life around" and what a "good opportunity" it would be for him. While Janet was inclined to support his application, echoing Ms. Crane's words saying, "This might be his chance to really turn his life around," Jennifer was not convinced. Instead Jennifer elaborated on the GPA flexibility clause saying, "That was like if you were just a little bit below and his is quite below." She continued, "If we let him in, then everyone who didn't make it in, who didn't make the cut would be all upset."

Eventually Janet and Jennifer explain the backstory to their concern, telling me about a "borderline case years back." This contestant "checked all the boxes." He "had this really hard background" and "this was the chance for him to turn his life around." However, they tell me, after making the decision to let him participate, even though his grades and other aspects of his application were less than optimal, he went on to be, as far as they knew, the only contestant to not raise a single dollar for the philanthropy. Typically each contestant raises thousands of dollars through letter-writing campaigns to businesses, personal appeals to friends and family, and through the "cash barrels" they meticulously decorate and carry around for the duration of pageant season so that students can spontaneously donate spare change. Janet said that "about half" of the money that participants raise "is in the kids' hands at any given time." In fact, coordinator meetings are regularly interrupted by contestants coming in to deposit their fundraising results. However, Jennifer said of this contestant, "We think he lost money." His cash barrel "came in with no money, which is impossible." Jennifer and Janet suspected that instead of donating the money from his cash barrel, he took it for his own use. Janet tried to be understanding, saying, "It makes sense because his family didn't have money so of course he would do this. It makes sense."

The logic of this pageant, that of philanthropy in general, is one that relies upon students not only having access to others with money to spare, but on not needing that money themselves.[13] For students who don't have robust financial resources, this means that they are already at a disadvantage, because they are not the sort of student for whom this pageant has been designed—a student who has financial resources enough such that they can raise money and donate it to others. This lack of financial resources is a part of why Tony's application is less competitive than others' in the first place. His financial resources and time were needed by his family, in a way that some more well-resourced students simply wouldn't experience. The inability to participate in the pageant reflected other times that Tony's class status made it difficult to be fully involved in the life of the school. American High, like some other schools, charges fifty dollars a year for a parking pass (regardless of the fact that there is plenty of parking around the school). Because Tony did not have money for a parking pass, he racked up several tickets over the course of the year. He was unable to pay these tickets and, as a result, was told he would not be able to "walk" at graduation. That is, he would not be allowed to don a gown, have his name called in front of friends and family, and receive a diploma from Principal Walt in the public graduation ceremony. This, in turn, led to feelings of anger, frustration, and defeat, because, as his Science Academy award indicates, he had worked incredibly hard to be a successful student during his time at American.

Unfortunately, his lack of class resources also shaped his ability to participate in the Eagle Pageant, as eventually Janet and Jennifer denied his application because of their overriding concern about how upset other people would be about his candidacy. Jennifer repeatedly worried that other applicants would find the process to be unfair if Tony was allowed to be on the ballot given his low GPA. It seems that his presence may call into question the meritocracy upon which the pageant relied. However, this meritocracy didn't, it seems, reflect worthiness so much as it reflected, in this instance, classed privilege. As scholar Natasha Warikoo's research suggests, a belief that we are operating in a meritocracy "serves as an ideological tool that allows elites to maintain their position in society."[14] In the case of the Eagle Pageant, this means that a focus on a particular interpretation of "fairness" excludes less privileged students. A focus like this one on worthiness and merit can both obscure and justify inequality in a way that validates the status elites enjoy both in and out of schools.

Pageant Families

Family participation is central to the pageant process. Pageant contestants are regularly reminded to "get your family on board." Janet, for instance, told interested contestants that "you need to reach out to your families. They will be helping you out with fundraisers and maybe introducing you to their friends who can help too. It's a bit of a financial commitment. Bring pizzas to meetings. You need to buy T-shirts and sweatshirts." While young folks are not turned away because of a lack of financial resources, the pageant process does rely on the family's donation of financial and labor resources. The gendered division of labor in the pageant itself mirrors a gendered division of labor often found in the families whose children participate in it. This philanthropy, in other words, depends on the classed and gendered resources provided by an "intact" nuclear family.

Kat's shifting living situation and unstable home life revealed the way pageant events themselves rely on participants' familial and financial stability. Over drinks at a local Starbucks, Macy told me, "It's kind of messed up. Like Kat lives by herself, she pays rent. Her mom and dad are separated. She lived with her dad for a little bit." However, Kat and her father had a falling out, so she left and "lived on her own, and she couldn't afford it. Then she moved in with her cousin. But she still can barely afford it, to pay rent and pay for gas." This living situation posed particular problems during the annual "kidnapping" event. Each year the pageant coordinators "kidnap" contestants, or surprise them while they are still asleep or in bed, and take them out for breakfast. Because of Kat's changing housing situation the coordinators couldn't find her house to kidnap her. Macy said that "we were looking for Kat's house somewhere in the Northside area. But she didn't live there anymore, because she had moved. And I really was confused. So we went to the apartments that are by South Street where she lives now. We couldn't even find her apartment. So, we had to call her." On this call, Hannah gave up trying to "kidnap" Kat and instead asked her, "Want to just meet us at the restaurant? You could just meet us there." Macy shook her head at Hannah's lack of effort, saying, "It wasn't even a surprise for Kat at that point, which it was supposed to be. You're supposed to surprise them. So, she was really sad. Like, she had a coordinator who hated her and she didn't live with her parents. She was at a real disadvantage." Hannah had made it clear from the start of Kat's participation that she did not want a girl participating as a contestant. Her comments occasionally reflected this perspective when, for instance, over the course of the pageant she regularly referred to the participants as "the contestants and Kat," a phrase that served as a regular reminder of Kat's multiple lines of gendered, familial, and classed difference.

To make sure that Kat had a good pageant experience and to minimize the impact of Hannah's treatment, Macy sent the rest of the coordinators along to the restaurant and went to Kat's apartment to pick her up. Macy said that when she got to the restaurant, Hannah gave her "a hard time" when she walked in late with Kat. "There was barely even a seat for Kat," Macy said. "There was a place setting right next to me, but no seat. So, Kat had to take one from another table. She sat next to me, and I felt really bad." I couldn't help but remember Macy's discomfort at the coordinator's meeting when she couldn't find a seat there too. It may be that Macy's bodily difference, in addition to the fact that her mother hailed from a working-class background, led Macy to be more attuned than others to Kat's marginalization, and that perhaps informed her attempts to mitigate it. This was just one of many times Kat's financial and familial resources affected her pageant participation. When the group would go out to eat after rehearsals, for instance, Kat frequently lacked the money to do so. Sometimes she opted out of these events and other times her fellow contestants footed the bill.

The importance of classed family resources and the intergenerational gendered division of labor became especially clear at one of the most popular events of pageant season, the Bunco fundraiser. During Bunco night, the normally quiet school library erupted with cheers, laughter, and general merriment as grandparents, siblings, and parents of coordinators and contestants found their seats at tables of four to play a chaotic dice game that involved luck, movement, yelling, and at some points a flying stuffed animal. As the White school secretary, Barbara, tried to explain the rules of the game, attendees talked, joked, and played with the dice, pens, notepads, and Hershey's candies scattered on the tables. The assembled group was almost entirely White and several wore patriotic or conservative symbols not commonly seen at American—an American flag shirt, a Reagan–Bush T-shirt, and a sweatshirt sporting the name of a local evangelical Christian college. The game got underway as Barbara concluded her instructions by thanking "the girls" for their hard work in putting the fundraiser together and "the boys" for their publicity efforts. During the game, coordinators and contestants walked around handing out brownies, cookies, and drinks, and selling raffle tickets for the colorful cakes made by participants, or as I came to understand throughout the course of the night, their mothers or girlfriends. Mothers of contestants loudly joked about how "the boys" relied on them for baking help. Henry's mom said, shaking her head, that "he called me last night saying he needed me to take him out to get ingredients for the cake." In response, Austin's mom laughingly said that his girlfriend simply made the cake for him.

As I settled into a table to prepare for what became a long night of losing at Bunco, losses that involved my getting moved further and further away from the winner's table at the front of the room, Andrea and Corey, the White parents of contestant Austin's girlfriend, greeted me kindly. They have played at this Bunco fundraiser for the past several pageant seasons. After talking about college and parenting for a bit, I asked if their younger son will be a contestant in the pageant when he is eligible. They both laughed as Andrea said, "He will be!" while Corey stated, "He doesn't have a choice!" Other contestant and coordinators echoed this sort of parental expectation. One coordinator-hopeful even said, "I have to be here [at the pageant meeting] or my mom would smack me right across the face!" Pageant is an intergenerational tradition, and perhaps one that a certain class of parents encourages because of the prestige it indicates on college applications and resumes.

The night continued as raucously as it began with players laughing, yelling, and moving from table to table. When, at the end of the evening, the cakes were raffled off, Leo's grandma, an elderly but sprightly woman, won the first one. Another player yelled, "Keeping it in the family!" as she jumped up and grabbed a multilayered cake featuring a *Grease* logo. Most of the participants had several family members, girlfriends, and boyfriends, and sometimes multiple generations of their family at Bunco night, families that helped with cakes and shelled out money for raffle tickets. The time, financial resources, and labor required by these philanthropic events depends on classed and gendered familial resources. These resources not only sustain the pageant process, they are also forms of privilege that are obfuscated by ideologies of merit that marginalize young folks who do not have these resources.

Parents, and especially mothers, provide the labor necessary to sustain this philanthropy. They sewed costumes, organized social events, and crafted pageant decorations. Some of this gendered labor was organized in a mandatory family meeting shortly before the night of the pageant, a meeting that encapsulated many of the gendered and classed dynamics that characterize the philanthropy. At this meeting, parents, seated on folding plastic chairs in the back of a restaurant owned by the parents of one contestant, discussed the last-minute details of the event. These parents were so intensely involved throughout the course of pageant season that Janet skipped introductions, saying, "You all know each other by now." She congratulated the parents on how hard their kids had worked over the past few months saying how "amazing it is that these high school students can ever raise twenty-five thousand dollars!" Chris's mom added, acknowledging the multiple clubs, sports, and church groups that most of the participants are engaged in, "Even with everything else they have going on!" Janet reviewed the fundraisers the young folks had put on, telling them to remind "the boys" to write thank-you notes to those who had donated money.

As they discussed which fundraisers "the boys" needed to write those thank-you notes for, the talk turned to the recent Carl's Jr. fundraiser. Reportedly passersby had responded negatively to the signs that coordinators and participants had held up and the stickers they had passed out with the Eagle Pageant motto "Save the Babies" on them. Jennifer said, incredulously, "People were giving them the finger and honking." It seems that these passersby understood this slogan to be related to "pro-life" messaging, as I did. The parents present, however, did not share this interpretation. Kyle's mom shook her head, commenting, "I didn't even think of that, wow!" Jennifer calmed the parents by dismissing these complaints, reassuring them, "People will always have something to complain about." Rather than seeing this slogan, one that is regularly used in anti-abortion messaging, as one that could be read as an attack on women's bodily integrity, the parents, Janet, and Jennifer instead seemed to reduce it to a matter of complaint, a reduction that served to minimize that interpretation, much like the language of "offense" minimized interpretations of racial harm regarding spirit weeks or theme nights at football games.

At this meeting, as with events involving contestants themselves, Jennifer, Janet, and the parents continually referred to "the boys." At one point Janet said, "the boys . . . and the girls . . ." looking pointedly at Kat's mom—sorry I'm trying so hard this year!" Kyle's mom used similar phrasing, even as she tried to correct herself saying, "Some of the boys . . . boys and girls, but it was mostly the boys . . . ," looking over at Kat's mom, leaning forward shooting out her arm as if to point her out and include her and to shush her all at the same time. Across the room Austin's mother commented on the gendered shift in pageant contestants saying, "It's a new era." Unlike most of the other quite talkative parents, Kat's mother did not speak through the whole meeting, save for asking Austin's dad for a pen so she could take notes. It may indeed be a "new era," but it's a new era that still relies on gendered labor and familial resources, a reliance that shifted little in the face of name and contestant changes.

During the meeting contestants' moms divided up the work still to be done for the pageant. Austin's mom volunteered to organize the post-pageant sleepover, saying she was in charge each time her older sons participated in the pageant. Kyle's mom volunteered to purchase flowers for the contestants to give to the coordinators at the end of the event. Casey's mom volunteered to sew special straps into his costume to hold it in place. Jennifer reminded them that at the end of the pageant "the boys" should say something nice about the coordinators, "unless," she paused, "they have nothing to say." Rolling her eyes, she continued, "not that I'm bitter or anything . . ." explaining that her "husband ranked low in congeniality points" when she was a senior coordinator and he was a contestant. From sewing, to baking, to buying flowers, to hosting overnights, to reminding the young men to say something nice to the coordinators at the end, these mothers do the gendered familial labor, labor that reflects the gendered work of the coordinators.

One mother, Carole, critiqued and resisted the expectation of gendered labor. Carole, a teacher and mother of a former pageant coordinator, asked me, shaking her head, "Have you met these mothers?" Because she had a full-time and consuming job, Carole did not do the cake-baking or crafting expected of pageant moms. However, this refusal shaped her daughter's experience with the pageant. Carole said both the lead coordinator and her mother gave her daughter a hard time because "her mom doesn't participate enough." Shaking her head she said, "I mean, I didn't want to spend six hours on a Saturday making decorations! C'mon!" While she eventually grudgingly promised to help out by selling tickets, Carole insisted, "But I wouldn't come early or stay late." Carole is a dedicated teacher who works hard to meet her students' needs. To add this sort of gendered philanthropic labor on top of her already intense work schedule is not only impossible, but, as her comments suggest, a bit insulting.

From the need to have a stable home, to the necessity of having a family with leisure time and disposable income, to the gendered labor of mothers, the creation of a student citizen requires more than simply classed resources; it requires classed and gendered familial resources. These families play an important role in the exclusionary processes that characterize the rest of this philanthropy by providing the sort of classed and gendered resources necessary for the pageant process, classed and gendered resources that, perhaps, give these young folks the sense that they can "change the world." The creation of the student citizen entails obfuscating those familial, financial, and gendered resources with an ideology of meritocracy that benefits this already privileged group of young folks.

Pageant as Tolerance Ritual

On the evening of the pageant itself for the first time ever a sign reading "Eagle Pageant" rather than "Mr. Eagle" hung above the stage. The coordinators, as well as some of their friends, had been released from their classes that Friday to decorate the auditorium with *Grease*-themed décor—pink and white balloons, large black music notes, and records featuring the contestants' names. Thirty minutes before the doors were slated to open, a line of seventy or so people snaked through the school courtyard. While those folks waited, Gracie and Rachel, clad like the other coordinators in form-fitting short black dresses, stood by a "VIP Entrance" greeting contestants' families and escorting them to a VIP room filled with hors d'oeuvres and drinks. Gracie encouraged them to "Go eat! There's a ton of food. Eat and feel special." Kyle's mom laughingly said to her family, "We're very important people, I told you!"

After the rest of the audience was admitted to the auditorium, the pageant continued as it had in years past. George, the emcee and a former Mr. Eagle himself, welcomed the attendees, introduced representatives from the Kids Aid organization, and provided commentary between the dances, skits, and songs. The contestants opened the show by running down the aisles to perform an extended dance routine to a 1950s medley, complete with Casey dressed as Sandy in a yellow sweater and skirt set rolling over the backs of the other dancers. Contestants performed a series of sketches for the talent portion of the night, sketches featuring a duet from the musical *Into the Woods,* a stand-up routine mocking kale-eating and kids named Rainbeaux, a choreographed dance to a popular hip-hop song, a routine featuring human-sized puppets strapped to a contestant, a lip-synch to Queen's hit song "Another One Bites the Dust," and, of course, the dance from *Mean Girls.* Kat's performance concluded the talent portion of the show. Wearing a long-sleeved red shirt and black pants, sitting on a stool, she quietly read the Dr. Seuss book *Marvin K. Mooney Will You Please Go Now!* into a microphone to subdued audience applause, the muted nature of the reaction standing in contrast to the loud cheers that followed the other contestants' performances.

As the event came an end, the contestants concluded the evening by singing a song of thanks to the coordinators, beginning by handing them bouquets of flowers purchased by Leo's mom, as a grand piano was wheeled onto the stage. Ryan thanked the coordinators for showing "so much care for us and night after night, yelling at us during practices, getting all the posters hung" while Austin, at the piano, began to play the opening bars of the song "Seasons of Love" from the musical *Rent.* Together and only slightly off-key, the contestants sang a set of rewritten lyrics in tribute to the coordinators' hard work, "It's for the kiiiiiiiids/It's for the babiiiieeeees/How do you measure commitment to a cause?" When the contestants finished, Hannah thanked them by saying, "It's been a long and tough journey for all of you. Thank you for putting in the work on this pageant. Even though you didn't like to pay attention and you liked to talk. You worked so hard and we are so proud of all of you," as the audience uproariously applauded.

The choice of song and rewritten lyrics symbolize the way the pageant excludes and appropriates while justifying the status quo, even as participants seemingly endeavor to "change the world." The use of a song from a musical set in the midst of the AIDS epidemic, about the abysmal state of health care, as well as the toll of addiction, poverty, and gentrification, is rewritten to celebrate "dedication to a cause"—raising money for underfunded NICUs, NICUs where some infants may end up precisely because of some of the issues critiqued in that musical: unequal access to health care and a lack of a robust social safety net. From the differential treatment of "important" people to the humorous deployment of drag, to the muted response to Kat's performance, to Hannah's gender-based chiding at the end of the event, to the song of thanks itself, the pageant evening encapsulated the way this philanthropic process reinforces gendered norms, validates social hierarchies, and focuses more on good feelings than on addressing social inequities.

The pageant process can tell us something about who matters, how exclusion works, the work that ideologies about meritocracy do, and how ideas about merit can cloud and justify systemic inequalities. The process of the Eagle Pageant is what we might think of as a "tolerance ritual."[15] Tolerance rituals are those social processes that seem inclusive and open to all, but the very appearance of inclusivity covers up the mechanism by which they exclude less privileged, less "normal," less mainstream Others. The shift in the name from Mr. Eagle to the Eagle Pageant, for instance, seems like an inclusive shift, but the set of normative processes that constitute the pageant remain the same—from the gendered division of labor to the

gendered nature of humor, to the unwritten classed and familial resources needed for participation. Programs like these "cover over the
workings of power"[16] as they exclude, not through explicit rules and
regulations, but through the very organization of the program itself.
It's an event that appears to be open to all, but functions to marginalize non-normatively sized, not sustainably housed, not middle class,
not straight, not traditionally gendered, not White participants. As
Wendy Brown writes, "Tolerance can thus work as a disciplinary
strategy of liberal individualism" in that this program appears to be
open to everyone, but the merit-based participation process actually
functions to exclude those students who do not benefit from intersectional race, gender, class, and sexual privilege.[17]

It may be tempting, but too easy to read the pageant as a simple
regressive gendered ritual, a regressive ritual that might be changed
by shifting to a more inclusive name. However, when viewed as a
"tolerance ritual," it seems that, much like the Powder Puff football
game, the pageant involves more complicated social dynamics. The
pageant exemplifies how young, White, affluent men are constructed
as exceptionally meritorious, and how young, mostly White, affluent
women can leverage the girl-boss feminism they use to combat harassment to maintain other forms of privilege.[18] In this way, the pageant process illustrates the intersectional construction of a student
citizen at the school—students who are gender normative, middle- or
upper-middle-class, White, and are able to deploy organizational resources to meet their goals. Unlike the students who walk out of
school to protest gun violence or work for the realization of the Black
Lives Matter display, the Eagle Pageant participants address a social
problem in a way that doesn't challenge systemic inequalities. That
is, throughout the course of the pageant, things like poverty, racial
disparities in health care, or women's health in general, all factors
that can contribute to preterm births, were never addressed. Even
the particular choice of song to conclude the pageant suggests a dis-

connect between concerns of inequality and the philanthropy itself. Unlike the students who pushed for systemic change, work that is often labeled as "political," these young folks were repeatedly released from class to do non-school activities and were continually being told that they were role models in ways that bolster a sense that they and their work are important and that, indeed, they "can change the world."

The Eagle Pageant symbolizes the way social problems are solved, or thought to be solved, in a regime of kindness. This type of apolitical work, involving a kindness and feel-good generosity central to philanthropic efforts, elides inequality while doing good and seeming to make a difference in the world for those who need it. Placing the experiences of pageant participants alongside those of the young folks throughout this book—the GSA youth who put on the drag show, the gun control protestors, the students in the BSU—can tell us something about how to create a system that supports young people who are working for systemic change. How, perhaps, to empower these young folks such that they all feel like they can "change the world." In looking at their experiences as well as at the stories of the staff who support them, we can unpack a regime of kindness, dismantle a politics of protection, and begin to craft a politics of care.

6   The Politics of Care

"If our posters are being taken down, that's for sure a 'no' on an-nouncements," Jessa said as the Climate Action Club tried to figure out how to publicize their participation in the international student strike to demand government action on climate change, the strike they had been told they could not advertise on school grounds be-cause it was "political." Cameron asked, "If we can't put them up on campus, where can we put them?" Mario suggested, "Put them up at the bus stop!" Colin asked, "Do the sidewalks count?" Barely looking up from the pile of papers she was grading, Ms. Bay held up her cell phone and said to them, "I just want to point out that you have these devices . . . ," trailing off as she set it down. She returned to grading papers, saying to me, "I'm basically pretending I don't hear them," as the club continued to plan.

Inspired by Ms. Bay's suggestion to advertise the event online, club members began brainstorming excitedly. Jessa asked, "Is there an American High Facebook page?" No one seemed to know, which is not a big surprise since young folks tend not to use Facebook, a site they associate with their parents and grandparents. Instead they be-gan to discuss their own club's social media presence. Colin asked the group, "Do we have a Climate Action Club page?" When Jessa re-sponded that they did not, Cameron suggested they make one, saying,

"What if we made our own Instagram and advertised it there?" Thinking they could also use their own social media accounts, Jo, an Asian sophomore, asked, "Should I just take a picture of that," pointing at one of their advertising posters, "and put it in my story?" The members of Climate Action Club seemed to lack the easy familiarity with and expertise about social media advertising and organizing exhibited by the Eagle Pageant coordinators. So when their posters were taken down, they struggled to figure out how to advertise their event without the philanthropic cultural capital or easy assumption of school resources displayed by the Eagle Pageant coordinators.

Similarly, unlike the exclusivity of the Eagle Pageant, a central goal of the more racially, class-, and gender-diverse Climate Action Club was to ensure that the event would be accessible to as many young folks as possible. For example, as the club members strategized about publicity, they also tried to make sure the event would be inclusive in terms of transportation. Jo commented, "If there's a lot of people, there needs to be, like, access to get there." Jessa, fortunately, had managed to secure a number of free bus passes. She handed them out to the group so club members could distribute them to march participants who need transportation. Watching them ensure this level of accessibility, Ms. Bay slipped me a note saying, "these kids are our future and I love them."

They spent the rest of the meeting creating signs for the march. Colin reminded everyone as they wrote to "make sure to put Climate Action Club *American High* on it. We want to make it clear that we are from American. Everyone thinks we are from Timber High." Attendees moaned in agreement as Jo added, "We get swept under the rug because of Timber." Jo's comment echoes the critique leveled by the students Coach Ted had helped by calling the newspaper to correct their misattribution when American students had been labeled as Timber students at another protest. Whiter and wealthier, Timber High students regularly receive more attention than

American students do in the community when they organize protests or engage in civic activities. Frustrated that American High students were often overlooked in this way, Ms. Bay told me, "They are okay with a certain kind of kid who looks a certain way protesting." Ms. Bay's comment captures the racialized and classed dynamics that characterize the way some young folks are recognized and supported for their efforts to change the world—and some are not.

When the day of the walkout arrived, about fifty students gathered at "the rock" during third period. Some carried the signs they made during the club meeting, signs that read, "We are inheriting the world," "Be a queen go green," and "When the earth is crying out for help will you listen?" Jessa, leading the protest, said, delightedly, "I did not think this many people were going to come!" Her co-leader, Colin, explained the march plans to the group, saying that everyone should "go to the bus stop," take the bus "to downtown and then march from there. If you don't have a bus pass or change, I've got a bunch of passes for people. I'm so proud of all of you who came out here because I know it's so scary!" Colin's exhortation captured the emotional conflict experienced by some young folks at American as they made decisions about whether or not to participate in these civic actions, decisions that may result in lower grades and disciplinary procedures.

Decisions like these do not have to be scary. They are made scary by the same set of intersecting inequalities that sustain the high social status of the Eagle Pageant participants. For some young folks, young folks who are not as White, wealthy, high status, straight, or normatively gendered as the Eagle Pageant participants, engaging in collective action can not only feel scary, it can feel confusing. By quietly offering "off the record" advice, Ms. Bay not only signals her support for these young folks to engage in social action, but she works to impart some of the cultural capital so easily deployed by higher status students at the school to the Climate Action Club members. We can think Ms. Bay's efforts to support them as part of what Ethan, earlier in the book, referred to as her "weird, nonpsychotic" love.

This type of love is both related to, and provides an important alternative to, a regime of kindness. We have seen this love displayed by adults throughout the book. Craig showed it when he set up a "Culture Corner" against the wall of the student lounge to house displays celebrating (and explaining) events like Kwanzaa, Passover, Día de Muertos, or Hoodies Up Day (a day memorializing the life of Trayvon Martin). Nella demonstrated it when she hosted (as she does annually) a panel of speakers on the Black Lives Matter movement and invited trans and queer activists to speak to her classes. Max displayed it when he took time out of his day to talk to GSA members about what it means to grow up to be a happy, thriving trans man. These practices exemplify the love that bell hooks exhorts people to practice. This love may be kind, but this love is not the same as a regime of kindness. A regime of kindness centers good feelings and elides inequalities, inequalities that are confronted, acknowledged, and countered by what bell hooks calls a "love ethic." These staff members exemplify this love ethic, connecting feelings and practice to, in the words of hooks, "create a more just society."[1]

This love is not the natural outcome of a regime of kindness at American High. It isn't the "be kind" of the messaging on signs surrounding the school. It isn't the niceness exemplified by the poster in the girls' bathroom. It isn't a love that is the opposite of hate. It's love grounded in an understanding of historical and contemporary social inequalities. It's a love that empowers young folks to challenge organizational orderings of gendered, sexual, racial, and classed inequalities even as those young folks see the rewards of working within rather than against such a system. It's love as action. The love that these staff members display, supporting and creating organizational space for young folks to push back against a logic of the politics of protection, a logic that locates harm in individual and unpredictable experiences divorced from systemic, institutionalized inequalities. This love is central to a politics of care, a politics that puts humans and human needs at the center of institutions, organizations, and policy. Scholars Gregg Gonsalves and Amy Kapczynski have called for an "embrace of a broad based vision of a new politics of care" in the wake of the COVID-19 pandemic and the racialized, classed, and gendered tolls it took and continues to take.[2] They suggest that this politics would "address the deep structural roots of problems" and be "one organized around a commitment to universal provision for human needs." The stories of inequalities at American High suggest ways we might begin to center a politics of care rather than a politics of protection in our organizations, institutions, and communities.

No Room for Inequality

"There's bigotry, but it's below the surface. It's hidden, and we don't talk about it because the narrative around Evergreen is just that we're progressive, and liberal, and we're so ahead of everybody else. And anything that challenges that . . . is sort of shushed, almost," said Sarah when she told me about American High. In documenting the experiences of young folks at American, this book tells the story of how this shushing happens, a shushing that renders inequality "below the surface," covered, perhaps, by a regime of kindness. The drag show, discussions of safety and harm, the MLK assembly, the Black Lives Matter display, girls' stories of harassment and assault, and pageant season all exemplify the varied and shifting manifestations of this "shushing," manifestations that suggest that inequality is being addressed, but substituting, instead, language about bullying, kindness, diversity, and merit. Processes of the politics of protection, processes including benign diversity, racialized emotions, girl-boss feminism, notions of meritocracy, and student citizenship, all do the work of hiding social inequality often while seeming to address it.

When we see inequality as an issue of individual hate, bias, prejudice, or in Sarah's words, bigotry, we can miss the way it operates in organizations like American High and in social institutions in general. These processes, the processes that make systemic inequalities look like individual ones, do the work of reproducing inequality with little overt hate or formal exclusion while simultaneously covering up this reproduction. Even in an organization where inequality is seen as undesirable, normalizing processes like that of the student citizen reproduce inequality without explicit processes of marginalization. Thus inequality at a school that has no room for hate becomes a matter of highlighting exceptional threats, individual feelings, individual solutions, and rituals of tolerance among young people and staff, rather than addressing the mundane and everyday ways inequality is instantiated.[3]

In their book, *Despite the Best Intentions*, Amanda Lewis and John Diamond ask how schools with the best intentions, schools like American High, may reproduce racial inequality. Part of the answer, they suggest, lies in the fact that "white parents' commitment to diversity is a shallow one."[4] Similar shallow commitments reverberate throughout the community of Evergreen and are concretized at American High. The district's equity coordinator exhibits a shallow commitment to diversity when she suggests that a queer tradition may lead to the victimization of trans youth. The silence around the MAGA hat-wearers is a shallow commitment to racial equality. Telling girls that "your body your choice" is a viable strategy to prevent sexual assault is a shallow commitment to gender equality. A focus on changing event names and not their content is a shallow commitment to gendered, raced, and classed equalities.

The process of avoiding politics is central to this shallow commitment. Invoking politics as a boundary—when a staff member takes a knee in support of Black lives, when a White male teacher expresses concern for increasing discrimination and bias, when students plan a school walkout in support of the environment, when students strategize to stand silently to protest school gun violence, when students and staff want to put up a Black Lives Matter display—ensures that commitments to equality remain symbolic and not, perhaps, costly to those who benefit from it. Avoiding politics means that a benign, nonthreatening diversity is valued—as long as it can be folded into some sort of sanitized high school project.

This sanitized high school project benefits some members of the school community more than others. Organizational scholar Joan Acker suggests that organizations are set up to benefit and meet the needs of a particular group of imagined organizational actors, actors she calls "ideal workers."[5] She describes these workers as married middle-class men who reap organizational rewards. What American High shows us is that schools, like workplaces, may be set up to benefit and meet the needs of "ideal students," students like the student citizens who participate in the Eagle Pageant. Part of developing a politics of care is setting up schools that benefit and meet the needs of all students, rather than rewarding those deemed most meritorious, when that merit stands in for racial, class, gender, and sexual privilege.[6]

A Politics of Care

My kids like to swap stories about a beloved guidance counselor, Gail, a counselor who worked at the middle school that all three of them attended. None of them saw Gail in any official capacity, for help with school, learning, or social or emotional challenges, but all three of them, like many of their classmates, formed an important bond with her. Gail, like Craig, was stationed at the heart of their school. Rather than occupying the edge of a planter, however, Gail had a full classroom-turned-office overflowing with couches, fidget toys, stuffed animals, board games, and delightful chaos. She'd walk the hallways inviting kids to play silly games at lunch like "Cuppy Cups" and "Cups on Your Head." Middle schoolers would line up to play, laughing uproariously as they tried to stack tiny dice using large plastic cups instead of their hands or toss small items into cups precariously balanced on each other's heads. Gail's door was rarely closed and young folks would move in and out of her classroom/office to check in, say hi, rest, and get help with problems big and small.

It's not an accident that my kids share not only fond memories of Gail, but of middle school in general—a notoriously difficult schooling phase. I think this is, in part, because Gail, her office, and its location represent a tangible example of a politics of care. Her physical and organizational location in the school systemize the care that Craig worked so hard to enact at American. Gail's care was organizationally supported and enabled. Quite literally at the heart of that middle school was an adult whose job it was to connect, care for, and meet the needs of young folks. Unlike Craig, Gail was not a security guard. Unlike Craig, she had her own office, not a planter or a shared office with the armed campus police officer. Unlike Craig, who goes beyond (and perhaps contradicts) his job description to wrap students in a "circle of care" by connecting them with cultural, nutritional, and educational resources, this sort of care was Gail's job. A politics of care does not rely on the "weird nonpsychotic love" of individual staff; it is built into the logic of a community, organization, or institution.

To fully engage in a politics of care requires movement from what scholar Nancy Fraser calls practices of "recognition" to those of "redistribution." Recognition practices entail the sort of surface inclusion represented by the MLK assembly, anti-bullying efforts, or the Powder Puff and Eagle Pageant name changes. Practices of redistribution, on the other hand, recognize the inequalities that structure these needs for recognition, emphasizing a more equitable diffusion of resources, opportunities, support, and status rather than name changes or surface inclusion. Such an approach systematizes care, rather than providing symbolic gestures in lieu of resources or relying on individual effort or generosity. It is not the responsibility of schools to reorient society around redistribution, of course, but as the experiences of young folks and staff throughout this book highlight, there are ways for individual schools to move toward a politics of care, specifically in terms of school rituals, sex education, teacher support, course content, mental health, and student activism.

Rituals like assemblies, talent shows, and sports games are a central part of the social life of schools. They build solidarity and school spirit, and they allow students to laugh together (and sometimes at staff) and to cheer each other on. These rituals, like rituals in general, also convey a set of meanings and values.[7] They can reflect and sustain certain understandings of social norms and say something important about who matters in the social life of a school. In this sense, easy name changes without attendant content changes in both Powder Puff and the Eagle Pageant leave in place messages about gender, race, and class. However, this doesn't have to be the case. A Power Tough Football game could be a fundraiser in which students who don't play football are coached by the football team to play flag football as the student body cheers them on and the band plays kazoos, for instance. Something like the Eagle Pageant may require more extensive shifts given the various barriers to participation across lines of gender, race, and class. In that case, ongoing reflections about the nature of rituals such as these in terms of the messages they send about what matters, and about who is included in them, may be a part of moving toward a system that supports all young folks, not just privileged ones. Similarly, when young folks agitate for all school events that call attention to issues of inequality and/or the ability to participate in cultural traditions, as was the case with the Black Lives Matter display or the drag show, messages about systemic inequality need to be addressed, not curtailed by a language concerned only with offense (i.e., not hurting anyone's feelings, or bullying). Otherwise these offenses, feelings, and bullying will continue to be seen as individual-level harms divorced from issues of patterned inclusion or exclusion.

The young people's activism documented throughout this book exemplifies a call for a politics of care. Certainly, part of being young may be pushing back against adult authority through this type of activism. Such activism, however, may also be an important part of civic engagement, part of what it means to be a member of a community and to work together to change that community.[8] Schools are unique organizations in that age is a cultural and legal category that renders some organizational members much less agentic than others.[9] As such, young folks at American feel like they are risking grades and disciplinary action for engaging in it. But, as the behavior of the principal at Timber High suggests, this need not be the case. Rather than fostering a culture of fear and uncertainty, this principal enabled young people's civic engagement through a simple and temporary schedule change. Other schools have been more robust in their support of student activism, orienting curricula and assemblies around calls for justice and equity, rather than curtailing these topics with a boundary drawn by a conception of the political.[10] While a school administration may not take a stand on a given topic, certainly organizational systems can be developed to support and not penalize young folks for participating in this type of civic engagement.

Oregon is one of the twenty-nine states that requires students receive comprehensive sex education (or sex education that addresses abstinence and safer sex practices) that is LGBTQ inclusive and incorporates some content about what constitutes healthy relationships. This sort of sex education is important, as research suggests that comprehensive sex education leads to a variety of positive outcomes, from an appreciation of sexual diversity and healthier relationships to the prevention of dating violence and sexual abuse.[11]

However, even by Coach Ted's own admission, he was not sufficiently trained in this topic, such that a queer student had to teach the class on sexual diversity. At a school like American, a school with high levels of social trust between students and staff, this solution seemed to work relatively well in the short term, but queer youth should not have to bear the burden of educating others about sexual diversity. Similarly, given that a personal, complicated, and life-shaping issue like sexual assault is dealt with in an assembly setting, led by two staff members with little training on the topic, it is little surprise that young women themselves suggest that the training is not helpful. A growing body of studies on these sorts of one-off trainings, in fact, suggests that they often do little to address the problem of harassment or assault and may, in some cases, even result in outcomes that make the problem worse.[12] One such study even indicated that some types of training around sexual harassment and assault might make survivors *less* likely to report their experiences to staff. Additionally, studies on bystander intervention suggest that such trainings have little effect on the perpetration of sexual assault itself.[13] Student experiences at American, when paired with research like this, suggest that education about sexual violence prevention should be provided by trained experts, using research-backed strategies and, importantly, should address the way this violence is shaped by raced, classed, gendered, and sexualized inequalities. Additionally, sex education, even sex education that includes brief discussions of enthusiastic consent, needs to more explicitly include content addressing sexual pleasure itself.[14]

Increasingly, schools like American High are attending to the mental health of students. This attention, however, often treats mental health as if it exists outside the structural conditions in which people live, work, and learn. Organizations, for instance, frequently provide feel-good wellness programs that focus on things like "self-care" rather than attending to the social dynamics that can give rise to or exacerbate mental health challenges. In schools, mental health is too often tied to concerns over safety that are grounded in a logic of securitization. While mental health care is absolutely an issue of safety, tying it to systems of punishment, like the "tip line" through which students can report concerns, make it one of securitization. In fact, the people who are most connected to many of the students at American and who do much of the daily work to care for them are actually employed as security guards and tasked with school discipline. Mental health needs to be dealt with in a nonpunitive, restorative way, one that takes into account how systemic inequalities, and in the case of American High, systemic racial inequalities, can take a greater toll on some students than others.

Alternatives to these securitized responses to mental health are emerging. Programs, for instance, like those in Oklahoma, Connecticut, and Oregon use state, federal, and city funds to put together mobile mental health care teams specifically for young people, programs that do not directly report to school authorities or police departments.[15] These innovative programs are a way to prioritize young people's mental health needs without threats of school or police punishment, needs that have reached crisis levels as the pandemic has eased, needs for which the federal government is increasingly providing funding.[16]

Additionally, rather than being dealt with through a "tip line," things like peer-to-peer aggression may be better responded to with restorative justice approaches. Craig received permission a few times to use a restorative justice approach (something for which he had sought training) with students who were having difficulties with one another. He beamed when he told me about how successful the intervention was. His experience is borne out by research that suggests that restorative justice practices can reduce racial inequities in punishment, inequities that take a toll on Black and Brown youth. Restorative justice practices can systematize the sort of trusting relationships people like Craig have worked so hard to build.[17] Similarly, girls need a way to deal with sexual harassment and misogyny that can avoid putting the girls themselves at risk. Schools need a staff member who has a working familiarity with gender equity and sexual harassment. At American High, not a single girl noted to me the availability of an administrator in the school who they felt was safe to speak with about these concerns.

As the experiences of youth of color in the Teen Action Committee show, mental health is tied to and needs to be understood in light of systemic inequalities. As such, curricula and school programing around racial inequality need to go beyond a focus on benign diversity and feel-good responses. The history and contemporary nature of racial inequality needs to be present in curriculum and programming. Such a focus needs to be present throughout the curriculum, such that young folks cannot simply check out of these discussions. Some states, like California (and more recently Oregon, though after this study was completed), have taken steps to systematize this type of education, by requiring that ethnic studies be a standard part of school curriculum. Research indicates that learning about racial inequality has a beneficial effect on all young people—for instance, reducing racism among White students and increasing a sense of agency among students of color.[18] Learning the whole of a racialized history rather than focusing on individual, often color-blind discussions of kindness and hate would help, not only to create agentic and involved citizens who can work toward equity and justice, but to support the mental health of youth of color.

A politics of care involves what scholar Jennifer Freyd calls prioritizing institutional courage over institutional betrayal.[19] It involves putting the needs of the most vulnerable at the center of organizational concerns. As this book shows, it requires avoiding the easy work of feel-good kindness or securitized approaches to safety and health. It involves relying less on one-time events, emotional assemblies, or fear-based trainings. It involves education, education that entails hard work and sometimes retraining. It's education that may not always feel good.[20] It's an education that involves continual reflection, uncomfortable (for some) conversations, and systematizing the care that some staff members go out of their way to provide for students.

The things I am writing about here—inequalities regarding class, race, gender, and sexuality—are bigger than schools. We already task schools with too much and cannot expect them to solve society-wide problems like these. Public schools, as we saw during the course of the COVID-19 pandemic, already do so much more than just educate. They serve as social service agencies and safety nets for young people in a society that continually pares down social services elsewhere. They receive too little federal funding and are often staffed by overworked, caring, and exhausted employees. I make these suggestions with the hope that schools can serve as a partial example of what a politics of care might look like in communities, organizations, and social institutions in general, *not* to suggest that it is the responsibility of public schools to imagine or institute such a politics.

That said, sociologists are not known for their ability to solve problems.[21] We are known for our ability to point them out and then critique whatever solutions someone else proposes. But I am an optimist. I think we can build communities, organizations, and institutions that work for people, that care for people. But these communities, organizations, and institutions are not self-sustaining. They depend on our work, revision, reflection, and maintenance. This work requires those of us who benefit from inequality to distribute those benefits instead of hoarding them.

Citizens for the Future

Public schools have long been at the center of social and political battles in the United States.[22] "Schools," as Heather McGhee and

Victor Ray write, are not just for making "young people into edu-cated, productive adults," they "are also for making Americans." Since their inception, schools have been seen as a way to "Ameri-canize" young folks, especially those young folks who were seen as a threat to the country's moral fabric—historically immigrant youth, working-class youth, and youth of color.[23]

I think a look at American High suggests that this Americaniza-tion process is still happening, albeit in a slightly different way. Con-temporary processes of Americanization have to do with accepting a particular social system, one based on individual effort and reward—a social system that sees inequality as a moral or personal failure, not a systemic one. American High shows us who this system rewards, how the inequalities in this system are made less visible, and what happens when people challenge this system. The reason the battles over public schools get so heated is because these battles are much bigger than one school or even the system of education itself. These battles are about the Americanization process. These are battles over the nature of who we are as a society, how much inequality we are willing to accept, and who we allow to suffer because of it. These are battles over what type of country we think the United States is and should be.

Schools are battlegrounds, even schools where there is no room for hate, schools like American High. While the book bans popping up in state after state and the laws prohibiting lessons about racism and policies targeting trans young folks are not yet affecting Ameri-can High, these policies are animated by similar logics to those that shape American High, logics that draw a boundary of the political around what is appropriate for schools and what is not. In the wake of a recent sweeping book ban in Oklahoma, for instance, a teacher was disciplined for making a "political" statement in her classroom by putting up a sign over the banned books, a sign stating that they were banned. In Florida, parental fears about "politicizing schools" helped to pass laws that restrict the extent to which topics of race, gender, or sexuality can even be raised in schools. Across the country, parental claims of "political indoctrination" continue to echo at schoolboard meetings as parents protest the inclusion of trans youth in the social life of schools. These school-based conflicts are about inequality, its causes, and its solutions.[24]

When we cannot talk openly of inequality in school settings, it constrains our ability to challenge laws that target already marginalized young folks. When diversity becomes not a problem of inequality but of difference, then arguments about harm stemming from systemic exclusion make little sense. Tolerance, in this approach, is applied equally to all identities or perspectives, whether or not those identities or perspectives were or continue to be legally or socially excluded. This is the work that is done by avoiding "the political." When we call something political, what we really mean is that it has to do with inequality and power, but the conflation of the political with "the partisan" obscures this meaning. Schools are political organizations, but they need not be partisan ones.

Schools are not the singular cause of nor are they the singular solution to inequality. They are, however, where young people learn what it means to be a citizen, what it means to be an American. So if we want to make Americans, we need to prepare young people for citizenship by equipping them with a robust language to discuss experiences, causes, and consequences of systemic inequality. When political talk and action is banned, it leaves a void that gets filled with a regime of kindness. What the community at American High has shown us is that kindness is not the solution to inequality, but creating space for and empowering young folks to understand and address inequality might be a start.

Appendix: Research Note

Doing research in a high school as a forty-something meant that I often felt like Steve Buscemi in that now famous meme in which he wears a hoodie, a backwards baseball cap, and a skateboard slung over his shoulder as he walks down a locker-lined hallway greeting students by saying, "How do you do, fellow kids?" As I wrote in the preface, when I entered American High School, no one mistook me for a student, unlike when I did research at another high school in the early 2000s. With my skinny jeans, earth-toned cardigans, glasses, and long layered brown hair, I more easily blended in with the moms of American High students who volunteered on campus from time to time. Indeed, comparisons to moms came from students and teachers alike. For instance, when I first began to hang out with the coordinators of the Eagle Pageant, I teared up when the young women told me about the fundraiser and the pediatric unit it benefits. As the mother of two NICU babies myself, I unsuccessfully fought the tears as the coordinators told me about the fundraisers they put on, from Bunco to dodgeball to car washes. Seeing me dab at my eyes, Betsy, a junior coordinator, piped up and said, "I was in the NICU too! And my mom always cries too!" At that point, fairly early in my research, I knew that my role in this ethnography would be different than my role in previous ethnographies of young folks where I tended to be seen as an older, but not yet motherly, figure.

For someone who has long researched youth, this shift posed a bit of a challenge. In previous research I had written about adopting a "least gendered identity."[1] In that earlier work, I sported short hair, wore baggy cargo pants, black boots, and black shirts, a presentation of self that marked me as a bit of a tomboy, and certainly as queer. For some of us, however, a gendered presentation of self can change with age. In my midforties, my gender became something I jokingly

[195]

referred to as "Stitch Fix Soccer Mom," to capture the sort of White suburban middle-class woman I had somehow become. Similarly, it no longer felt authentic to try to embody, as other researchers have in research with young folks, a "least adult identity."[2] When I thought about attempting such a strategy, all I could see was that Steve Buscemi meme (or really any of those movies where adults try to pass themselves off as teens—21 *Jump Street* or *Never Been Kissed* come immediately to mind). After years of working and researching with young folks, what I had come to learn was that what goes a long way in terms of building trust with them is authenticity. Showing up earnestly and in good faith to say "I'm interested in telling a story that reflects your experience. What is your experience?" forges connection and builds rapport more effectively than, in my experience at least, trying to distance oneself from adulthood.

This research involved, as such ethnography often does, a series of decisions, decisions that included ones about how to present myself. I made these decisions by focusing on a goal of authenticity. I was honest about who I was, a professor at a college where I teach sociology. I am a mom of three kids. I have a wife. And two dogs. Like many of the adults at American High with whom young folks had good relationships, I tried to have a sense of humor about myself, like on the day that Anna looked at my sandals and noticed a large, dried drop of purple nail polish. "CJ," she laughed, "did you paint your toe nails WITH YOUR SHOES ON?" Indeed I had. I laughed along with her and the other students who found my rushed attempts at beauty humorous.

That said, this decision about authenticity also posed some challenges. I have a particular set of moral and ethical commitments to increasing social equality. These commitments could alienate some young folks who have different perspectives about the social world. So I decided to do at American High what I try to do in my own classroom. Instead of sharing my own perspective in response to questions, I endeavored to share what research suggests to be true, such that students, in the case of my classroom, or young folks, in the case of American High, could make their own decisions about the world. For instance, one day Tony came running over to me as I sat on the edge of the planter in the student lounge, dragging a friend along with him. He said, as he approached, "CJ! Matt thinks there are only two genders. Tell him he's wrong!" But, of course, I wasn't interested in telling Matt or other young folks they were wrong. I was and continue to be interested in learning from their perspectives. So, instead, I shared what anthropological and sociological research suggests about how gendered categories are constructed and shift over time—while affirming that a lot of people feel like Matt does, that there are two genders. While I may have disappointed Tony because I couldn't help him win his argument, instead I provided him and Matt information about what the research suggests, letting them work it out themselves.

As part of this authenticity, I aimed to be a resource in classes for students and teachers alike, drawing on my own experience or knowledge to help as needed. Nella, for instance, would sometimes ask me about my own experience as a student or a professor. On the day of the active shooter training, for example, she asked, "CJ do you have any stories?" This question surprised me and I had to think about it for a few seconds before I was able to say, "No I don't, actually. It didn't happen when I was in high school." For a moment I had a hard time believing that what I was saying was a true statement, trying to remember what school was like when we weren't being trained to defend ourselves from mass shootings. I continued by saying, "And they give us no training at the university to deal with these sorts of things. It's a good thing my students know, because I certainly don't."

In some way I had little choice but to be authentic. A quick Google search would bring up my public writings and talks about gendered and sexual inequalities. Several of the teachers at American High had read my work, including my first school ethnography, in their graduate programs. In fact, at one point a student teacher began working in a few of the classes I regularly sat in on. When we were introduced, he recognized my name immediately. He spent the rest of the day telling students, "Do you know who she is? She's famous!" Of course, I'm "famous" in a certain academic ecology, not in the world of the young folks at American High. Thankfully his pronouncements provided another opportunity to laugh at myself by commenting to the young folks who were certain that I was, in fact, not famous that they were right. "I'm not actually famous," I told them to much laughter; "I'm nerd famous." It's my sense that this sort of self-deprecation helped, because it was more in line with how young folks often saw me, as, in the words of one student, "that random lady who is around." Early in my time at American High, Coach Ted kindly agreed to let me introduce myself to his class. The agenda, which he typically wrote on the board, contained the following line, "Item 1: C.J. Presentation." Brett, sitting in the corner, loudly asked, "What's a C.J. Presentation?" Nicole who sat in front of him turned around and said, "It's that random lady who is around." I chuckled. Fortunately by the end of the two years I spent at American, I was less a random lady who was around and more recognizable as a researcher of and a resource for students. Nicole, herself, went on to share extensive insights about the social world at American High, insights that helped me understand the dynamics of racial inequality there.

In addition to being as authentic as possible, I tried to make it clear that I was on the side of the students, that I was not there to get them in trouble, and that I was there to help as much as I could. I didn't report vaping, cell phone use in class, or skipping school. I did try to help out when needed. When the BSU needed pizza picked up for a meeting, I offered to go get it. When extra hands were needed at Ohana night for setup, I provided some. When young folks encountered financial aid roadblocks because of their parents' immigration status, I put them in touch with folks at a local university who could help. As has been my experience researching with young people in other settings, what I found was that repeatedly showing up and being supportive builds trust. It helps young people realize you are not there to surveil or get them in trouble but because you want to tell their stories.

While my goal was to document young people's experiences in this book, I also saw myself reflected in their stories. To deal with the weight of the stories that girls told me about sexual harassment I often ran miles on trails at the end of the day with tears running down my face. The tears were a sign of mourning for my own adolescence, an adolescence characterized by similar harassment, but also for how little had changed since I had researched schools in the early 2000s. When the queer youth celebrated at the drag show, I celebrated with them, elated at their inclusion, visibility, and joy. While I write here about White racial ignorance, I spent much of this research imperfectly confronting my own ignorance, attempting to listen, learn, and provide an analysis that reflected the reality of the young folks of color at American.

Though I took notes on and interviewed folks for two years, the research process for this book began a full year before I began formal recordings. When I first approached Principal Walt about this project, I knew he was familiar with my previous research as well as some of the public writing I had done on issues of gender and sexual inequality in and out of schools. We had several meetings to discuss the parameters of this research and my interest in understanding what it was like to be a teenager in this particular historical moment. I offered help wherever needed on campus, as I usually do when I propose to do research in a school. I offered to provide writing support, college advice, or serve in other capacities in which help was needed, but I asked not to be put in a position of power over students. As a school-based researcher, it was important to me that I not be in a position to dole out punishments or rewards to students the way staff are. My aim was to be seen as a sort of neutral, if somewhat weird, observer who was always happy to lend a hand or an ear. After several meetings, Principal Walt approved this project and it was subsequently approved by the district office that oversaw external research projects.

I began research at American High in the fall after I gained approval for the project. I carried around little fliers that I handed out to American High community members with my contact information and the topic of the research project. I let people know I was a professor of sociology and was happy to answer any questions about college or what it's like to study high schoolers. I regularly used the language of "I'm writing about what life is like for high schoolers today" to explain the project.

I completed over two years of ethnographic observations with a total of over five hundred hours, plus fifty-one formal interviews with students, parents, and staff at American High School as well as countless informal interviews. I observed football games, classes, dances, club meetings, assemblies, youth-led protests, after-school events, and social media posts. I also analyzed a decade of yearbooks in the school library. Two to three days each week I could be found sitting next to Craig on his planter, in Nella's class, or at an after-school event carrying a purple pen and small notebook, as old fashioned as that seems at this point. While I conducted formal interviews in addition to these observations, I'm ambivalent about the type of data produced by formal interviews in a project such as this. The more I interview young folks from various backgrounds, the more I'm convinced that formal recorded interviews reward a particular classed, gendered, and aged disposition that makes me question how useful they are in this type of research. I can think of multiple times when a young person wouldn't say much in a formal interview as the iPad was recording but three days later talked nonstop about life, relationships, and struggles as we sat on a bench, with no recording equipment around, in the central quad. As such, most of the stories in this book are not drawn from those formal interviews conducted in local coffee shops or in library meeting rooms.

I wrote this book with a deep concern that I protect the identities of the folks involved as best I could. Most of the names in the book are ones participants chose themselves, and a few I assigned. I changed genders, ages, ethnicities, and combined and separated some respondents in order to protect the privacy of individuals in a way that does not change the claims or the findings in this book. I changed dates and details as well as combined events and locations in order to further maintain privacy.

Less than a year after I left the world of American High, our world shifted in ways few of us anticipated as the COVID-19 pandemic swept across the globe. Schools closed and then moved online. We sheltered in place and tried to figure out how to move forward in a changed world. This book was drafted in the context of that pandemic, in an uninsulated room above the garage that had been turned into my office, my wife's classroom, and my lecture hall while our kids watched their classmates appear in digital squares on iPads as they learned about math,

English, and science. I'm grateful for that room, for the financial resources that meant we were able to live comfortably during the lockdown, and for the quiet dark two-hour window starting at 5:30 a.m. when I had time to write. The racial, gendered, and classed inequalities documented in this book were thrown into stark relief as the economic and health toll of the virus became clear. I think writing the book in that social context added an intensity to the claims I make about inequality in the text, not because these claims became any more important, but because evidence of the life-or-death toll wrought by inequality became inescapable, even for the most privileged among us. Hopefully the stories of these young folks can help us to unpack the inequalities that predated the pandemic and to develop strategies to solve them in the future.

Notes

Preface

1. Alexandra Alter and Elizabeth A. Harris, "Attempts to Ban Books Are Accelerating and Becoming More Divisive," *New York Times*, September 16, 2022.

Chapter 1

1. Names of people, places, and events have all been changed. Identifying characteristics of people, places, and events have also been altered when possible to protect privacy. This means that the timelines of some events have also been changed and occasionally repeating events have been treated as singular.

2. A note on language: I try to mirror the language that folks at American High use to refer to themselves and others in terms of race, gender, sexuality, and other identifiers as best I can. As such, I typically use Latina and Latino, which were the terms they used, reserving Latinx for gender-fluid or trans young folks.

3. "School Anti-Bullying," *Human Rights Campaign*, January 19, 2022, https://www.hrc.org/resources/state-maps/school-anti-bullying.

4. The #MeToo movement, while initially begun in the early 2000s, had yet to gain popularity when I started my research; it went viral a few months into this project.

5. Mizuko Ito et al., *Hanging Out, Messing Around, and Geeking Out: Kids Living and Learning with New Media* (Cambridge, MA: MIT Press, 2013).

6. Ruth Milkman, "A New Political Generation: Millennials and the Post-2008 Wave of Protest," *American Sociological Review* 82, no. 1 (2017): 1–31, https://doi.org/10.1177/0003122416681031.

7. Vanessa Romo and Martina Stewart, "Trump Embroiled in 2 Controversies about Professional Sports, Race, and Culture," *NPR,* September 24, 2017.

8. While imperfect and halting, things like expanding marriage rights, increased health-care coverage, some immigration reform, as well as some increased gun control measures, may be thought of as examples of these social shifts.

9. Andrew J. Perrin, *Citizen Speak: The Democratic Imagination in American Life,* Morality and Society Series (Chicago: University of Chicago Press, 2006), https://press.uchicago.edu/ucp/books/book/chicago/C/bo3750684.html.

10. Perrin, *Citizen Speak.*

11. Nina Eliasoph, *Avoiding Politics: How Americans Produce Apathy in Everyday Life,* Cambridge Cultural Social Studies (Cambridge, UK: Cambridge University Press, 1998).

12. Perrin, *Citizen Speak.*

13. Jay MacLeod, *Ain't No Makin' It: Aspirations and Attainment in a Low Income Neighborhood* (Boulder, CO: Westview Press, 1987).

14. Jeffrey Guhin, "Why Study Schools?," in *Handbook of Classical Sociological Theory,* edited by S. Abrutyn and O. Lizardo (Cham, Switzerland: Springer International, 2021), 381–97; Natasha Kumar Warikoo, *The Diversity Bargain: And Other Dilemmas of Race, Admissions, and Meritocracy at Elite Universities* (Chicago: University of Chicago Press, 2016).

15. We have even gone so far as to make this a medical issue. Doctors attempted to develop a drug that could solve, for instance, the problem of racism. James Thomas and David Brunsma, "Oh, You're Racist? I've Got a Cure for That!" *Ethnic and Racial Studies* 37, no. 9 (2014): 1467–85, doi: 10.1080/01419870.2013 .783223.

16. "Race, Religion, and Political Affiliation of Americans' Core Social Networks," *PRRI* (blog), August 3, 2016, https://www.prri.org/research/poll-race -religion-politics-americans-social-networks/.

17. S. Michael Gaddis and Raj Ghoshal, "Searching for a Roommate: A Correspondence Audit Examining Racial/Ethnic and Immigrant Discrimination among Millennials," *Socius* 6 (December 14, 2020): https://doi.org/10.1177 /2378023120972287.

18. Gaddis and Ghoshal, "Searching for a Roommate."

19. Donald Tomaskovic-Devey and Dustin Robert Avent-Holt, *Relational Inequalities: An Organizational Approach* (New York: Oxford University Press, 2019).

20. Joan Acker, "Hierarchies, Jobs, Bodies: A Theory of Gendered Organizations," *Gender & Society* 4, no. 2 (1990): 139–58, https://www.jstor.org

/stable/189609; Victor Ray, "A Theory of Racialized Organizations," *American Sociological Review* 84, no. 1 (January 25, 2019): 26–53, https://doi.org/10.1177/0003122418822335; C. J. Pascoe, *"Dude, You're a Fag": Masculinity and Sexuality in High School* (Berkeley: University of California Press, 2007).

21. James M. Thomas, "Diversity Regimes and Racial Inequality: A Case Study of Diversity University," *Social Currents* 5, no. 2 (April 1, 2018): 140–56, https://doi.org/10.1177/2329496517725335.

22. Émile Durkheim, *Moral Education: A Study in the Theory and Application of the Sociology of Education* (New York: Free Press of Glencoe, 1961).

23. David F. Labaree, "Public Goods, Private Goods: The American Struggle over Educational Goals," *American Educational Research Journal* 34, no. 1 (1997): 39–82, 41, https://doi.org/10.3102/00028312034001039.

24. Joseph Jay Tobin, *Preschool in Three Cultures: Japan, China, and the United States* (New Haven, CT: Yale University Press, 1989); Emily Handsman, "From Virtue to Grit: Changes in Character Education Narratives in the U.S. from 1985 to 2016," *Qualitative Sociology* 44, no. 2 (2021): 271–91, https://doi.org/10.1007/s11133-021-09475-2; Kate Henley Averett, *The Homeschool Choice: Parents and the Privatization of Education* (New York: New York University Press, 2021); Guhin, "Why Study Schools?"

25. Robert Crosnoe, *Fitting In, Standing Out: Navigating the Social Challenges of High School to Get an Education* (New York: Cambridge University Press, 2011), https://doi.org/10.1017/CBO9780511793764.

26. Amanda E. Lewis and John Hammond, *Despite the Best Intentions: How Racial Inequality Thrives in Good Schools*, Transgressing Boundaries (New York: Oxford University Press, 2015); Prudence L. Carter, *Stubborn Roots: Race, Culture, and Inequality in U.S. and South African Schools* (New York: Oxford University Press, 2012); R. L'Heureux Lewis-McCoy, *Inequality in the Promised Land: Race, Resources, and Suburban Schooling* (Stanford, CA: Stanford University Press, 2014); Amy Best, *Prom Night: Youth, Schools and Popular Culture* (New York: Routledge, 2000); Julie Bettie, *Women without Class: Girls, Race, and Identity* (Oakland: University of California Press, 2014); Pamela Perry, *Shades of White: White Kids and Racial Identities in High School* (Durham, NC: Duke University Press, 2002); Warikoo, *The Diversity Bargain*.

27. Andrew Nalani, Hirokazu Yoshikawa, and Prudence L. Carter, "Social Science–Based Pathways to Reduce Social Inequality in Youth Outcomes and Opportunities at Scale," *Socius* (2021), doi: 10.1177/23780231211020236.

28. While it is traditional to discuss at length the identities of those formally interviewed for a project such as this, what I found over the course of this research

was that those interviews were, at best, supplemental to the ethnographic research from which most of the data are drawn. Interviews entail a particular gendered, classed, and importantly age-based mode of interaction that is not always appropriate for research with a diverse group of young folks.

29. The importance of calls for care in schools has a long history. Often such calls focus more on formal educational process and less on the social life of the school. See, for example, Nel Noddings, *The Challenge to Care in Schools: An Alternative Approach to Education,* 2nd ed. (New York: Teachers College Press, 2005).

30. Joan C. Tronto, *Moral Boundaries: A Political Argument for an Ethic of Care* (New York: Routledge, 1993).

31. Barbara Ehrenreich, *Bright-Sided: How Positive Thinking Is Undermining America* (New York: Picador, 2010).

Chapter 2

1. N'dea Moore-Petinak et al., "Active Shooter Drills in the United States: A National Study of Youth Experiences and Perceptions," *Journal of Adolescent Health* 67, no. 4 (October 1, 2020): 509–13, doi:10.1016/j.jadohealth.2020.06.015.

2. Mai ElSherief et al., "Impacts of School Shooter Drills on the Psychological Well-Being of American K-12 School Communities: A Social Media Study," *Humanities and Social Sciences Communications* 8, no. 1 (2021): 1–14, doi: 10.1057/s41599-021-00993-6.

3. This class is what is known as an "advisory" class, a class that meets intermittently to meet programming needs like registration or school mandated trainings.

4. ElSherief et al., "Impacts of School Shooter Drills."

5. Even as I edit this paragraph, tears come to my eyes as I am reminded not only of that classroom, or the time I crouched with my twin five-year-olds in the corner of a darkened classroom when my parent volunteer hours coincided with an active shooter drill, but also of all the images of terrified students running out of schools with their hands over their heads when once again a gunman had opened fire in a school.

6. Associated Press, "From Columbine to Robb, 169 Dead in US Mass School Shootings," *US News & World Report,* May 25, 2022, https://www.usnews.com/news/us/articles/2022-05-24/a-look-at-some-of-the-deadliest-us-school-shootings.

7. Alexis Stern and Anthony Petrosino, *What Do We Know about the Effects of School-Based Law Enforcement on School Safety?* (San Francisco: WestEd, 2018).

8 Nicole Nguyen, *A Curriculum of Fear: Homeland Security in U.S. Public Schools* (Minneapolis: University of Minnesota Press, 2016), https://journals.sagepub.com/doi/10.1177/0094306118755396dd.

9. Cindi Katz, "Banal Terrorism, Spatial Fetishism, and Everyday Insecurity," in *Violent Geographies: Fear, Terror, and Political* Violence, edited by Derek Gregory and Allan Pred (New York: Routledge, 2007), 349–62.

10. Melvin D. Livingston, Matthew F. Rossheim, and Kelli Stidham Hall, "A Descriptive Analysis of School and School Shooter Characteristics and the Severity of School Shootings in the United States, 1999-2018," *Journal of Adolescent Health* 64, no. 6 (June 1, 2019): 797–99, https://doi.org/10.1016/j.jadohealth.2018.12.006; Delbert S. Elliott, "Lessons from Columbine: Effective School-Based Violence Prevention Strategies and Programmes," *Journal of Children's Services* 4, no. 4 (2009): 53–62; Daniel P. Mears, Melissa M. Moon, and Angela J. Thielo, "Columbine Revisited: Myths and Realities about the Bullying-School Shootings Connection," *Victims & Offenders* 12, no. 6 (November 2, 2017): 939–55, https://doi.org/10.1080/15564886.2017.1307295; Randy Borum et al., "What Can Be Done about School Shootings?: A Review of the Evidence," *Educational Researcher* 39, no. 1 (January 1, 2010): 27–37, https://doi.org/10.3102/0013189X09357620.

11. In her research on drag balls, Amy Stone calls this education a form of "comfort work," in which queer folks manage potentially disreputable parts of queer culture through education of non-queer folk, often family members, who are witnessing it. Amy L. Stone, "When My Parents Came to the Gay Ball: Comfort Work in Adult Child–Parent Relationships," *Journal of Family Issues* 42, no. 5 (2021): 1116–37, doi: 10.1177/0192513X20935497.

12. Laurie A. Greene, *Drag Queens and Beauty Queens: Contesting Femininity in the World's Playground* (New Brunswick, NJ: Rutgers University Press, 2021).

13. Greene, *Drag Queens and Beauty Queens.*

14. Sara Warner, *Acts of Gaiety: LGBT Performance and the Politics of Pleasure* (Ann Arbor: University of Michigan Press, 2012); Andrea Pauline Herrera, "Alien Femininities: Transcending Gender through Drag in an Aesthetically Restrictive Culture" (PhD diss., University of Oregon, 2020); Amy Stone, *Queer Carnival: Festivals and Mardi Gras in the South* (New York: NYU Press, 2022).

15. Increasingly these types of drag shows, and drag in general, are being targeted by conservative activists as a form of child abuse.

16. Each student club requires a staff advisor, a requirement that can become challenging to meet when staff are already overburdened or when staff members leave the school. Rose, for instance, left American for another school in the middle of my research and the GSA could not find another queer-identified staff member to advise it. Seth, a straight-identified White man, ended up taking it on, but the students were frustrated, not at all with him, but with the lack of leadership from a queer adult.

17. J. G. Kosciw et al., *The National School Climate Survey: The Experiences of Lesbian, Gay, Bisexual, Transgender, and Queer Youth in Our Nation's Schools* (New York: GLSEN, 2020).

18. Kosciw et al., *The National School Climate Survey.*

19. Kosciw et al., *The National School Climate Survey.*

20. Please note that the data was gathered before the recent dramatic increase in anti-trans and "don't say gay" laws that were passed throughout the country.

21. Kosciw et al., *The National School Climate Survey.*

22. The few students I spoke with who had reported "tips" to this line said they did not know where this information went or what was done with it, only that they could share the information anonymously, in a way they couldn't with teachers or administrators.

23. Catherine Connell, *School's Out: Gay and Lesbian Teachers in the Classroom* (Oakland: University of California Press, 2015).

24. J. R. Latham, "Axiomatic: Constituting 'Transexuality' and Trans Sexualities in Medicine," *Sexualities* 22, nos. 1–2 (February 1, 2019): 13–30, https://doi.org/10.1177/1363460717740258.

25. Amy Best, *Prom Night: Youth, Schools and Popular Culture* (New York: Routledge, 2000).

26. Kristen Schilt and Laurel Westbrook, "Doing Gender, Doing Heteronormativity: 'Gender Normals,' Transgender People, and the Social Maintenance of Heterosexuality," *Gender & Society* 23 (2009): 440; Jack Halberstam, *Female Masculinity* (Durham, NC: Duke University Press, 1998).

27. C. J. Pascoe, "Bullying as a Social Problem: Interactional Homophobia and Institutional Heteronormativity," in *The Sociology of Bullying: Power, Status and Aggression among Adolescents,* edited by Christopher Donoghue (New York: NYU Press, 2022), 76–94.

28. Joyce M. Bell and Douglas Hartmann, "Diversity in Everyday Discourse: The Cultural Ambiguities and Consequences of 'Happy Talk,'" *American Sociological Review* 72, no. 6 (December 2007): 895–914, 910.

29. Jean M. Twenge et al., "Age, Period, and Cohort Trends in Mood Disorder Indicators and Suicide-Related Outcomes in a Nationally Representative Dataset, 2005–2017," *Journal of Abnormal Psychology* 128, no. 3 (April 2019): 185–99, https://doi.org/10.1037/abn0000410.

30. Marc S. Atkins et al., "Toward the Integration of Education and Mental Health in Schools," *Administration and Policy in Mental Health and Mental Health Services Research* 37, no. 1 (March 1, 2010): 40–47, doi: 10.1007/s10488-010-0299-7.

31. Anthony Fulginiti et al., "Sexual Minority Stress, Mental Health Symptoms, and Suicidality among LGBTQ Youth Accessing Crisis Services," *Journal of Youth and Adolescence* 50, no. 5 (May 2021): 893–905, doi: 10.1007/s10964-020-01354-3; Amanda M. Pollitt et al., "Predictors and Mental Health Benefits of Chosen Name Use among Transgender Youth," *Youth & Society* 2019 (June 2019), https://doi.org/10.1177/0044118X19855898; Arnold H. Grossman and Anthony R. D'Augelli, "Transgender Youth: Invisible and Vulnerable," *Journal of Homosexuality* 51, no. 1 (2006): 111–28, http://dx.doi.org/10.1300/J082v51n01_06.

32. Jacob Bor et al., "Police Killings and Their Spillover Effects on the Mental Health of Black Americans: A Population-Based, Quasi-Experimental Study," *Lancet* 392, no. 10144 (2018): 302–10, doi: 10.1016/S0140-6736(18)31130-9.

33. Shervin Assari et al., "Racial Discrimination during Adolescence Predicts Mental Health Deterioration in Adulthood: Gender Differences among Blacks," *Frontiers in Public Health* 5 (2017), https://www.frontiersin.org/article/10.3389/fpubh.2017.00104; American Psychological Association, "Addressing the Mental Health Needs of Racial and Ethnic Minority Youth," 2017, https://www.apa.org/pi/families/resources/mental-health-needs.pdf; Emergency Task Force on Black Youth Suicide and Mental Health, "Ring the Alarm: The Crisis of Black Youth Suicide in America," Report to Congress from the Congressional Black Caucus, December 17, 2019, https://watsoncoleman.house.gov/suicidetaskforce/; Rajeev Ramchand, Joshua A. Gordon, and Jane L. Pearson, "Trends in Suicide Rates by Race and Ethnicity in the United States," *JAMA Network Open* 4, no. 5 (2021): e2111563, doi: 10.1001/jamanetworkopen.2021.11563.

34. Trevor Project, *National Survey on LGBTQ Youth Mental Health,* 2022 https://www.thetrevorproject.org/survey-2022/; Human Rights Campaign Foundation, "Dismantling a Culture of Violence," 2018 https://reports.hrc.org/dismantling-a-culture-of-violence.

35. Kelly M. Hoffman et al., "Racial Bias in Pain Assessment and Treatment Recommendations, and False Beliefs about Biological Differences between Blacks and Whites," *Proceedings of the National Academy of Sciences* 113, no. 16 (2016): 4296–4301, doi: 10.1073/pnas.1516047113.

36. Christina Caron and Julien James, "Why Are More Black Kids Suicidal? A Search for Answers," *New York Times,* November 18, 2021, https://www.nytimes.com/2021/11/18/well/mind/suicide-black-kids.html; Bettina L. Love, *We Want to Do More than Survive: Abolitionist Teaching and the Pursuit of Educational Freedom* (Boston: Beacon Press, 2019).

37. Seth Abrutyn and Anna S. Mueller, "Toward a Cultural-Structural Theory of Suicide: Examining Excessive Regulation and Its Discontents," *Sociological Theory* 36, no. 1 (2018): 48–66, doi: 10.1177/0735275118759150.

38. Sara Ahmed, *On Being Included: Racism and Diversity in Institutional Life* (Durham, NC: Duke University Press, 2012), 3.

39. Calvin Morrill and Michael C. Musheno, *Navigating Conflict: How Youth Handle Trouble in a High-Poverty School* (Chicago: University of Chicago Press, 2018).

40. Morrill and Musheno, *Navigating Conflict.*

41. Eliasoph, *Avoiding Politics.*

Chapter 3

1. Mary E. Pattillo, "Church Culture as a Strategy of Action in the Black Community," *American Sociological Review* 63, no. 6 (1998): 767–84. doi: 10.2307/2657500.

2. Cynthia Miller-Idriss, *Hate in the Homeland: The New Global Far Right* (Princeton, NJ: Princeton University Press, 2020).

3. Mary C. Waters, *Ethnic Options: Choosing Identities in America* (Berkeley: University of California Press, 1990).

4. Affinity groups are clubs that, in the language of the student handbook, allow "students of shared affinity to connect."

5. Eduardo Bonilla-Silva, "Feeling Race: Theorizing the Racial Economy of Emotions," *American Sociological Review* 84, no. 1 (February 1, 2019): 1–25, https://doi.org/10.1177/0003122418816958.

6. Sarah Mayorga-Gallo, "The White-Centering Logic of Diversity Ideology," *American Behavioral Scientist* 63, no. 13 (November 1, 2019): 1789–1809, https://doi.org/10.1177/0002764219842619.

7. bell hooks, *All about Love: New Visions* (New York: William Morrow, 2000), 13.

8. Cynthia Enloe, *Bananas, Beaches and Bases: Making Feminist Sense of International Politics.* (Oakland: University of California Press, 2000).

9. Rita Kohli and Daniel G. Solórzano, "Teachers, Please Learn Our Names! Racial Microaggressions and the K-12 Classroom," *Race Ethnicity and Education* 15, no. 4 (2012): 441–62, https://doi.org/10.1080/13613324.2012.674026.

10. Jennifer C. Mueller, "Racial Ideology or Racial Ignorance? An Alternative Theory of Racial Cognition," *Sociological Theory* 38, no. 2 (June 1, 2020): 142–69, https://doi.org/10.1177/0735275120926197.

11. Casey Stockstill and Grace Carson, "Are Lighter-Skinned Tanisha and Jamal Worth More Pay? White People's Gendered Colorism toward Black Job Applicants with Racialized Names," *Ethnic and Racial Studies* 45, no. 5 (2022): 896–917, doi: 10.1080/01419870.2021.1900584.

12. Mueller, "Racial Ideology or Racial Ignorance?"

13. Danielle Sarver Coombs et al., "Flag on the Play: Colin Kaepernick and the Protest Paradigm," *Howard Journal of Communications* 31, no. 4 (August 7, 2020): 317–36, https://doi.org/10.1080/10646175.2019.1567408; Jules Boykoff and Ben Carrington, "Sporting Dissent: Colin Kaepernick, NFL Activism, and Media Framing Contests," *International Review for the Sociology of Sport* 55, no. 7 (November 1, 2020): 829–49, https://doi.org/10.1177/1012690219861594.

14. Marcos Pizarro and Rita Kohli, "'I Stopped Sleeping': Teachers of Color and the Impact of Racial Battle Fatigue," *Urban Education* 55, no. 7 (September 1, 2020): 967–91, https://doi.org/10.1177/0042085918805788; Susan Kemper Patrick and Francisco Arturo Santelli, "Exploring the Relationship between Demographic Isolation and Professional Experiences of Black and Latinx Teachers," *Journal of Education Human Resources* 40, no. 2 (March 2022): 138–68, doi: 10.3138/jehr-2021-0042.

15. Ann Ferguson, *Bad Boys: Public Schools in the Making of Black Masculinity* (Ann Arbor: University of Michigan Press, 2000).

16. Ferguson, *Bad Boys*

17. The movement has undergone shifts in the years since this research was performed in terms of vision, projects, governance, and fundraising.

18. Warikoo, *The Diversity Bargain*.

19. Marlese Durr, "What Is the Difference between Slave Patrols and Modern Day Policing? Institutional Violence in a Community of Color." *Critical Sociology* 41, no. 6 (2015): 873–79. doi: 10.1177/0896920515594766.

20. Eduardo Bonilla-Silva, "The Structure of Racism in Color-Blind, 'Post-Racial' America," *American Behavioral Scientist* 59, no. 11 (October 1, 2015): 1358–76, https://doi.org/10.1177/0002764215586826.

21. Frank Edwards, Hedwig Lee, and Michael Esposito, "Risk of Being Killed by Police Use of Force in the United States by Age, Race–Ethnicity, and Sex." *Proceedings of the National Academy of Sciences* 116, no. 34 (2019): 16793–98. doi: 10.1073/pnas.1821204116.

22. bell hooks, *Outlaw Culture: Resisting Representations* (New York: Routledge, 1994), https://www.routledge.com/Outlaw-Culture-Resisting-Representations/hooks/p/book/9780415389587.

23. Importantly, Kwanzaa is not a religion, but a celebration of African-American culture grounded in the Black activism of the 1960s.

24. Dorothy Roberts, *Killing the Black Body: Race, Reproduction, and the Meaning of Liberty* (New York: Knopf Doubleday, 2014).

25. Angela Valenzuela, *Subtractive Schooling: U.S.-Mexican Youth and the Politics of Caring* (Albany: State University of New York Press, 1999).

26. Toya Jones Frank et al., "Exploring Racialized Factors to Understand Why Black Mathematics Teachers Consider Leaving the Profession," *Educational Researcher* 50, no. 6 (2021): 381–91. doi: 10.3102/0013189X21994498.

27. Ray, "A Theory of Racialized Organizations."

28. Amanda E. Lewis, *Race in the Schoolyard: Negotiating the Color Line in Classrooms and Communities,* Series in Childhood Studies (Piscataway, NJ: Rutgers University Press, 2003).

29. Bonilla-Silva, "Feeling Race."

30. hooks, *All about Love.* 55.

Chapter 4

1. "Powderpuff (Sports)," 2023, *Wikipedia.*

2. Dan Cassino and Yasemin Besen-Cassino, *Gender Threat: American Masculinity in the Face of Change* (Stanford, CA: Stanford University Press, 2021).

3. Tristan Bridges and C. J. Pascoe, "Hybrid Masculinities: New Directions in the Sociology of Men and Masculinities," *Sociology Compass* 8, no. 3 (2014): 246–58, https://doi.org/10.1111/soc4.12134.

4. Well under 1 percent of high school football players are girls. "More Girls Are Playing Tackle Football," NFL Football Operations, January 9, 2020, https://operations.nfl.com/gameday/analytics/stats-articles/more-girls-are-playing-tackle-football/.

5. Sarah Banet-Weiser, *Empowered: Popular Feminism and Popular Misogyny* (Durham, NC: Duke University Press, 2018).

6. Jennifer S. Hirsch and Shamus Khan, *Sexual Citizens: A Landmark Study of Sex, Power, and Assault on Campus* (New York: W. W. Norton & Company, 2020).

7. Andréa Becker, Jessie V. Ford, and Timothy J. Valshtein, "Confusing Stalking for Romance: Examining the Labeling and Acceptability of Men's (Cyber)

Stalking of Women," *Sex Roles* 85, no. 1 (July 1, 2021): 73–87, https://doi.org/10.1007/s11199-020-01205-2.

8. Laura's House is a local domestic violence shelter.

9. To the extent that false accusations do exist, they are typically by White women against men of color and are a form not of reverse sexism but of white supremacy. Dana A. Weiser, "Confronting Myths About Sexual Assault: A Feminist Analysis of the False Report Literature: False Reports," *Family Relations* 66, no. 1 (2017): 46 60, doi: 10.1111/fare.12235.

10. Sarah Sobieraj, *Credible Threat: Attacks against Women Online and the Future of Democracy* (New York: Oxford University Press, 2020).

11. Carol Brooks Gardner, *Passing By: Gender and Public Harassment* (Berkeley: University of California Press, 1995).

12. Sobieraj, *Credible Threat*.

13. Gardner, *Passing By*; Sobieraj, *Credible Threat*.

14. "Youth Statistics. Internet & Social Media," ACT for Youth, April 5, 2022, http://actforyouth.net/adolescence/demographics/internet.cfm; Emily A. Vogels, Risa Gelles-Watnick, and Navid Massarat, *Teens, Social Media and Technology 2022*, Pew Research Center, August 10, 2022, https://www.pewresearch.org/internet/2022/08/10/teens-social-media-and-technology-2022/.

15. Gardner, *Passing By*; Sobieraj, *Credible Threat*.

16. Mizuko Itō et al., *Hanging Out, Messing Around, and Geeking Out*; Amy Adele Hasinoff, *Sexting Panic: Rethinking Criminalization, Privacy, and Consent*, Feminist Media Studies (Urbana: University of Illinois Press, 2015), https://academic.oup.com/illinois-scholarship-online/book/20077.

17. Tara's comment reflects what some studies have found· the number of male friends a girl has changes her likelihood of sexual victimization—as does, as other girls suggest, drinking behavior. John Stogner et al., "Peer Group Delinquency and Sexual Victimization: Does Popularity Matter?," *Women & Criminal Justice* 24, no. 1 (January 1, 2014): 62–81, https://doi.org/10.1080/08974454.2013.842520.

18. Richard Weissbourd et al., *The Talk: How Adults Can Promote Healthy Relationships and Prevent Misogyny and Sexual Harassment* (Cambridge, MA: Harvard Graduate School of Education, 2017).

19. Christopher Uggen and Amy Blackstone, "Sexual Harassment as a Gendered Expression of Power," *American Sociological Review* 69, no. 1 (2004): 64–92, doi: 10.1177/000312240406900105.

20. Joel David Vallett, "The Diffusion of Erin's Law: Examining the Role of the Policy Entrepreneur," *Policy Studies Journal* 49, no. 2 (2021): 381–407, https://doi.org/10.1111/psj.12396.

21. This is a problem because research indicates that sexual violence takes different forms in queer communities than it does in straight ones. "Sexual Assault and the LGBTQ Community," HRC Foundation, retrieved September 19, 2022, https://www.hrc.org/resources/sexual-assault-and-the-lgbt-community.

22. Hirsch and Khan, *Sexual Citizens.*

23. Katie M. Edwards et al., "Preventing Teen Relationship Abuse and Sexual Assault through Bystander Training: Intervention Outcomes for School Personnel," *American Journal of Community Psychology* 65, nos. 1–2 (2020): 160–72, https://doi.org/10.1002/ajcp.12379.

24. This program was not created by the staff at American High.

25. This is not to say that bystander intervention programs do not work, but that the format of this one is not optimal. Katie M. Edwards et al., "Feasibility and Acceptability of a High School Relationship Abuse and Sexual Assault Bystander Prevention Program: School Personnel and Student Perspectives," *Journal of Interpersonal Violence* 36, nos. 13–14 (July 1, 2021): NP7070–85, https://doi.org/10.1177/0886260518824655.

26. Carly Parnitzke Smith and Jennifer J. Freyd, "Institutional Betrayal," *American Psychologist* 69, no. 6 (2014): 575–87, doi: 10.1037/a0037564.

27. Elizabeth A. Armstrong, Miriam Gleckman-Krut, and Lanora Johnson, "Silence, Power, and Inequality: An Intersectional Approach to Sexual Violence," *Annual Review of Sociology* 44, no 1 (2018): 99–122, doi: 10.1146/annurev-soc-073117-041410.

28. Hirsch and Khan, *Sexual Citizens;* Tara N. Richards et al., "Sex-Based Harassment in the United States' K–12 Schools: Rates and Predictors of Allegations, Student Reporting, and Student Discipline," *Journal of School Violence* 20, no. 4 (October 2, 2021): 402–16, https://doi.org/10.1080/15388220.2021.1920423.

29. Chloe Grace Hart, "Trajectory Guarding: Managing Unwanted, Ambiguously Sexual Interactions at Work," *American Sociological Review* 86, no. 2 (April 1, 2021): 256–78, https://doi.org/10.1177/0003122421993809.

30. The United Nations defines gender-based violence as "harmful acts directed at an individual based on their gender," UNHCR, https://www.unhcr.org/en-us/gender-based-violence.html.

31. Karen A. Cerulo and Janet M. Ruane, "Future Imaginings: Public and Personal Culture, Social Location, and the Shaping of Dreams," *Sociological Forum* 36, no. S1 (2021): 1345–70, doi: 10.1111/socf.12765.

32. Jamie L. Small, "'Jocks Gone Wild': Masculinity, Sexual Bullying, and the Legal Normalization of Boys' Victimization," *Social Problems* (August 30, 2021): spab030, https://doi.org/10.1093/socpro/spab030.

33. Pascoe, *"Dude, You're a Fag."*

34. Peggy Orenstein, *Boys & Sex: Young Men on Hookups, Love, Porn, Consent, and Navigating the New Masculinity* (New York: Harper, 2020).

35. Mary Nell Trautner, Jessica Hoffman, and Elizabeth Borland, "Periods, Penises, and Patriarchy: Perspective Taking and Attitudes about Gender among Middle School, High School, and College Students," *Socius* (May 2022), doi: 10.1177 /23780231221100378.

36. Donna Eder, *School Talk: Gender and Adolescent Culture* (New Brunswick, NJ: Rutgers University Press, 1995).

37. Meredith G. F. Worthen, "The Young and the Prejudiced? Millennial Men, 'Dude Bro' Disposition, and LGBTQ Negativity in a US National Sample," *Sexuality Research and Social Policy* 18, no. 2 (June 1, 2021): 290–308, https://doi .org/10.1007/s13178-020-00458-6. (Some research suggests that this change has been overstated or at least is more complicated than it first appears.)

38. Pascoe, *"Dude, You're a Fag"*; Eder, *School Talk.*

39. Paige L. Sweet, "The Sociology of Gaslighting," *American Sociological Review* 84, no. 5 (2019): 851–75, https://doi.org/10.1177/0003122419874843.

40. Sweet, "The Sociology of Gaslighting," 851–75.

41. Shauna Pomerantz, Rebecca Raby, and Andrea Stefanik, "Girls Run the World?: Caught between Sexism and Postfeminism in School," *Gender & Society* 27, no. 2 (2013): 185–207, https://doi.org/10.1177/0891243212473199.

Chapter 5

1. Pierre Bourdieu, *Distinction: A Social Critique of the Judgement of Taste* (Cambridge, MA: Harvard University Press, 1984); Annette Lareau, *Unequal Childhoods: Class, Race, and Family Life,* 2nd ed. (Berkeley: University of California Press, 2011).

2. Annette Lareau, "Cultural Knowledge and Social Inequality," *American Sociological Review* 80, no. 1 (2015): 1–27, doi: 10.1177/0003122414565814.

3. Oluwakemi M. Balogun, *Beauty Diplomacy: Embodying an Emerging Nation* (Stanford, CA: Stanford University Press, 2020).

4. Maxine Leeds Craig, *Sorry I Don't Dance: Why Men Refuse to Move* (New York: Oxford University Press, 2013).

5. Pascoe, *"Dude, You're a Fag."*

6. Pascoe, *"Dude, You're a Fag."*

7. Marjorie L. DeVault, *Feeding the Family: The Social Organization of Caring as Gendered Work,* Women in Culture and Society (Chicago: University of Chicago

Press, 1991); Pamela Stone, *Opting Out? Why Women Really Quit Careers and Head Home* (Berkeley: University of California Press, 2007).

8. Richard E. Behrman, Adrienne Stith Butler, and Institute of Medicine (US) Committee on Understanding Premature Birth and Assuring Healthy Outcomes, eds., *Preterm Birth: Causes, Consequences, and Prevention* (Washington, DC: National Academies Press, 2007), https://www.ncbi.nlm.nih.gov/books/NBK11388/.

9. INCITE! Women of Color Against Violence, *The Revolution Will Not Be Funded: Beyond the Non-Profit Industrial Complex,* repr. (Durham, NC: Duke University Press Books, 2017).

10. Anand Giridharadas, *Winners Take All: The Elite Charade of Changing the World* (New York: Knopf, 2018).

11. This adds to what we already know about the way class is reproduced in the social, rather than the academic, life of schools. See, for instance, Paul E. Willis, *Learning to Labour: How Working Class Kids Get Working Class Jobs* (Farnborough, UK: Saxon House, 1977); Lareau, *Unequal Childhoods;* Shamus Khan, *Privilege: The Making of an Adolescent Elite at St. Paul's School,* Princeton Studies in Cultural Sociology (Princeton, NJ: Princeton University Press, 2011).

12. While James did end up attending the meeting, he did not follow through with the application process as he ended up withdrawing from school.

13. Ira Silver, "Disentangling Class from Philanthropy: The Double-Edged Sword of Alternative Giving," *Critical Sociology* 33, no. 3 (2007): 537–49, doi: 10.1163/156916307X189013.

14. Warikoo, *The Diversity Bargain,* 14.

15. Brown, *Regulating Aversion,* 44.

16. Brown, *Regulating Aversion,* 47.

17. Brown, *Regulating Aversion,* 47.

18. Michela Musto, "Brilliant or Bad: The Gendered Social Construction of Exceptionalism in Early Adolescence," *American Sociological Review* 84, no. 3 (2019): 369–93, doi: 10.1177/0003122419837567.

Chapter 6

1. hooks, *All about Love,* 22.

2. Boston Review, *The Politics of Care* (Cambridge, MA: Verso, 2020), 19.

3. Wendy Brown, *Regulating Aversion: Tolerance in the Age of Identity and Empire* (Princeton, NJ: Princeton University Press, 2006).

4. Lewis and Diamond, *Despite the Best Intentions.*

5. Acker, "Hierarchies, Jobs, Bodies," 139–58.

6. Murray Milner, *Freaks, Geeks, and Cool Kids: American Teenagers, Schools, and the Culture of Consumption* (New York: Routledge, 2004).

7. Durkheim, *Moral Education;* Pascoe, *"Dude, You're a Fag"*; Douglas E. Foley, *Learning Capitalist Culture: Deep in the Heart of Tejas,* 2nd ed. (Philadelphia: University of Pennsylvania Press, 2010).

8. Nicolás Riveros and Nick Fernald, *Student Walkouts: Responding to Civil Disobedience* (Cambridge, MA: Harvard Graduate School of Education, n.d.); Andreana Clay, *The Hip-Hop Generation Fights Back: Youth, Activism and Post-Civil Rights Politics* (New York: New York University Press, 2012).

9. Hava Rachel Gordon, *We Fight To Win: Inequality and the Politics of Youth Activism,* Series in Childhood Studies (Piscataway, NJ: Rutgers University Press, 2009).

10. Wayne Au and Jesse Hagopian, "How One Elementary School Sparked a Citywide Movement to Make Black Students' Lives Matter," *Rethinking Schools,* 2017, https://rethinkingschools.org/articles/how-one-elementary-school -sparked-a-citywide-movement-to-make-black-students-lives-matter/.

11. Eva S. Goldfarb and Lisa D. Lieberman, "Three Decades of Research: The Case for Comprehensive Sex Education," *Journal of Adolescent Health* 68, no. 1 (2021): 13–27, doi: 10.1016/j.jadohealth.2020.07.036.

12. Dalton Miller-Jones and Marilyn Marks Rubin, "Achieving Equity in Education: A Restorative Justice Approach," *Journal of Public Management & Social Policy* 27, n. 1, art. 3 (2020): 27–43, https://digitalscholarship.tsu.edu/jpmsp/vol27/iss1/3.

13. Heather Hensman Kettrey, Robert A. Marx, and Emily E. Tanner-Smith, "Effects of Bystander Programs on the Prevention of Sexual Assault among Adolescents and College Students: A Systematic Review," *Campbell Systematic Reviews* 15, nos. 1-2 (2019): e1013, doi: 10.4073/csr.2019.1; Htun et al., "Effects of Mandatory Sexual Misconduct Training on University Campuses," *Socius* 8 (2022), doi: 10.1177/23780231221124574.

14. Leslie M. Kantor and Laura Lindberg, "Pleasure and Sex Education: The Need for Broadening Both Content and Measurement," *American Journal of Public Health* 110, no. 2 (2020): 145–48, doi: 10.2105/AJPH.2019.305320.

15. Stephanie Hepburn, "Youth Mobile Response: A Tool for Decriminalizing Mental Health," #CrisisTalk, 2022, https://talk.crisisnow.com/youth-mobile -response-a-tool-for-decriminalizing-mental-health/.

16. "Project AWARE (Advancing Wellness and Resiliency in Education)," April 2022, https://www.samhsa.gov/grants/grant-announcements/sm-22-001.

17. Miller-Jones and Rubin, "Achieving Equity in Education."

18. Matthew D. Nelsen, "Cultivating Youth Engagement: Race & the Behavioral Effects of Critical Pedagogy," *Political Behavior* 43, no. 2 (2021): 751–84, doi: 10.1007/s11109-019-09573-6; Julie M. Hughes, Rebecca S. Bigler, and Sheri R. Levy, "Consequences of Learning about Historical Racism Among European American and African American Children," *Child Development* 78, no. 6 (2007): 1689–1705, doi: 10.1111/j.1467-8624.2007.01096.x.

19. Jennifer J. Freyd and Alec M. Smidt, "So You Want to Address Sexual Harassment and Assault in Your Organization? Training Is Not Enough; Education Is Necessary," *Journal of Trauma & Dissociation* 20, no. 5 (2019): 489–94, doi: 10.1080/15299732.2019.1663475.

20. Freyd and Smidt, "So You Want to Address Sexual Harassment and Assault in Your Organization?"

21. Adam Gamoran, "Sociology's Role in Responding to Inequality: Introduction to the Special Collection," *Socius* 7 (2021): doi: 10.1177/23780231211020201.

22. Aaron Kupchik, *Homeroom Security: School Discipline in an Age of Fear,* Youth, Crime, and Justice 6 (New York: New York University Press, 2010).

23. Lewis and Diamond, *Despite the Best Intentions,* 161.

24. Schools like American High are helpful in understanding the dimensions of these conflicts because they are "meso level institutions" that demonstrate how inequality is reproduced and resisted in everyday interactions and organizational practices. Tomaskovic-Devey and Avent-Holt, *Relational Inequalities.*

Appendix

1. Amy L. Best, ed., *Representing Youth: Methodological Issues in Critical Youth Studies* (New York: NYU Press, 2007).

2. Nancy Mandell, "The Least-Adult Role in Studying Children," *Journal of Contemporary Ethnography* 16, no. 4 (1988): 433–67, https://doi.org/10.1177/0891241688164002.

Bibliography

Abrutyn, Seth, and Anna S. Mueller. "Toward a Cultural-Structural Theory of Suicide: Examining Excessive Regulation and Its Discontents." *Sociological Theory* 36, no. 1 (2018): 48–66. doi: 10.1177/0735275118759150.

Acker, Joan. "Hierarchies, Jobs, Bodies: A Theory of Gendered Organizations." *Gender & Society* 4, no. 2 (1990): 139–58. https://www.jstor.org/stable/189609.

Ahmed, Sara. *On Being Included: Racism and Diversity in Institutional Life.* Durham, NC: Duke University Press, 2012. https://doi.org/10.1215/9780822395324.

———. "Whiteness and the General Will: Diversity Work as Willful Work." *PhiloSOPHIA* 2, no. 1 (April 1, 2012): 1–20. muse.jhu.edu/article/486618

Alter, Alexandra, and Elizabeth A. Harris. "Attempts to Ban Books Are Accelerating and Becoming More Divisive." *New York Times,* September 16, 2022. https://www.nytimes.com/2022/09/16/books/book-bans.html.

American Psychological Association. "Addressing the Mental Health Needs of Racial and Ethnic Minority Youth," 2017. https://www.apa.org/pi/families/resources/mental-health-needs.pdf.

Armstrong, Elizabeth A., Miriam Gleckman-Krut, and Lanora Johnson. "Silence, Power, and Inequality: An Intersectional Approach to Sexual Violence." *Annual Review of Sociology* 44, no. 1 (2018): 99–122. doi: 10.1146/annurev-soc-073117-041410.

Assari, Shervin, Ehsan Moazen-Zadeh, Cleopatra Howard Caldwell, and Marc A. Zimmerman. "Racial Discrimination during Adolescence Predicts Mental Health Deterioration in Adulthood: Gender Differences among Blacks." *Frontiers in Public Health* 5 (2017). https://www.frontiersin.org/article/10.3389/fpubh.2017.00104.

Associated Press. "From Columbine to Robb, 169 Dead in US Mass School Shootings." *US News & World Report,* May 25, 2022. https://www.usnews .com/news/us/articles/2022-05-24/a-look-at-some-of-the-deadliest-us -school-shootings.

Atkins, Marc S., Kimberly E. Hoagwood, Krista Kutash, and Edward Seidman. "Toward the Integration of Education and Mental Health in Schools." *Administration and Policy in Mental Health and Mental Health Services Research* 37, no. 1 (March 1, 2010): 40–47. https://doi.org/10.1007/s10488-010-0299-7.

Au, Wayne, and Jesse Hagopian. "How One Elementary School Sparked a Citywide Movement to Make Black Students' Lives Matter. Rethinking Schools, 2017. https://rethinkingschools.org/articles/how-one-elementary -school-sparked-a-citywide-movement-to-make-black-students-lives-matter/.

Averett, Kate Henley. *The Homeschool Choice: Parents and the Privatization of Education.* New York: New York University Press, 2021.

Bailey, Marlon M. *Butch Queens up in Pumps: Gender, Performance, and Ballroom Culture in Detroit.* Triangulations: Lesbian/Gay/Queer Theater/Drama /Performance. Ann Arbor: University of Michigan Press, 2013.

Balogun, Oluwakemi M. *Beauty Diplomacy: Embodying an Emerging Nation.* Stanford, CA: Stanford University Press, 2020.

Banet-Weiser, Sarah. *Empowered: Popular Feminism and Popular Misogyny.* Durham, NC: Duke University Press, 2018.

Becker, Andréa, Jessie V. Ford, and Timothy J. Valshtein. "Confusing Stalking for Romance: Examining the Labeling and Acceptability of Men's (Cyber) Stalking of Women." *Sex Roles* 85, no. 1 (July 1, 2021): 73–87. https://doi .org/10.1007/s11199-020-01205-2.

Behrman, Richard E., Adrienne Stith Butler, and Institute of Medicine (US) Committee on Understanding Premature Birth and Assuring Healthy Outcomes, eds. *Preterm Birth: Causes, Consequences, and Prevention.* Washington, DC: National Academies Press, 2007. https://www.ncbi.nlm. nih.gov/books/NBK11388/.

Bell, Joyce M., and Douglas Hartmann. "Diversity in Everyday Discourse: The Cultural Ambiguities and Consequences of 'Happy Talk.'" *American Sociological Review* 72, no. 6 (December 2007): 895–914. https://doi .org/10.1177/000312240707200603.

Best, Amy L. *Prom Night: Youth, Schools, and Popular Culture.* New York: Routledge, 2000.

———, ed. *Representing Youth: Methodological Issues in Critical Youth Studies.* New York: NYU Press, 2007.

Bettie, Julie. *Women without Class: Girls, Race, and Identity*. Oakland: University of California Press, 2014.

Blumer, Herbert. *Symbolic Interactionism: Perspective and Method*. Englewood Cliffs, NJ: Prentice-Hall, 1969.

Bonilla-Silva, Eduardo. "Feeling Race: Theorizing the Racial Economy of Emotions." *American Sociological Review* 84, no. 1 (February 1, 2019): 1–25. https://doi.org/10.1177/0003122418816958.

———. "The Structure of Racism in Color-Blind, 'Post-Racial' America." *American Behavioral Scientist* 59, no. 11 (October 1, 2015): 1358–76. https://doi.org/10.1177/0002764215586826.

Bor, Jacob, Atheendar S. Venkataramani, David R. Williams, and Alexander C. Tsai. "Police Killings and Their Spillover Effects on the Mental Health of Black Americans: A Population-Based, Quasi-Experimental Study." *Lancet* 392, no. 10144 (2018): 302–10. doi: 10.1016/S0140-6736(18)31130-9.

Borum, Randy, Dewey G. Cornell, William Modzeleski, and Shane R. Jimerson. "What Can Be Done about School Shootings? A Review of the Evidence." *Educational Researcher* 39, no. 1 (January 1, 2010): 27–37. https://doi.org/10.3102/0013189X09357620.

Boston Review. *The Politics of Care: From COVID-19 to Black Lives Matter*. Cambridge, MA: Verso, 2020.

Bourdieu, Pierre. *Distinction: A Social Critique of the Judgement of Taste*. Cambridge, MA. Harvard University Press, 1984.

Boykoff, Jules, and Ben Carrington. "Sporting Dissent: Colin Kaepernick, NFL Activism, and Media Framing Contests." *International Review for the Sociology of Sport* 55, no. 7 (November 1, 2020): 829–49. https://doi.org/10.1177/1012690219861594.

Bridges, Tristan, and C. J. Pascoe. "Hybrid Masculinities: New Directions in the Sociology of Men and Masculinities." *Sociology Compass* 8, no. 3 (2014): 246–58. https://doi.org/10.1111/soc4.12134.

Bridges, Tristan, and Tara Leigh Tober. "Mass Shootings and Masculinity." In *Feminist Frontiers*, 10th ed., edited by Verta Taylor, Nancy Whittier, and Leila J. Rupp. Lanham, MD: Rowman & Littlefield, 2019.

Brown, Wendy. *Regulating Aversion: Tolerance in the Age of Identity and Empire*. Princeton, NJ: Princeton University Press, 2006.

Calarco, Jessica McCrory. *Negotiating Opportunities: How the Middle Class Secures Advantages in School*. New York: Oxford University Press, 2018.

Caron, Christina, and Julien James. "Why Are More Black Kids Suicidal? A Search for Answers." *New York Times,* November 18, 2021. https://www .nytimes.com/2021/11/18/well/mind/suicide-black-kids.html.

Carter, Prudence L. *Stubborn Roots: Race, Culture, and Inequality in U.S. and South African Schools.* New York: Oxford University Press, 2012.

Cassino, Dan, and Yasemin Besen-Cassino. *Gender Threat: American Masculinity in the Face of Change.* Stanford, CA: Stanford University Press, 2021.

Cerulo, Karen A., and Janet M. Ruane. "Future Imaginings: Public and Personal Culture, Social Location, and the Shaping of Dreams." *Sociological Forum* 36, no. S1 (2021): 1345–70. doi: 10.1111/socf.12765.

Clay, Andreana. *The Hip-Hop Generation Fights Back: Youth, Activism and Post-Civil Rights Politics.* New York: NYU Press, 2012.

Connell, Catherine. *School's Out: Gay and Lesbian Teachers in the Classroom.* Oakland: University of California Press, 2015.

Coombs, Danielle Sarver, Cheryl Ann Lambert, David Cassilo, and Zachary Humphries. "Flag on the Play: Colin Kaepernick and the Protest Paradigm." *Howard Journal of Communications* 31, no. 4 (August 7, 2020): 317–36. https:// doi.org/10.1080/10646175.2019.1567408.

Craig, Maxine Leeds. *Sorry I Don't Dance: Why Men Refuse to Move.* Illustrated edition. New York: Oxford University Press, 2013.

Crosnoe, Robert. *Fitting In, Standing Out: Navigating the Social Challenges of High School to Get an Education.* New York: Cambridge University Press, 2011. https://doi.org/10.1017/CBO9780511793264.

DeVault, Marjorie L. *Feeding the Family: The Social Organization of Caring as Gendered Work.* Women in Culture and Society. Chicago: University of Chicago Press, 1991.

Diefendorf, Sarah, and C. J. Pascoe. "In the Name of Love: Whiteness, Emotion Work and Resource Distribution in Racialized Organizations." Presented at American Sociological Association Annual Conference (online), August 10, 2021.

Diefendorf, Sarah, and Tristan Bridges. "On the Enduring Relationship between Masculinity and Homophobia." *Sexualities* 23, no. 7 (October 1, 2020): 1264–84. https://doi.org/10.1177/1363460719876843.

Dobbin, Frank, Daniel Schrage, and Alexandra Kalev. "Rage against the Iron Cage: The Varied Effects of Bureaucratic Personnel Reforms on Diversity." *American Sociological Review* 80, no. 5 (2015): 1014–44, https://doi.org /10.1177/0003122415596416.

Durkheim, Émile. *Moral Education: A Study in the Theory and Application of the Sociology of Education.* New York: Free Press of Glencoe, 1961.

Durr, Marlese. "What Is the Difference between Slave Patrols and Modern Day Policing? Institutional Violence in a Community of Color." *Critical Sociology* 41, no. 6 (2015): 873–79. doi: 10.1177/0896920515594766.

Eder, Donna. *School Talk: Gender and Adolescent Culture.* New Brunswick, NJ: Rutgers University Press, 1995.

Edwards, Frank, Hedwig Lee, and Michael Esposito. "Risk of Being Killed by Police Use of Force in the United States by Age, Race–Ethnicity, and Sex." *Proceedings of the National Academy of Sciences* 116, no. 34 (2019): 16793–98. doi: 10.1073/pnas.1821204116.

Edwards, Katie M., Emily A. Waterman, Katherine D. M. Lee, Lorelei Himlin, Kirby Parm, and Victoria L. Banyard. "Feasibility and Acceptability of a High School Relationship Abuse and Sexual Assault Bystander Prevention Program: School Personnel and Student Perspectives." *Journal of Interpersonal Violence* 36, nos. 13–14 (July 1, 2021): NP7070–85. https://doi.org/10.1177/0886260518824655.

Edwards, Katie M., Stephanie N. Sessarego, Kimberly J. Mitchell, Hong Chang, Emily A. Waterman, and Victoria L. Banyard. "Preventing Teen Relationship Abuse and Sexual Assault through Bystander Training: Intervention Outcomes for School Personnel." *American Journal of Community Psychology* 65, nos. 1–2 (2020): 160–72. https://doi.org/10.1002/ajcp.12379.

Edwards, Torrie K., and Catherine Marshall. "Undressing Policy: A Critical Analysis of North Carolina (USA) Public School Dress Codes." *Gender and Education* 32, no. 6 (August 17, 2020): 732–50. https://doi.org/10.1080/09540 253.2018.1503234.

Ehrenreich, Barbara. *Bright-Sided: How Positive Thinking Is Undermining America.* New York: Picador, 2010.

Eliasoph, Nina. *Avoiding Politics: How Americans Produce Apathy in Everyday Life.* Cambridge Cultural Social Studies. Cambridge, UK: Cambridge University Press, 1998.

Elliott, Delbert S. "Lessons from Columbine: Effective School-Based Violence Prevention Strategies and Programmes." *Journal of Children's Services* 4, no. 4 (2009): 53–62. doi: 10.5042/JCS.2010.0021.

ElSherief, Mai, Koustuv Saha, Pranshu Gupta, Shrija Mishra, Jordyn Seybolt, Jiajia Xie, Megan O'Toole, Sarah Burd-Sharps, and Munmun De Choudhury. "Impacts of School Shooter Drills on the Psychological Well-Being of American K-12 School Communities: A Social Media Study." *Humanities and Social Sciences Communications* 8, no. 1 (2021): 1–14. doi: 10.1057/s41599-021-00993-6.

Emergency Task Force on Black Youth Suicide and Mental Health. "Ring the Alarm: The Crisis of Black Youth Suicide in America." Report to Congress from The Congressional Black Caucus, December 17, 2019. https://watsoncoleman.house.gov/suicidetaskforce/.

Enloe, Cynthia. *Bananas, Beaches and Bases: Making Feminist Sense of International Politics*. Berkeley: University of California Press, 2000.

Ferguson, Ann. *Bad Boys: Public Schools in the Making of Black Masculinity*. Ann Arbor: University of Michigan Press, 2000.

Fine, Gary Alan, and Ugo Corte. "Group Pleasures: Collaborative Commitments, Shared Narrative, and the Sociology of Fun." *Sociological Theory* 35, no. 1 (2017): 64–86. https://doi.org/10.1177/0735275117692836.

Foley, Douglas E. *Learning Capitalist Culture: Deep in the Heart of Tejas*, 2nd ed. Philadelphia: University of Pennsylvania Press, 2010.

Frank, Toya Jones, Marvin G. Powell, Jenice L. View, Christina Lee, Jay A. Bradley, and Asia Williams. "Exploring Racialized Factors to Understand Why Black Mathematics Teachers Consider Leaving the Profession." *Educational Researcher* 50, no. 6 (2021): 381–91. doi: 10.3102/0013189X21994498.

Freyd, Jennifer J., and Alec M. Smidt. "So You Want to Address Sexual Harassment and Assault in Your Organization? Training Is Not Enough; Education Is Necessary." *Journal of Trauma & Dissociation* 20, no. 5 (2019): 489–94. doi: 10.1080/15299732.2019.1663475.

Fulginiti, Anthony, Harmony Rhoades, Mary Rose Mamey, Cary Klemmer, Ankur Srivastava, Garrett Weskamp, and Jeremy T. Goldbach. "Sexual Minority Stress, Mental Health Symptoms, and Suicidality among LGBTQ Youth Accessing Crisis Services." *Journal of Youth and Adolescence* 50, no. 5 (May 2021): 893–905. https://doi.org/10.1007/s10964-020-01354-3.

Gaddis, S. Michael, and Raj Ghoshal. "Searching for a Roommate: A Correspondence Audit Examining Racial/Ethnic and Immigrant Discrimination among Millennials." *Socius* 6 (January 1, 2020). https://doi.org/10.1177/2378023120972287.

Gamoran, Adam. "Sociology's Role in Responding to Inequality: Introduction to the Special Collection." *Socius* 7 (2021). doi: 10.1177/23780231211020201.

Gardner, Carol Brooks. *Passing By: Gender and Public Harassment*. Berkeley: University of California Press, 1995.

Gaskin, Gerard H. *Legendary: Inside the House Ballroom Scene*. Durham, NC: Duke University Press, 2013.

Giridharadas, Anand. *Winners Take All: The Elite Charade of Changing the World*. New York: Knopf, 2018.

Goldfarb, Eva S., and Lisa D. Lieberman. "Three Decades of Research: The Case for Comprehensive Sex Education." *Journal of Adolescent Health* 68, no. 1 (2021): 13–27. doi: 10.1016/j.jadohealth.2020.07.036.

Gordon, Hava Rachel. *We Fight To Win: Inequality and the Politics of Youth Activism.* Series in Childhood Studies. Piscataway, NJ: Rutgers University Press, 2009.

Gordon, Hava Rachel, and Jessica K. Taft. "Rethinking Youth Political Socialization: Teenage Activists Talk Back." *Youth & Society* 43, no. 4 (2011): 1499–1527. https://doi.org/10.1177/0044118X10386087.

Gray, Mary. *Out In the Country: Youth Media and Queer Visibility in Rural America.* New York: NYU Press, 2009.

Greene, Laurie A. *Drag Queens and Beauty Queens: Contesting Femininity in the World's Playground.* New Brunswick, NJ: Rutgers University Press, 2021.

Grossman, Arnold H., and Anthony R. D'Augelli. "Transgender Youth: Invisible and Vulnerable." *Journal of Homosexuality* 51, no. 1 (2006): 111–28. http://dx.doi.org/10.1300/J082v51n01_06.

Guenther, Katja M. "How Volunteerism Inhibits Mobilization: A Case Study of Shelter Animal Advocates." *Social Movement Studies* 16, no. 2 (March 4, 2017): 240–53. https://doi.org/10.1080/14742837.2016.1252668.

Guhin, Jeffrey. "Why Study Schools?" In *Handbook of Classical Sociological Theory,* edited by S. Abrutyn and O. Lizardo, 381–97. Cham, Switzerland: Springer International, 2021.

Hagerman, Margaret A. *White Kids: Growing Up with Privilege in a Racially Divided America.* New York: NYU Press, 2018.

Haines, Rebecca J., Carla T. Hilario, Emily K. Jenkins, Cara K. Y. Ng, and Joy L. Johnson. "Understanding Adolescent Narratives About 'Bullying' through an Intersectional Lens: Implications for Youth Mental Health Interventions." *Youth & Society* 50, no. 5 (July 2018): 636–58. https://doi.org/10.1177/0044118X15621465.

Halberstam, J. *Female Masculinity.* Durham, NC: Duke University Press, 1998.

———. "Oh Behave! Austin Powers and the Drag Kings." *GLQ: A Journal of Lesbian and Gay Studies* 7, no. 3 (2001): 425–52. muse.jhu.edu/article/12172.

Handsman, Emily. "From Virtue to Grit: Changes in Character Education Narratives in the U.S. from 1985 to 2016." *Qualitative Sociology* 44, no. 2 (2021), 271–91. https://doi.org/10.1007/s11133-021-09475-2. muse.jhu.edu/article/12172.

Hart, Chloe Grace. "Trajectory Guarding: Managing Unwanted, Ambiguously Sexual Interactions at Work." *American Sociological Review* 86, no. 2 (April 1, 2021): 256–78. https://doi.org/10.1177/0003122421993809.

Harvey, Peter Francis. "'Make Sure You Look Someone in the Eye': Socialization and Classed Comportment in Two Elementary Schools." *American Journal of Sociology* 127, no. 5 (2022): 1417–59. doi: 10.1086/719406.

Hasinoff, Amy Adele. *Sexting Panic: Rethinking Criminalization, Privacy, and Consent.* Feminist Media Studies. Urbana: University of Illinois Press, 2015. https://academic.oup.com/illinois-scholarship-online/book/20077.

Hepburn, Stephanie. "Youth Mobile Response: A Tool for Decriminalizing Mental Health." *#CrisisTalk,* May 10, 2022. https://talk.crisisnow.com /youth-mobile-response-a-tool-for-decriminalizing-mental-health/.

Herrera, Andrea Pauline. "Alien Femininities: Transcending Gender through Drag in an Aesthetically Restrictive Culture." PhD diss., University of Oregon, 2020.

Hirsch, Jennifer S., and Shamus Khan. *Sexual Citizens: A Landmark Study of Sex, Power, and Assault on Campus.* New York: W. W. Norton & Company, 2020.

Hlavka, Heather R. "Normalizing Sexual Violence: Young Women Account for Harassment and Abuse." *Gender & Society* 28, no. 3 (June 1, 2014): 337–58. https://doi.org/10.1177/0891243214526468.

Hoffman, Kelly M., Sophie Trawalter, Jordan R. Axt, and M. Norman Oliver. "Racial Bias in Pain Assessment and Treatment Recommendations, and False Beliefs about Biological Differences between Blacks and Whites." *Proceedings of the National Academy of Sciences* 113, no. 16 (2016): 4296–4301. doi: 10.1073/pnas.1516047113.

hooks, bell. *All about Love: New Visions.* New York: William Morrow, 2000.

———. *Outlaw Culture: Resisting Representations.* New York: Routledge, 1994. https://www.routledge.com/Outlaw-Culture-Resisting-Representations /hooks/p/book/9780415389587.

Htun, Mala, Francesca R. Jensenius, Melanie Sayuri Dominguez, Justine Tinkler, and Carlos Contreras. "Effects of Mandatory Sexual Misconduct Training on University Campuses," *Socius* 8 (2022). doi: 10.1177/23780231221124574.

Hughes, Julie M., Rebecca S. Bigler, and Sheri R. Levy. "Consequences of Learning about Historical Racism among European American and African American Children." *Child Development* 78, no. 6 (2007): 1689–1705. doi: 10.1111/j.1467-8624.2007.01096.x.

Human Rights Campaign Foundation. "Dismantling a Culture of Violence," updated October 2021. https://reports.hrc.org/dismantling-a-culture-of-vio-lence.

Huopalainen, Astrid, and Suvi Satama. "'Writing' Aesth-ethics on the Child's Body: Developing Maternal Subjectivities through Clothing Our Children."

Gender, Work and Organization 27, no. 1 (January 2020): 98–116. https://onlinelibrary.wiley.com/doi/10.1111/gwao.12404.

INCITE! Women of Color Against Violence. *The Revolution Will Not Be Funded: Beyond the Non-Profit Industrial Complex.* Reprint. Durham, NC: Duke University Press Books, 2017.

Ito, Mizuko, Sonja Baumer, Matteo Bittanti, danah boyd, Rachel Cody, Becky Herr Stephenson, Heather A. Horst et al. *Hanging Out, Messing Around, and Geeking Out: Kids Living and Learning with New Media.* Cambridge, MA: MIT Press, 2013.

Kantor, Leslie M., and Laura Lindberg. "Pleasure and Sex Education: The Need for Broadening Both Content and Measurement." *American Journal of Public Health* 110, no. 2 (2020): 145–48. doi: 10.2105/AJPH.2019.305320

Katz, Cindi. "Banal Terrorism: Spatial Fetishism and Everyday Insecurity." In *Violent Geographies: Fear, Terror and Political Violence,* edited by Derek Gregory and Allan Pred, 349–62. New York: Routledge, 2007.

Kempei Patrick, Susan, and Francisco Arturo Santelli. "Exploring the Relationship between Demographic Isolation and Professional Experiences of Black and Latinx Teachers." *Journal of Education Human Resources* 40, no. 2 (March 2022): 138–68. https://doi.org/10.3138/jehr-2021-0042.

Kettrey, Heather Hensman, Robert A. Marx, and Emily E. Tanner-Smith. "Effects of Bystander Programs on the Prevention of Sexual Assault among Adolescents and College Students. A Systematic Review." *Campbell Systematic Reviews* 15, nos. 1–7 (2019): e1013. doi: 10.4073/csr.2019.1.

Khan, Shamus. *Privilege: The Making of an Adolescent Elite at St. Paul's School.* Princeton Studies in Cultural Sociology. Princeton, NJ: Princeton University Press, 2011.

Kohli, Rita, and Daniel G. Solórzano. "Teachers, Please Learn Our Names!: Racial Microaggressions and the K-12 Classroom." *Race Ethnicity and Education* 15, no. 4 (2012): 441–62. doi:10.1080/13613324.2012.674026.

Kosciw, J. G., C. M. Clark, N. L. Truong, and A. D. Zongrone. *The 2019 National School Climate Survey: The Experiences of Lesbian, Gay, Bisexual, Transgender, and Queer Youth in Our Nation's Schools.* New York: GLSEN, 2020. https://www.glsen.org/research/2019-national-school-climate-survey.

Kupchik, Aaron. *Homeroom Security: School Discipline in an Age of Fear.* Youth, Crime, and Justice 6. New York: NYU Press, 2010.

Labaree, David F. "Public Goods, Private Goods: The American Struggle over Educational Goals." *American Educational Research Journal* 34, no. 1 (1997): 39–82. https://doi.org/10.3102/00028312034001039.

Lareau, Annette. "Cultural Knowledge and Social Inequality." *American Sociological Review* 80, no. 1 (2015): 1–27. doi: 10.1177/0003122414565814.

———. *Unequal Childhoods: Class, Race, and Family Life,* 2nd ed. Berkeley: University of California Press, 2011.

Latham, J. R. "Axiomatic: Constituting 'Transexuality' and Trans Sexualities in Medicine." *Sexualities* 22, nos. 1–2 (February 1, 2019): 13–30. https://doi.org/10.1177/1363460717740258.

Lewis, Amanda E. *Race in the Schoolyard: Negotiating the Color Line in Classrooms and Communities.* Series in Childhood Studies. Piscataway, NJ: Rutgers University Press, 2003.

Lewis, Amanda E., and John B. Diamond. *Despite the Best Intentions: How Racial Inequality Thrives in Good Schools.* New York: Oxford University Press, 2015.

Lewis-McCoy, R. L'Heureux. *Inequality in the Promised Land: Race, Resources, and Suburban Schooling.* Stanford, CA: Stanford University Press, 2014.

Livingston, Melvin D., Matthew E. Rossheim, and Kelli Stidham Hall. "A Descriptive Analysis of School and School Shooter Characteristics and the Severity of School Shootings in the United States, 1999–2018." *Journal of Adolescent Health* 64, no. 6 (June 1, 2019): 797–99. https://doi.org/10.1016/j.jadohealth.2018.12.006.

Love, Bettina L. *We Want to Do More Than Survive: Abolitionist Teaching and the Pursuit of Educational Freedom.* Boston: Beacon Press, 2019.

MacLeod, Jay. *Ain't No Makin It: Aspirations and Attainment in a Low Income Neighborhood.* Boulder, CO: Westview Press, 1987.

Mandell, Nancy. "The Least-Adult Role in Studying Children." *Journal of Contemporary Ethnography* 16, no. 4 (1988): 433–67. https://doi.org/10.1177/0891241688164002.

Mayorga-Gallo, Sarah. "The White-Centering Logic of Diversity Ideology." *American Behavioral Scientist* 63, no. 13 (November 1, 2019): 1789–1809. https://doi.org/10.1177/0002764219842619.

Mears, Daniel P., Melissa M. Moon, and Angela J. Thielo. "Columbine Revisited: Myths and Realities about the Bullying–School Shootings Connection." *Victims & Offenders* 12, no. 6 (November 2, 2017): 939–55. https://doi.org/10.1080/15564886.2017.1307295.

Meyer, Elizabeth J. *Gender, Bullying, and Harassment: Strategies to End Sexism and Homophobia in Schools.* New York: Teachers College Press, 2009. https://eric.ed.gov/?id=ED527279.

Milkman, Ruth. "A New Political Generation: Millennials and the Post-2008 Wave of Protest." *American Sociological Review* 82, no. 1 (2017): 1–31. doi: 10.1177/0003122416681031.

Miller-Idriss, Cynthia. *Hate in the Homeland: The New Global Far Right.* Princeton, NJ: Princeton University Press, 2020.

Miller-Jones, Dalton, and Marilyn Marks Rubin. "Achieving Equity in Education: A Restorative Justice Approach." *Journal of Public Management & Social Policy* 27, no. 1 (2020): 22–43. https://digitalscholarship.tsu.edu/jpmsp/vol27/iss1/3.

Milner, Murray. *Freaks, Geeks, and Cool Kids: American Teenagers, Schools, and the Culture of Consumption.* New York: Routledge, 2004.

Moore-Potinak, N'dea, Marika Waselewski, Blaire Alma Patterson, and Tammy Chang. "Active Shooter Drills in the United States: A National Study of Youth Experiences and Perceptions." *Journal of Adolescent Health* 67, no. 4 (October 1, 2020): 509–13. https://doi.org/10.1016/j.jadohealth.2020.06.015.

"More Girls Are Playing Tackle Football," NFL Football Operations, January 9, 2020. https://operations.nfl.com/gameday/analytics/stats-articles/more-girls-are-playing-tackle-football/.

Morrill, Calvin, and Michael C. Musheno. *Navigating Conflict: How Youth Handle Trouble in a High-Poverty School.* Chicago: University of Chicago Press, 2018.

Mueller, Jennifer C. "Racial Ideology or Racial Ignorance? An Alternative Theory of Racial Cognition." *Sociological Theory* 38, no. 2 (June 1, 2020): 142–69. https://doi.org/10.1177/0735275120926197.

Musto, Michela. "Brilliant or Bad: The Gendered Social Construction of Exceptionalism in Early Adolescence." *American Sociological Review* 84, no. 3 (2019): 369–93. doi: 10.1177/0003122419837567.

Mowatt, Rasul A. "Lynching as Leisure: Broadening Notions of a Field." *American Behavioral Scientist* 56, no. 10 (October 1, 2012): 1361–87. https://doi.org/10.1177/0002764212454429.

Nalani, Andrew, Hirokazu Yoshikawa, and Prudence L. Carter. "Social Science-Based Pathways to Reduce Social Inequality in Youth Outcomes and Opportunities at Scale." *Socius* 7 (2021). doi: 10.1177/23780231211020236.

Nelson, Matthew D. "Cultivating Youth Engagement: Race & the Behavioral Effects of Critical Pedagogy." *Political Behavior* 43, no. 2 (2021): 751–84. doi: 10.1007/s11109-019-09573-6.

Nguyen, Nicole. *A Curriculum of Fear: Homeland Security in U.S. Public Schools.* Minneapolis: University of Minnesota Press, 2016. https://academic.oup.com/minnesota-scholarship-online/book/23534.

Noddings, Nel. *The Challenge to Care in Schools: An Alternative Approach to Education,* 2nd ed. New York: Teachers College Press, 2005.

Orenstein, Peggy. *Boys & Sex: Young Men on Hookups, Love, Porn, Consent, and Navigating the New Masculinity.* New York: Harper, 2020.

Pascoe, C. J. "Bullying as a Social Problem: Interactional Homophobia and Institutional Heteronormativity." In *The Sociology of Bullying: Power, Status, and Aggression among Adolescents,* edited by Christopher Donaghue. New York: NYU Press, 2022.

———. *"Dude, You're a Fag": Masculinity and Sexuality in High School.* Berkeley: University of California Press, 2007.

———. "Notes on a Sociology of Bullying: Young Men's Homophobia as Gender Socialization." *QED: A Journal in GLBTQ Worldmaking,* Inaugural Issue (2013): 87–104. https://doi.org/10.14321/qed.0087.

Pattillo, Mary E. "Church Culture as a Strategy of Action in the Black Community." *American Sociological Review* 63, no. 6 (1998): 767–84. doi:10.2307/2657500.

Pérez, Raúl. "Racism without Hatred? Racist Humor and the Myth of 'Color-blindness.'" *Sociological Perspectives* 60, no. 5 (October 1, 2017): 956–74. https://doi.org/10.1177/0731121417719699.

———. "Racist Humor: Then and Now." *Sociology Compass* 10, no. 10 (2016): 928–38. https://doi.org/10.1111/soc4.12411.

Perrin, Andrew J. *Citizen Speak: The Democratic Imagination in American Life.* Morality and Society Series. Chicago: University of Chicago Press, 2006. https://press.uchicago.edu/ucp/books/book/chicago/C/bo3750684.html.

Perry, Pamela. *Shades of White: White Kids and Racial Identities in High School.* Durham, NC: Duke University Press, 2002.

Pizarro, Marcos, and Rita Kohli. "'I Stopped Sleeping': Teachers of Color and the Impact of Racial Battle Fatigue." *Urban Education* 55, no. 7 (September 1, 2020): 967–91. https://doi.org/10.1177/0042085918805788.

Pollitt, Amanda M., Salvatore Ioverno, Stephen T. Russell, Gu Li, and Arnold H. Grossman. "Predictors and Mental Health Benefits of Chosen Name Use among Transgender Youth." *Youth & Society* 2019 (June 2019). doi: 10.1177 /0044118X19855898.

Pomerantz, Shauna, Rebecca Raby, and Andrea Stefanik. "Girls Run the World?: Caught between Sexism and Postfeminism in School." *Gender & Society* 27, no. 2 (2013): 185–207. https://doi.org/10.1177/0891243212473199.

"Powderpuff (Sports)." *Wikipedia,* 2023.

"Project AWARE (Advancing Wellness and Resiliency in Education)," April 2022. https://www.samhsa.gov/grants/grant-announcements/sm-22-001.

Raby, Rebecca. "'Tank Tops Are Ok but I Don't Want to See Her Thong': Girls' Engagements with Secondary School Dress Codes."

Youth & Society 41, no. 3 (2010): 333–56. https://doi.org/10.1177/0044118X09333663.

"Race, Religion, and Political Affiliation of Americans' Core Social Networks." PRRI, August 3, 2016. https://www.prri.org/research/poll-race-religion-politics-americans-social-networks/.

Ramchand, Rajeev, Joshua A. Gordon, and Jane L. Pearson. "Trends in Suicide Rates by Race and Ethnicity in the United States." *JAMA Network Open* 4, no. 5 (2021): e2111563. doi: 10.1001/jamanetworkopen.2021.11563.

Ray, Victor. "A Theory of Racialized Organizations." *American Sociological Review* 84, no. 1 (February 1, 2019): 26–53. https://doi.org/10.1177/0003122418822335.

Reddy-Best, Kelly L., and Eunji Choi. "'Male Hair Cannot Extend below Plane of the Shoulder' and 'No Cross Dressing': Critical Queer Analysis of High School Dress Codes in the United States." *Journal of Homosexuality* 67, no. 9 (2020): 1290–1340. https://doi.org/10.1080/00918369.2019.1585730.

Richards, Tara N., Kathryn Holland, Katherine Kafonek, and Jordana Navarro. "Sex-Based Harassment in the United States' K-12 Schools: Rates and Predictors of Allegations, Student Reporting, and Student Discipline." *Journal of School Violence* 20, no. 4 (October 2, 2021): 402–16. https://doi.org/10.1080/15388220.2021.1920423.

Ringrose, Jessica, and Emma Renold. "Normative Cruelties and Gender Deviants: The Performative Effects of Bully Discourses for Girls and Boys in School." *British Educational Research Journal* 36, no. 4 (2010): 573. doi: 10.1080/01411920903018117.

Riveros, Nicolás, and Nick Fernald. *Student Walkouts: Responding to Civil Disobedience.* Cambridge, MA: Harvard Graduate School of Education, n.d. https://www.justiceinschools.org/files/playpen/files/school_walkouts.pdf.

Roberts, Dorothy. *Killing the Black Body: Race, Reproduction, and the Meaning of Liberty.* New York: Knopf Doubleday, 2014.

Romo, Vanessa, and Martina Stewart. "Trump Embroiled In 2 Controversies about Professional Sports, Race, and Culture." *NPR*, September 24, 2017. https://www.npr.org/2017/09/24/553214114/trump-embroiled-in-two-controversies-about-professional-sports-race-and-culture.

Rupp, Leila J., and Verta Taylor. *Drag Queens at the 801 Cabaret.* Chicago: University of Chicago Press, 2003.

Savin-Williams, Ritch C. *The New Gay Teenager.* Cambridge, MA: Harvard University Press, 2009. https://doi.org/10.4159/9780674043138.

Schilt, Kristen, and Laurel Westbrook. "Doing Gender, Doing Heteronormativity: 'Gender Normals,' Transgender People, and the Social Maintenance of

Heterosexuality." *Gender & Society* 23 (2009): 440. doi: 10.1177 /0891243209340034.

"School Anti-Bullying." *Human Rights Campaign,* January 19, 2022. https:// www.hrc.org/resources/state-maps/school-anti-bullying.

Schwalbe, Michael, Sandra Godwin, Daphne Holden, Douglas Schrock, Shealy Thompson, and Michele Wolkomir. "Generic Processes in the Reproduction of Inequality: An Interactionist Analysis." *Social Forces* 79, no. 2 (2000): 419–52. https://doi.org/10.2307/2675505.

"Sexual Assault and the LGBTQ Community." *Human Rights Campaign,* retrieved September 19, 2022. https://www.hrc.org/resources/sexual -assault-and-the-lgbt-community.

Silver, Ira. "Disentangling Class from Philanthropy: The Double-Edged Sword of Alternative Giving." *Critical Sociology* 33, no. 3 (2007): 537–49. doi: 10.1163/156916307X189013.

Simon, Mara, and Laura Azzarito. *Race Talk in White Schools: Re-Centering Teachers of Color.* Lanham, MD: Lexington Books, 2020.

Small, Jamie L. "'Jocks Gone Wild': Masculinity, Sexual Bullying, and the Legal Normalization of Boys' Victimization." *Social Problems,* August 30, 2021. https://doi.org/10.1093/socpro/spab030.

Smith, Carly Parnitzke, and Jennifer J. Freyd. "Institutional Betrayal." *American Psychologist* 69, no. 6 (2014): 575–87. doi: 10.1037/a0037564.

Sobieraj, Sarah. *Credible Threat: Attacks against Women Online and the Future of Democracy.* New York: Oxford University Press, 2020.

Stein, Nan. "Bullying as Sexual Harassment." In *The Jossey-Bass Reader on Gender in Education,* edited by Susan M. Bailey, 409–28. San Francisco: Jossey-Bass, 2002.

Stern, Alexis, and Anthony Petrosino. *What Do We Know about the Effects of School-Based Law Enforcement on School Safety?* San Francisco: WestEd, 2018. https://www.wested.org/resources/effects-of-school-based-law -enforcement-on-school-safety.

Stockstill, Casey, and Grace Carson. "Are Lighter-Skinned Tanisha and Jamal Worth More Pay? White People's Gendered Colorism toward Black Job Applicants with Racialized Names." *Ethnic and Racial Studies* 45, no. 5 (2022): 896–917. doi: 10.1080/01419870.2021.1900584.

Stogner, John, J. Mitchell Miller, Bonnie S. Fisher, Eric A. Stewart, and Christopher J. Schreck. "Peer Group Delinquency and Sexual Victimization: Does Popularity Matter?" *Women & Criminal Justice* 24, no. 1 (January 1, 2014): 62–81. https://doi.org/10.1080/08974454.2013.842520.

Stone, Amy L. *Queer Carnival: Festivals and Mardi Gras in the South*. New York: NYU Press, 2022.

———."When My Parents Came to the Gay Ball: Comfort Work in Adult Child–Parent Relationships." *Journal of Family Issues* 42, no. 5 (2021): 1116–37. doi: 10.1177/0192513X20935497.

Stone, Pamela. *Opting Out? Why Women Really Quit Careers and Head Home*. Berkeley: University of California Press, 2007.

Sweet, Paige L. "The Sociology of Gaslighting." *American Sociological Review* 84, no. 5 (2019): 851–75. https://doi.org/10.1177/0003122419874843.

Taft, Jessica K. *Rebel Girls: Youth Activism and Social Change Across the Americas*. New York: NYU Press, 2010.

Thomas, James M. "Diversity Regimes and Racial Inequality: A Case Study of Diversity University." *Social Currents* 5, no. 2 (April 1, 2018): 140–56. https://doi.org/10.1177/2329496517725335.

Thomas, James, and David Brunsma. "Oh, You're Racist? I've Got a Cure for That!" *Ethnic and Racial Studies* 37, no. 9 (2014): 1467–85. doi: 10.1080/01419870.2013./83223.

Thornberg, Robert. "School Bullying and Fitting into the Peer Landscape: A Grounded Theory Field Study." *British Journal of Sociology of Education* 39, no. 1 (January 2, 2018): 144–58. https://doi.org/10.1080/01425692.2017.1330680.

Tobin, Joseph Jay. *Preschool in Three Cultures: Japan, China, and the United States*. New Haven, CT: Yale University Press, 1989.

Tomaskovic-Devey, Donald, and Dustin Robert Avent-Holt. *Relational Inequalities: An Organizational Approach*. New York: Oxford University Press, 2019.

Trautner, Mary Nell, Jessica Hoffman, and Elizabeth Borland. "Periods, Penises, and Patriarchy: Perspective Taking and Attitudes about Gender among Middle School, High School, and College Students." *Socius* 8 (2022). doi: 10.1177/23780231221100378.

Trevor Project. *National Survey on LGBTQ Youth Mental Health*, 2022. https://www.thetrevorproject.org/survey-2022/.

Tronto, Joan C. *Moral Boundaries: A Political Argument for an Ethic of Care*. New York: Routledge, 1993.

Twenge, Jean M., A. Bell Cooper, Thomas E. Joiner, Mary E. Duffy, and Sarah G. Binau. "Age, Period, and Cohort Trends in Mood Disorder Indicators and Suicide-Related Outcomes in a Nationally Representative Dataset, 2005–2017." *Journal of Abnormal Psychology* 128, no. 3 (April 2019): 185–99. https://doi.org/10.1037/abn0000410.

Uggen, Christopher, and Amy Blackstone. "Sexual Harassment as a Gendered Expression of Power." *American Sociological Review* 69, no. 1 (2004): 64–92. doi: 10.1177/000312240406900105.

Valenzuela, Angela. *Subtractive Schooling: U.S.-Mexican Youth and the Politics of Caring.* Albany: State University of New York Press, 1999.

Vallett, Joel David. "The Diffusion of Erin's Law: Examining the Role of the Policy Entrepreneur." *Policy Studies Journal* 49, no. 2 (2021): 381–407. https://doi.org/10.1111/psj.12396.

Vogels, Emily A., Risa Gelles-Watnick, and Navid Massarat. *Teens, Social Media and Technology* 2022. Pew Research Center, August 10, 2022. https://www.pewresearch.org/internet/2022/08/10/teens-social-media-and-technology-2022/.

Warikoo, Natasha Kumar. *The Diversity Bargain: And Other Dilemmas of Race, Admissions, and Meritocracy at Elite Universities.* Chicago: University of Chicago Press, 2016.

Warner, Sara. *Acts of Gaiety: LGBT Performance and the Politics of Pleasure.* Ann Arbor: University of Michigan Press, 2012.

Waters, Mary C. *Ethnic Options: Choosing Identities in America.* Berkeley: University of California Press, 1990.

Weiser, Dana A. "Confronting Myths About Sexual Assault: A Feminist Analysis of the False Report Literature." *Family Relations* 66, no. 1 (2017): 46–60. doi: 10.1111/fare.12235.

Weissbourd, Richard, Trisha Ross Anderson, Alison Cashin, and Joe McIntyre. *The Talk: How Adults Can Promote Healthy Relationships and Prevent Misogyny and Sexual Harassment.* Cambridge, MA: Harvard Graduate School of Education, 2017.

Willis, Paul E. *Learning to Labour: How Working Class Kids Get Working Class Jobs.* Farnborough, UK: Saxon House, 1977.

Wiltse, Jeff. *Contested Waters: A Social History of Swimming Pools in America.* Chapel Hill: University of North Carolina Press, 2007. https://doi.org/10.5149/9780807888988_wiltse.

Worthen, Meredith G. F. "The Young and the Prejudiced? Millennial Men, 'Dude Bro' Disposition, and LGBTQ Negativity in a US National Sample." *Sexuality Research and Social Policy* 18, no. 2 (June 1, 2021): 290–308. https://doi.org/10.1007/s13178-020-00458-6.

"Youth Statistics: Internet & Social Media," ACT for Youth, April 5, 2022. http://actforyouth.net/adolescence/demographics/internet.cfm.

Index

achievement ideology, 21

Acker, Joan, 184

active shooter drills, 31–39, 197, 204n5

Ahmed, Sarah, 64–65

"all lives matter" message, 93–94

"all opinions count" vs. facts, 94, 113

"All You Can Rely on Is Yourself"
(student essay), 82

"American dream" (achievement
ideology/bootstraps ideology), 21

American High: academics of, 5–12;
"advisory" classes, 204n3; affinity
groups, 208n4; author's research
methodology of, xvii–xix; Be Nice
Club, 3, 132; Black Student Union
of, 67–68; Climate Action Club, 17,
68, 178–81; college-going experience class, 6–7; Daring Discussions
class, 10, 81–86, 94; demographics
of, 3–5, 9, 26–27, 179–80; Honors
Academy, 160–61; Human
Sexuality class/curricula, 8–10, 45,
49, 57–58; kindness culture of, 1–14;
location of, 26; as "meso level
institution," 216n24; Mr. Eagle
Pageant, 140; poster campaigns, 1,
5, 10, 67, 71, 76, 84–95, 113, 178–79;
Powder Puff game as "Power
Tough," 103–11, 210n4; security system of, 1–3, 10–11, 15, 27, 100, 189;
student clubs and staff advisors,
206n16; teacher-student socializing at, 7–8; teaching staff and racial
diversity, 73, 100, Teen Action
Committee (TAC), 57–63, 71, 190;
UPWARD class, 6–7, 156–57,
161–62; Women's/Human
Empowerment and Crafting Club,
111–12, 132, 155. See also class issues;
love and justice; Mr. Eagle Pageant;
politics of care; politics of protection; regime of kindness; sexism
and gendered harassment

"as/with" mantra, 9

authenticity in research, 196–97

avoidance, 137

"bathroom problem," 53–55

beauty pageant. See Mr. Eagle
Pageant

Bell, Joyce, 56

benevolent sexism, 108–11

Be Nice Club (American High), 3.
See also regime of kindness

demographics. *See* class issues

Despite the Best Intentions (Lewis and Diamond), 183

Diamond, John, 27, 183

diversity regime: benign diversity, defined, 70–72; defined, 24; diversity ideology, 71

drag shows: acceptability to school administration, 147, 151–59, 175, 177; activism against, 205n15; "comfort work" of, 205n11; politics of protection on, 40–48

Dude, You're a Fag: Masculinity and Sexuality in High School (Pascoe), xvi–xvii, 12

Ehrenreich, Barbara, 29

Eliasoph, Nina, 20

emotion: emotional intelligence (EQ) of teachers, 8; hurt feelings and language of offense, 76; love as emotion-based solution, 78; racialized emotions, 71; and safety management, 130–31. *See also* love and justice

Erin's Law, 117, 123, 124, 131, 134 35

ethnic studies curricula, 190

facial recognition technology, 27

"fag discourse" ("compulsive heterosexuality"), xv, xvi

financial issues: of class and preferential treatment, 153, 161–66, 170, 173; of school safety and stranger making, 64. *See also* class issues

football programs: coaching and care provided to students in, 8–10; political issues within kindness culture, 17–18; statistics of girls playing football, 210n4. *See also* Powder Puff

Fraser, Nancy, 185

Freyd, Jennifer, 122–24, 190

Gardner, Carol, 114–15

Gay/Straight Alliances (GSA), American High examples of. *See* drag shows; LGBTQ issues

Gay/Straight Alliances (GSA), inception and increase of, xvii

gender. *See* sexism and gendered harassment; sexuality and gender identity

Giridharada, Anand, 160

girl-boss feminism, 28, 110, 118, 121, 138–40

Gonsalves, Gregg, 187

The Good High School (Lightfoot), 101

gun violence: active shooter drills as politics of protection, 31–39, 197, 204n5; increase of, in late nineties, xiv; student activism on, 35; threats of, 128

"happy talk," 56

harassment. *See* bullying; race and benign diversity; sexism and gendered harassment

Hart, Chloe, 131

Hartmann, Douglas, 56

homophobia, xiii–xvii, 12

hooks, bell, 72, 96, 102, 181

Human Sexuality class/curricula (American High): emotional intelligence for teaching of, 8–10; on gender and sexual diversity, 45, 49; on pronouns, 57–58

humor: as bullying, 153; and gender reversal, 105–9, 141, 142, 150–51, 156–57, 175–76

positive thinking tradition, 29

poster campaigns (American High): for anti-bullying awareness, 1; for climate action awareness, 5, 178–79; for racial inequality awareness, 10, 67, 71, 76, 84–95, 113. *See also* race and benign diversity

Powder Puff: benevolent sexism in, 108–11; fundraising component of, 103, 108; gender reversal ritual of, 105–6; as "Power Tough," 106–11; statistics of girls playing football, 210n4

power: and gendered harassment response, 117; girl-boss feminism, 110, 118, 121, 138–40; and political issues within kindness culture, 20; uneven distribution in schools, 25–26; and Whiteness as social category, 10

pronouns and gender, 57–58, 60

public harassment, defined, 114–15

Queen Quixotic (drag queen), 40–42, 44

queer, terminology for, 49–50

race and benign diversity, 66–102; benign diversity, defined, 70–72; "checking-out" from anti-racist gestures, 83–84, 86–95; color-blind racism, 92; "critical race theory," xix; interracial romantic relationships, 22; kneeling protests of racism, 15–16, 72; Kwanzaa spirit week events, 99; in late eighties/ early nineties, xv–xvi; love in action for, 95–100, 181; mental health and politics of protection, 57–59, 62; microaggressions and response,

66–72; as political issue within kindness culture, 18–19; power and Whiteness as social category, 10; race and false accusations of sexual violence, 211n9; racialized emotions, 71; racism as "medical issue," 202n15; and schools as racialized organizations, 100–102; "sugarcoating," 28, 72–78; and White racial ignorance, 78–86. *See also* politics of protection; systemic inequality

"Race Card" (National Public Radio), 82

Ray, Victor, 100, 191–92

redistribution practices, 185–86

regime of kindness, 1–30; "all lives matter" as, 93–94; caring vs., 5, 24–30, 204n29; characteristics of, 1–14; hurt feelings vs. inequality, 76; and individual vs. systemic nature of inequality, 20–24, 29–30, 48–56, 63–65, 70–72, 95; inequality and obscurity by, 39; and language for harassment, 110–11; limitations of, xviii, 5, 28–30; vs. love as action, 181–82; Mr. Eagle Pageant as, 148, 175, 177; "political" concept within, 14–20; and positive thinking tradition, 29; and racialized emotions, 71; and social justice intention, xvii–xviii. *See also* love and justice

research methods, about, xvii–xix, 195–200, 201n2, 203–204n28

restorative justice, 89, 91, 189–90

River High, author's research of, xiii–xvii. *See also* American High

"Safe Schools Now" (Oregon Education Association), 37

Founded in 1893,
UNIVERSITY OF CALIFORNIA PRESS
publishes bold, progressive books and journals
on topics in the arts, humanities, social sciences,
and natural sciences—with a focus on social
justice issues—that inspire thought and action
among readers worldwide.

The UC PRESS FOUNDATION
raises funds to uphold the press's vital role
as an independent, nonprofit publisher, and
receives philanthropic support from a wide
range of individuals and institutions—and from
committed readers like you. To learn more, visit
ucpress.edu/supportus.